An Introduction to Conversation Analysis

An Introduction to Conversation Analysis

By Anthony J. Liddicoat

continuum

Continuum
The Tower Building
11 York Road
London SE1 7NX

80 Maiden Lane
Suite 704
New York, NY 10038

British Library Cataloguing-in-Publication Data
A catalogue record for this book is available from the British Library.

ISBN: HB: 978-0-8264-9114-5
     PB: 978-0-8264-9115-2

Typeset by YHT Ltd, London
Printed and bound in Great Britain by Biddles Ltd, Kings Lynn, Norfolk

For David Liddicoat

Contents

Acknowledgements

I would like to thank Belinda Collins, Marian May, Maurice Nevile, Johanna Rendle-Short and Yanyin Zhang for their useful feedback on this text and their help in refining it. I would also like to thank Charles Goodwin and Lawrence Erlbaum for permission to reproduce the image on p.41, which is taken from Goodwin, C. (2003), 'Pointing as situated practice', in S. Kita (ed.), *Pointing: Where Language, Culture and Cognition Meet* Mahwah, NJ: Lawrence Erlbaum (pp. 217–41).

1 Conversation and Conversation Analysis

Introduction

Conversation is one of the most prevalent uses of human language. All human beings engage in conversational interaction and human society depends on conversation in order to function:

> Social interaction is the primordial means through which the business of the social world is transacted, the identities of its participants are affirmed or denied, and its cultures are transmitted, renewed and modified.
>
> (C. Goodwin and Heritage, 1990: 283)

Conversation is the way in which people socialize and develop and sustain their relationships with each other. When people converse they engage in a form of linguistic communication, but there is much more going on in a conversation than just the use of a linguistic code. Much that is important in conversation is carried out by things other than language, including eye gaze and body posture, silences and the real-world context in which the talk is produced.

Conversation has received a great deal of attention from writers over a very long period of time; however, much of what has been written about conversation is prescriptive in nature and deals with the idea of what makes a 'good conversationalist' (see Burke, 1993). Such approaches to conversation take the form of a set of prescriptive rules which describe what a conversation should be. They present sets of social rules which indicate which topics are appropriate or how language is to be used for maximum effect. These principles of what constitutes good or appropriate conversation vary from culture to culture and change over time (Burke, 1993). Such approaches to conversation show little about conversation as a normal everyday human activity, but frame conversation as an elite activity governed by the conventions of 'polite society'. However, conversation is not solely an elite activity, but rather an everyday one, and it is important to understand how it is that people engage in this everyday activity as a structured social event.

The everyday nature of talk has often been denigrated as a subject for study, with linguists such as Chomsky (1965) seeing language used in actual instances of spontaneous communication as being in some way defective and negatively influenced by non-linguistic factors. Such views of language, however, divorce the linguistic system from its primary use in human communication. Given the fundamental role of conversation in human social life, it is important to understand conversation as a linguistic activity, and since the 1960s increasing importance has been given to the analysis of conversation as a field of study (Clayman and Maynard, 1995; C. Goodwin and Heritage, 1990; Heritage, 1989).

The development of conversation analysis

Conversation analysis is an approach to the study of talk in interaction which grew out of the ethnomethodological tradition in sociology developed by Harold Garfinkel (1964, 1967, 1988). Ethnomethodology as a field of sociology studies the common sense resources, practices and procedures through which members of a society produce and recognize mutually intelligible objects, events and courses of action. These main ideas for the approach were established in *Studies in Ethnomethodology* (Garfinkel, 1967). The core focus of ethnomethodology is small-scale social order seen through the common social knowledge of members of society of the forces that influence how individuals interpret the situations and messages they encounter in their social world. Garfinkel sought to study the social structure of everyday lived experience and to develop an understanding of 'how the structures of everyday activities are ordinarily and routinely produced and maintained' (Garfinkel, 1967: 35–6). Ethnomethodology also gave increased prominence to participants' understandings of social action and viewed the participants themselves as knowledgeable agents who attribute meaning to their social actions in ways which were central to the unfolding of those actions (Boden, 1990; Clayman and Maynard, 1995).

Ethnomethodology proceeds from an assumption that social order appears to be orderly, but is in reality potentially chaotic. For ethnomethodologists the social order is not a pre-existing framework, but rather it is constructed in the minds of social actors as they engage with society. As each member of a society encounters sense impressions and experiences, s/he must somehow organize them into a coherent pattern. Garfinkel (1967) suggests that the way individuals bring order to, or make sense of, their social world is through a psychological process, which he calls 'the documentary method'. This method firstly consists of selecting certain facts from a social situation that seem to conform to a pattern and then making sense of these facts in terms of the pattern. Once the pattern has been established, it can be used as a framework for interpreting new facts which arise within the situation. In the documentary method, context plays a vital role as people make sense of occurrences in the social world by reference to the context in which the occurrence appears: participants index an occurrence to its particular circumstances. Garfinkel argued that people constantly make use of the documentary method in their daily lives to create a 'taken-for-granted' understanding of the social world which they feel they 'know' and in which they can be 'at home'. They perceive the social world through a series of patterns they have built up for making sense of and coping with the variety of situations that they encounter in their lives.

This taken-for-granted nature of understandings of the social world implies that social knowledge is implicit and for this reason understandings of social knowledge cannot be elicited (Duranti, 1997). Instead, social organization can only be understood by examining actual instances of social interaction. In each instance of social interaction, members need to make available to others their understanding of the activities in which they are engaged and participants routinely monitor each other to confirm and test shared understandings of the activity as it unfolds. For this reason, in studying social interaction, ethnomethodology tends to ignore the information actually transmitted during interaction, concentrating more on how the interaction was performed. This is because the stance of ethnomethodology suggests that all meanings are, and can only ever be, subjective and that the only objective social reality, and therefore the only thing worth studying, is the reality of commonly understood methods of communication.

The emphasis on studying actual instances of social interaction is further developed in the work of Erving Goffman (1959, 1963, 1967, 1969, 1971, 1981), who asserted that the ordinary activities of daily life were an important subject for study. Goffman's work demonstrated that it was possible to study everyday events and situations and to discover from these non-trivial information about how human beings engage in sociality. He was able to show how matters of great social significance could be found in everyday activities. Goffman's approach to research was a qualitative one in which description and analysis were the primary tools for developing an understanding of social processes and this contrasted with much of the prevailing work in sociology and social psychology which favoured more quantitative approaches based on hypothesis testing. Goffman (1964) in particular drew attention to the need to study ordinary instances of speaking, which had in his view been neglected. He argued that:

> Talk is socially organized, not merely in terms of who speaks to whom in what language, but as a little system of mutually ratified and ritually governed face-to-face action, a social encounter.
>
> (Goffman, 1964: 65)

He argued that the study of speaking was not simply a matter of narrowly focused linguistic descriptions of language, but rather that interaction had its own system of rules and structures which were not intrinsically linguistic in nature. This means that the study of language in purely linguistic terms could not adequately account for the nature of language-in-use.

The work of Garfinkel and Goffman provided an impetus for the development of conversation analysis by establishing a concern for investigating the orderliness of everyday life and these were taken up by Harvey Sacks in his lectures on conversation from the early 1960s (Sacks, 1992). In these lectures, Sacks developed an approach to the study of social action which sought to investigate social order as it was produced through the practices of everyday talk. By the late 1960s and early 1970s, through the work of Harvey Sacks and his colleagues Emmanuel A. Schegloff and Gail Jefferson, conversation analysis began to emerge from sociology as an independent area of enquiry oriented towards understanding the organizational structure of talk which has influenced a number of the social science disciplines concerned with human communication (Lerner, 2004). Conversation analysis drew from ethnomethodology a concern for understanding how order was achieved in social interaction, and empirically based methodology based on micro-analytic studies (Clayman and Maynard, 1995).

Sacks' approach to the study of conversation is characterized by a view of talk as activity through which speakers accomplish things in interaction. Talk can, therefore, be strategically employed to achieve communicative goals. For Sacks, this strategic use of talk is not a set of rules or recipes by which actions are accomplished, but rather the production of interactional effects which are achieved through the use of talk in a particular context (Schegloff, 1992a). For Sacks, conversation was orderly and this order was manifested at all points (Sacks,

1992a). The orderly nature of talk results from the recognizable achievement of the same outcome through similar methods in similar contexts. Conversation then is realized through sets of practices which speakers can deploy in order to undertake particular actions in particular contexts and which will be recognized as achieving the appropriate action by other participants.

The core assumptions of conversation analysis are (cf. Psathas, 1995)

1. *Order is produced orderliness.* That is, order does not occur of its own accord nor does it pre-exist the interaction, but is rather the result of the coordinated practices of the participants who achieve orderliness and then interact.

2. *Order is produced, situated and occasioned.* That is, order is produced by the participants themselves for the conversation in which it occurs. The participants themselves orient to the order being produced and their behaviour reflects and indexes that order. This means that in analysing conversation as an academic activity, orderliness being documented is not externally imposed by the analyst, but internally accomplished by the participants. This observed order is not the result of a pre-formed conception of what should happen, nor is it a probabilistic generalization about frequencies.

3. *Order is repeatable and recurrent.* The patterns of orderliness found in conversation are repeated, not only in the talk of an individual speaker, but across groups of speakers. The achieved order is therefore the result of a shared understanding of the methods by which order is achievable.

These three formulations make it clear that conversation analysis assumes that there is overwhelming order in conversation. Conversation is neither random nor unstructured; however, the order observable in conversation does not imply an overarching uniformity in conversational structure which is generalizable across conversations (Wooffitt, 2005). Instead, the participants themselves construct conversations in orderly ways.

A key idea in conversation analysis is the notion of recipient design, which Sacks, Schegloff and Jefferson (1974) characterize as the most general principle of conversational interaction. Recipient design refers to the idea that participants in talk design their talk in such a way as to be understood by an interlocutor, in terms of the knowledge that participants assume they share (Sacks and Schegloff, 1979; Schegloff, 1972). This means that conversational contributions are designed with a recipient in mind and are designed as appropriate for that recipient. Recipient design is not simply a resource which speakers use to design talk, it is also a resource listeners can use in interpreting talk, as listeners are motivated to hear a turn that is designed for them, and participants track the trajectory of the talk to hear a turn if a turn is designed for them (Boden, 1994). This means that recipient design is a highly salient feature of talk and the organization of talk, and therefore one aspect of the produced orderliness of conversation. The task of the analyst is to discover and describe the produced orderliness which is created by conversationalists during conversation. Such an analysis allows the machinery of conversation to become visible, and it is the purpose of this book to describe this machinery of conversation – the sets of procedures which participants in conversation deploy in order to achieve orderly and ordered social interaction.

Conversation analysis, as the name of an approach to studying talk in interaction, is in some ways a misnomer for the approach, as the focus of conversation analysis is actually much larger than conversation as it is usually understood. In fact, while much work in conversation analysis has examined informal talk in everyday social settings, there is a growing body of work which has applied the same methodological and theoretical tools to talk in institutional contexts (see for example, Drew and Heritage, 1992; Drew and Sorjonen, 1997; Heritage, 1998, 2004). Conversation analysts do not see an inherent distinction between the formal and the informal, the everyday and the institutional; rather they see talk in interaction as a social process which is deployed to realize and understand the social situations in which talk is used. As Schegloff argues (1992b: 1296), 'talk-in-interaction is a primordial site of sociality on the one hand and, on the other hand, one of the (largely presupposed) preconditions for, and achievements of, organized life'. Conversation analysis therefore legitimately investigates all areas of socially motivated talk.

Conversation analysis as an approach to studying interaction

Conversation analysis studies the organization and orderliness of social interaction. In order to do this, it begins with an assumption that the conduct, including talk, of everyday life is produced as sensible and meaningful.

> The central goal of conversation analytic research is the description and explication of the competences that ordinary speakers use and rely on in participating in intelligible socially organized interaction. At its most

basic, this objective is one of describing the procedures by which conversationalists produce their own behaviour and understand that of
others.

(Heritage, 1984b: 1)

A fundamental assumption of such a programme of research is that
in engaging in talk, participants are engaging in socially organized
interaction. Human talk is a form of action, and is understood as action
by participants in the interaction. This talk is presented and understood as meaningful because participants share the same procedures
for designing and interpreting talk. Conversation analysis seeks to
understand these shared procedures which participants in an interaction use to produce and recognize meaningful action.

Action is meaningful only in context and context is seen as playing
two primary roles in interaction. Heritage (1984b) refers to this as the
context-shaped and the context-renewing significance of a speaker's
contribution. Talk is context-shaped in that talk responds to the context in which it is created. What participants say is shaped by and for
the context in which it occurs and each next bit of talk is understood in
the light of what has preceded it. This contextualization is an important procedure for understanding conversational contributions. At the
same time talk is context-renewing because talk shapes the context as
each next bit of talk constrains and affects what follows and influences
how further talk will be heard and understood. Each turn at talk is the
response to some previous talk and, by its utterance, provides a context
in which the next turn at talk will be heard. Context is, therefore,
dynamic and is renewed at each point in the talk. Conversationalists
design their talk to demonstrate the sense they have made of the
preceding talk and display, through the construction of their talk, their
understanding of the talk-so-far. Turns at talk are, therefore, publicly
available displays of understanding which allow for 'shared understandings' to be created and ratified (C. Goodwin and Goodwin, 1992).

While context is therefore vitally relevant to interaction, it is necessary to be cautious about what can legitimately be invoked as relevant
context. Schegloff (1992a) has indicated that context can be considered in two different ways. Context may be external to the interaction itself; this includes context in the form of social categories, social
relationships and institutional and cultural settings. The second is
internal to the interaction and is created by participants through their
talk. The core issue in thinking about context in these terms is the
extent to which aspects of context are relevant to the participants in
the interaction as they interact with each other. Schegloff (1992a)

argues that not all potentially knowable aspects of external context can be taken as being equally potentially relevant at any point in the interaction and, as such, the test of the analyst is to determine, on the basis of the interaction itself, which elements of context are displayed as relevant and consequential to the participants themselves. This means that context needs to be seen more as something which is invoked in interaction, rather than something which impacts on interaction.

Conversation analysis and method

The underlying assumptions of conversation analysis discussed so far have implications for the ways in which analysts work to develop accounts of language as social action. Firstly, the data for study must be actual talk occurring in actual contexts (Heritage, 1995). Conversation analysis is analysis of real-world, situated, contextualized talk. As conversational order is achieved order and the achievement is done through the deployment of practices in particular contexts, only naturally occurring instances of actual talk can provide the information necessary for developing an account of what occurs in talk. The use of actual instances of talk allows for the possibility of an examination of what speakers actually do when speaking, rather than producing an account of what speakers think they do (for example, as the result of introspection about language use). Conversation analysis uses a specimen approach in which each data segment used for developing an account of conversational behaviour is not a statement about reality but rather a part of the reality being studied (ten Have, 1999). As an empirical discipline, conversation analysis allows order to emerge from the data without an intervening layer of theoretical constructs and allows for the determination of the organizing principles that are used and oriented to by the speakers themselves.

Moreover, because talk is seen as organized and orderly and because this order is understood as constructed in a particular context for a particular conversation, conversation analysts work with recordings of spontaneously occurring talk. Recordings allow the talk to be subjected to multiple examinations and these allow details which may have been ignored or set aside to be taken up in later analyses.

Video and tape recordings are much richer sources of conversational data than other ways of capturing interaction (Heritage, 1984b, 1995). For example, note-taking and recall all necessarily involve some editing of the data, as not all of the minute details which are available to participants can be represented or recalled. Any attempt to construct a written version of a conversation will therefore obscure much of what made the conversation meaningful and orderly for the participants themselves. In fact, even the production of a written transcription based on recorded data involves some loss of detail and for conversation analysis the recording of the actual instance of interaction always remains the primary data. Pomerantz and Fehr (1997: 70) state that 'Conversation analysts strongly prefer to work from recordings of conduct' and argue that the advantages of recording are that it allows for the possibility of playing and replaying the interaction both for transcribing and developing an analysis, permits rechecking of the analysis against full detailed material and makes it possible to return to the data with new interests.

Using spontaneous data as a starting point, conversation analysis tends to proceed using 'unmotivated looking'; that is, repeated listenings to the same data in order to discover what is happening (Hopper, 1988; Psathas, 1995). Psathas (1990) notes that unmotivated looking involves the analyst being open to discovering what is going on in the data, rather than searching for a particular pre-identified or pre-theorized phenomenon. Unmotivated looking allows for noticing of an action being done in the talk and of the procedures through which the action is accomplished in the talk (Schegloff, 1996a). Schegloff (1996a: 172–3) argues that an account of action should be characterized by three methodological elements:

1. a formulation of the action being accomplished in the data, accompanied by exemplifications of the action from data and discussion of deviant cases as exemplifications of the underlying formulation being proposed;
2. a grounding of the formulation in the reality of the participants in order to demonstrate that the observation is not a construct of the analyst alone, but is understood and oriented to by the participants themselves;
3. an explication or analysis of how the practice observed yields the action being accomplished.

These requirements impose a high level of rigour on unmotivated looking and prevent conversation analytic accounts from becoming unstructured. This means that the starting point for analysis is open, but the procedures required once something has been noticed are highly rigorous. Once a phenomenon has been noticed, there are differing possibilities for exploring the phenomenon in order to construct an account. This may be done by exploring a single-case example or by establishing a collection of similar actions.

Single-case analysis involves looking at a conversation, or a segment of a conversation, in order to track in detail the various devices and strategies used by participants to accomplish a particular action (Schegloff, 1987a, 1988b). The analysis of a single case is in effect the starting point for any analysis, as single-case examples allow the analyst to examine how conversational practices operate in particular instances and allow for a description of these practices to begin. It allows the analyst to examine how an instance of conversation is orderly for its participants (Schegloff, 1968). As all conversational interaction is orderly and as each instance of conversation is a produced order which is achieved by particular participants in a particular conversation, each single conversation is the place in which order is produced. A single case of talk is a single case of achieved orderly interaction, which can be examined as such and which can reveal much about the procedures used to create this order. This means that the single case is derived from and manifests the competency that members have to produce orderly talk.

> That this particular social action occurred is evidence that the machinery for its production is culturally available, involves members' competencies, and is therefore possibly (and probably) reproducible.
>
> (Psathas, 1995: 50)

Any single case of orderly interaction is therefore an indication of the nature of members' competencies involved in creating order. As such, a single case is not like a sample drawn from a pre-existing collection of such cases and representative of those cases, but rather an entire, self-contained instance of produced order.

As the conversation analytic approach is concerned with identifying patterns of action, identifying instances of action through unmotivated looking and then moving to establishing collections of similar actions is an effective way of examining regularly occurring patterns. A collection can only proceed from a single-case analysis, as such an analysis is required to determine what a particular action is an instance of (Psathas, 1995). A collection is, therefore, a possible next step in analysis rather than an alternative analytic approach. Once a collection has been assembled it can be used to test the robustness of a particular description of action and to refine the analysis in the light of repeated instances of an action in different instances of interaction. The analysis of a collection allows the regularly occurring procedures for accomplishing a particular type of action to become clear and allows for differing trajectories for the accomplishment of the action to be seen.

When working with a collection of actions, it becomes necessary to consider how to quantify the results: is something frequent or infrequent in the data? In conversation analysis quantification is usually expressed by adjectival means (*commonly, overwhelmingly, regularly, typically, etc.*) rather than numerically, as totals, frequency counts or percentages (Schegloff, 1993). While it may seem useful to be able to provide a numerical quantity, the quantification of results is highly problematic in conversation analysis because of the nature of the instances being counted (Heritage, 1995). The collections used by conversation analysts are instances of highly contextualized talk and the collection allows for the possibility of examining in a systematic way patterns as they occur across differing contexts and with differing participants. This means that while there may be patterns which span contexts and participants, each context is unique: a collection is a collection of single instances rather than multiple examples of the same thing (Schegloff, 1993). The study of collections is therefore the study of multiple single-case examples, in which each next case demonstrates the systematic commonalities which exist across participants and contexts.

The analytical approach discussed here is an inductive one (ten Have, 1991; Heritage, 1988) which seeks to build an understanding of regularities in the way talk is organized from the study of actual instances of interaction. The analyst, however, does not stop at a description of regularities, but rather is required to show that regularities are methodically produced and oriented to by participants (Heritage, 1988). Regularities in conversation are then viewed as normative in that they affect the behaviour of participants in the interaction and participants display an orientation to regular procedures as the taken-for-granted orderliness of the social world. Of particular interest in the study of collections is the study of 'deviant' cases. In a conversation analytic perspective, deviant cases are not viewed as exceptions, but rather as indications of orderliness which have not yet been accounted for by the description (Schegloff, 1968). Any description of a regular pattern should be able to account for behaviours which do not conform to the normal course of action and these accounts should demonstrate how the deviant case is in some way orienting to the normal course of action. If an instance of interaction is a departure from an expected process then it needs to be shown how the participants in the interaction orient to the departure (Heritage,

1988). Deviant cases which do not appear to fit an analytic description are taken as evidence that the account is not yet maximally generalizable rather than being in some sense a deviant or defective instance.

Conclusion

Since conversation analysis was first developed in the 1960s, a coherent body of knowledge has emerged about the ways in which conversation is structured. This body of knowledge has been developed on the basis of a distinctive methodology which is based on the study of actually occurring examples of human interaction. One important part of this method is the written representation of spoken language in the form of transcripts, and this issue will be taken up in the next chapter. Understanding transcription is an important step to understanding the body of findings in conversation analysis because it gives an indication of what is considered by analysts in their study of talk.

The book then turns to an examination of the methods which participants in interaction regularly use to structure their talk. This examination is an account of the basic machinery of talk through which talk is designed and recognized as orderly. This basic machinery covers three broad areas of conversational organization. The first of these is how turns at talk are structured and managed by participants (Chapters 3 and 4). The second is the ways in which turns at talk are organized into conversation as sequences, and how basic sequences can be expanded to produce larger, coherent units of conversational action (Chapters 5 and 6). The third basic dimension of the machinery for producing orderly talk is the repair system which deals with breakdowns in the application of the machinery (Chapter 7). Once these three sets of processes have been discussed, the book will turn to investigate three areas of conversational difficulty – opening a conversation, closing a conversation and telling a story – and examine the mechanisms by which these difficulties are addressed.

2 Transcribing Conversation

The basic data for conversation analysis is naturally occurring talk. If such talk is to be used for detailed analysis it must first be recorded and then transcribed. However, transcripts of talk are only ever partial representations of the talk they record but they allow the analyst to see the transient and complex nature of talk captured in an easily usable, static format. This means that transcriptions are not substitutes for the original recordings but additional tools which can be used to help analyse and understand these recordings (Heritage, 1984b; Psathas and Anderson, 1990).

Transcripts however are not neutral and objective representations of talk. As Green, Franquiz and Dixon (1997: 172) note, a 'transcript is a text that "re"-presents an event; it is not the event itself. Following this logic, what is re-presented is data constructed by a researcher for a particular purpose, not just talk written down.' Transcripts are in every case subjective representations of the talk in which the transcriber has made decisions about what features of talk to include or exclude from the transcription. These decisions in turn have an influence on how the researcher perceives the structure of the interaction by making some features of the interaction more visible while obscuring others (Ochs, 1979). The subjective and created nature of transcriptions means that researchers may need to produce different transcriptions at different times in order to examine different aspects of the talk being transcribed and to see the talk according to evolving sets of ideas and foci. Mishler (1991), for example, demonstrates how the same inter-action can be transcribed differently for different purposes even by the same researcher.

Transcription is not a once-for-all-time representation of talk but rather an open-ended process in which the transcript changes as the researcher's insights into the talk are refined from ongoing analysis (Ehlich and Switala, 1976; Gumperz and Berenz, 1993). For these reasons, researchers in conversation analysis frequently retranscribe their data in order to see and hear different nuances in the interaction. Transcriptions, then, while indispensable for conversation analytic research, are only ever secondary data representing the primary data of the recorded interaction. They are used alongside recordings and are constantly updated as the result of repeated listening. Transcription then is not simply a representation of talk, but an analytic tool which helps the researcher to notice features of the talk being transcribed and to attend to detailed aspects of talk which may not be apparent outside the act of transcription (Heath and Luff, 1993).

In conversation analysis no level of detail is considered *a priori* to be irrelevant for the understanding of talk in interaction and this means that transcription is much more than the recording of the words produced by participants in interaction. In addition to knowing *what* has been said, the conversation analyst also needs to know many aspects of *how* it was said (ten Have, 1999). However, the need for detail in a transcription is also a potential problem (Cook, 1990). In transcribing talk, the transcriber needs to balance two considerations: (1) the high level of detail found in the talk itself and (2) the accessibility of the transcript to a range of potential audiences. The latter consideration means that the system should not have too many symbols which are unfamiliar to speakers of the language and which require a large amount of specialized knowledge in order to be useful (Heritage, 1984b). A transcript which is accessible to a range of readers provides a way of communicating (partial) information about the talk being studied in a written analysis of the talk.

In conversation analysis it is usual to use the transcription system which was first developed by Gail Jefferson (1985, 2004) for early work in conversation analysis and described for example in early works such as Sacks, Schegloff and Jefferson (1974). This transcription system is well suited to detailed analysis of talk and it has proved to be both a robust and a useful tool for understanding the ways in which language is used in social interaction.

Information external to the talk

In addition to a representation of the talk itself, it is important that a transcript also provides information about the circumstances in which the recording was produced. This information includes the time, date and place of the recording and identification of the participants (ten Have, 1999; Psathas and Anderson, 1990). In conversation analytic transcripts, the identification of participants is in some ways problematic. In most cases, participants in interaction are indicated by a name, as in extract (1) or a letter, as in extract (2).

(1) [Car Conversation]

```
Nick:    on-[which] day' s your anniversary?
Elvis:       [yeah?]
Sasha:   sixth. June.
Nick:    the sixth.
Elvis:   yeah,
```

(2) [UTCL J66.3 (Drummond, 1989)]

```
X:       Is that who we use to do those dividers
Y:       Yeah.
         (0.9)
Y:       [ and she ] said it took- they didn' t do- (.)
X:       [ Well    ]
Y:       very good proof reading or anything
```

In everyday interaction, such names or letters are usually adequate in conversation analysis for transcribing everyday interaction, in which the membership categories of the participants are only relevant to the extent to which they appear in the interaction as it unfolds (Psathas and Anderson, 1990). Naming participants is, however, potentially problematic for ethical reasons, as participants may be identifiable from the talk in the transcript. For this reason, transcripts often use pseudonyms to identify participants. Choosing a pseudonym can be difficult as the phonetic shape of the word allows for different possibilities in interaction. For example, consonants such as *l*, *m*, *s*, etc., can be lengthened readily whereas other consonants such as *p*, *t*, *k* are less easily lengthened. So for example, if an original interaction involves an articulation like:

(3) [UMN: 01:9:6]

```
H:       His name' s uh Ph:::ill:::.
```

where the : symbol indicates lengthening of the previous sound. This will be hard to capture with a pseudonym like *Pete*, as the transcription:

(3') [UMN: 01:9:6]

```
H:       His name' s uh P:::et:::e.
```

would indicate a very odd articulation as the stop *t* cannot be lengthened in the same way an *l* can. Similarly, sometimes conversationalists make word plays on names that may not be apparent when a pseudonym is used to replace the original form.

In institutional talk in which the membership categories to which participants belong are interactionally important, it is common to identify participants by their membership category, as in the following extract from a study of interaction in a small claims court.

```
(4) [Flooded council flat (Pomerantz, 1987)]
    Adj:      how if I can just ask you please one or two
              points in clari[fication
    Pla:                     [Sure. Yes that's what
              w[e' re here for
    Adj:       [of the issue:[s
    Pla:                     [Yes,
```

Here *Adj* stands for adjudicator and *Pla* stands for plaintiff and they encode the roles that the two have in the interaction under way. This transcript treats the identities of the participants in terms of who they are in the court, not who they are in more general terms. Moreover, unlike names, these terms do not indicate aspects of identity such as gender and so they privilege one (institutional) identity over other possible and possibly relevant identities. Watson (1997), in his critique of transcription of medical interactions, has argued that labelling participants according to such categories constrains readers to understand talk as being produced by 'doctors' or 'patients' without having established that such a categorization is warranted in the interaction. Ten Have (1999), however, argues that using names rather than categories for representing the participants is artificial given that the institutional identities of each is known to the other during the interaction. At the same time, labelling a doctor and patient using names (*John, Mary, Ms Smith*) also indexes a social identity which may not be relevant or appropriate to the interaction. The choice of an identifying form is not a neutral matter, but rather one in which the transcript must be seen as a constructed representation and choices convey connotations. Ten Have, therefore, notes that even the coding of elements external to the talk itself has analytic consequences and that these should be considered by the transcriber in the act of transcription.

A further problem for identifying speakers when using taped interactions is that it may not always be possible to determine who said something during the interaction. Where this is the case, a question mark is used to indicate the uncertainty, either with a name to indicate that the identity of the speaker is uncertain (5), or without to indicate that the speaker is unknown (6).

```
(5) [Lunch]
    Joy:       [ an' he was saying that he jus' didn' wanna
               go.
    Hal?:      [ °when?°]

(6) [Lunch]
    ?:         hhh.
```

Transcribing words

The first step in developing a transcription is to capture the words that the participants are saying (Psathas and Anderson, 1990). Writing down these words raises the question of how such words are to be represented in a written form. Languages usually have a standard orthography; that is, a set of established conventions for representing the words of a language and this standard orthography represents one way of writing the words spoken in the transcription. The standard orthography has the advantage that it is known to (literate) speakers of the language and, therefore, is easily understandable by non-specialist readers of the transcript. However, a standard orthography is not a neutral representation of the language but rather it contains a partial theory of the sounds and units of the language (Duranti, 1997) and is based on a particular variety of the language – the notional standard language (Liddicoat, 2005). This means that a transcript written in the standard orthography makes some pre-specified decisions about the boundaries of words and the pronunciation of the sounds in those words. For example the sentence:

(7) Why don't you take a break?

indicates a sequence of six identifiable words and attaches sound values to those words. Languages, however, do not typically have one simple pronunciation which is invariable for all speakers and in all situations and the question of what constitutes a word and what sounds are found in a word vary with geography and social context. A standard orthography cannot capture the variation in the ways in which things are said. In actual conversation, then, the sentence in (7) may be pronounced very differently from the way the standard orthography expects, and may be better rendered as something like:

(8) Whyncha take a break?

in which the first element is pronounced more or less as a single unit. Example (7) can be considered an idealization of language which is useful for communication across regions and social contexts, but (8) is a more accurate representation of what a speaker actually says in a particular context. Similar issues occur for dialect differences, whether regional or social, and the same standard orthography may represent widely varying pronunciations of the word, which may be relevant to understanding what happens in a conversation. There is therefore a tension between standard orthography, which promotes the readability of transcript and the actual words which are spoken in a particular way in a particular conversation. In order to be as faithful as possible to the words as spoken, many transcribers try to capture a close representation of what is said by modifying the spelling away from the standard version in order to be a more accurate representation of what is said.

Modifying spelling, however, is not without problems. Standard orthography, like any aspect of a standardized language tends to be viewed as the 'right' way to do things in the language and deviations from this may be stigmatized as sloppy, or undedicated or as negatively marked in other ways (Duranti, 1997; Jefferson, 1983; Liddicoat, 2005). The transcriber then has to face the issue when making a transcription of how to find a balance between representing speech accurately, representing it readably and representing it in a way which does not inappropriately stigmatize the speakers. The end result in the transcription is a choice between a range of possibilities:

1. Using standard orthography only and ignoring spoken language characteristics found in the speech. This means representing spoken language in a written language form and could possibly mean that features of talk which are interactionally salient are not included in the transcript. Such a transcript would usually depart too far from the actual spoken form to be useful for conversation analysis.

2. Using standard orthography for most of the transcript but using modified spelling where the spoken language is noticeably different from what is presented by the standard orthography. This means making a decision about whether a word or phrase should be represented using standard orthography or using a modified spelling. However, as the difference between standard written forms of language and non-standard or spoken forms is actually a continuum, it may be difficult to decide exactly what to modify

when transcribing a particular piece of talk. The result may be that there is a great deal of variation within the transcript and that the variation in writing does not always reflect the variation in the talk itself.

3. Using modified orthography throughout the transcript as consistently as possible to reflect actual use. This is a very good approach for the researcher, as it helps to promote noticing of the language features in the interaction and requires the transcriber to make careful decisions in representing the spoken language. However, such transcriptions can be very difficult for readers who have not been trained in transcription.

In the end, decisions about how to transcribe are subjective and are influenced by how the transcriber him/herself hears the talk and this is in part influenced by the transcriber's own starting position. For example, it is not uncommon to see words such as *ever* or *part* transcribed as *evuh* or *paht* by American transcribers who normally pronounce the post-vocalic *r* in these words and perceive it as missing in the pronunciation of English speakers who use varieties without these *r*s. However, for a speaker of British or other *r*-less varieties, the omission of the *r* would probably not be noticed and the words could be transcribed using the standard orthography. In the end, a transcriber has to decide on an approach which best suits his/her needs and audience, to make principled decisions about how far to modify the transcript and to use these decisions consistently in transcribing.

Transcribing prosody

The words of a language are spoken with stress, intonation and differences in volume and length of sounds which are interactionally important. For example, intonation can distinguish between questions and statements. Consider the difference between the ways in which the following sentences would be said:

(9) You have a pen?
    You have a pen.

Here the intonation contour is the primary aspect of the delivery of these sentences which marks their function in talk. In conventional English orthography, this difference in function is marked by punctuation. In a similar way, stress can be communicatively important, as it may be used for contrast or emphasis. Consider the differences in meaning which come when stressing different words in the sentence:

(10) He told me it was you.

In conventional orthography, stress is marked by underlining the stressed part of the word, or by writing it in italics. For example,

(11) He told me it was you.

shows a stress on the verb *told*.

When transcribing stress, there is a need to consider how much detail to use in the transcription. For example, English has both word stress and sentence stress. This means that in most English words there is a stressed syllable, while, in longer utterances, one or more words may have a greater stress than other words in the utterance. Most transcribers of English mark sentence stress but not word stress, as word stress is a predictable feature of English words. Other transcribers note sentence stress only when it deviates from the 'expected' stress in English – that is when a word which would not normally be stressed is stressed or where the stress is stronger than would be expected. As with modifying spelling, decisions about how to transcribe stress will depend on the individual transcriber, but it is important that the decisions taken help the reader to understand what is happening in the transcription.

When transcribing prosody, the usual conventions available to written languages are not adequate or useful for representing what happens in speech. Punctuation, for example, tends to show more about the function of a sentence than pronunciations. For example, both (12) and (12') are written with a question mark, but the intonation is different in each. For most English speakers, in (12) the intonation contour falls, while in (12') it rises.

(12) What did he do?
(12') You have a pen?

It is therefore necessary to develop specialized conventions to represent actual speech in transcripts. In the Jefferson system, many of the features for transcribing prosody are, in fact, punctuation symbols, but used in different ways. For example, length is shown by inserting a colon after the lengthened sound as in:

(13) [Sal 99:3:4:2]
```
Sal:      Yea:h,
Sue:      Yeah.
```

Here Sal's *yea:h* is said with a longer vowel and this sound is hearably longer than Sue's following *yeah*. When a sound is exceptionally long, more than one colon can be used. In extract (14), Elvis speaks both of the words with additional lengthening, while in (15), Ben's articulation of *to:* is lengthened, while that of *the:::* is very long, the additional colons showing that it is about twice as long as the sound in *to:*.

(14) [Car Conversation]
```
Elvis:    o:[:h no::.
```

(15) [AB:01:17]
```
Ben:      an so we wen' to: the::: La Paella restaurant
```

Punctuation symbols are also used to show intonation. In extract (9) above, the two utterances were distinguished by the intonation used. The first is said with a rising intonation, which marks it as a question, and the second with a falling intonation, which marks it as a statement. In the Jefferson transcription system, punctuation symbols are used to mark the intonation contours of talk:

.   a full stop marks a falling intonation.
?   a question mark marks a rising intonation.
,   a comma marks a slightly rising intonation, but is also used when the intonation contour is hearably incomplete, although this may sometimes be used for a level contour or even a slight fall. The basic hearing here is of an incomplete intonation contour.
¿   an upside-down question mark is used for intonation which rises more than a slight rise (,) but is not as sharp a rise or does not reach as high a pitch as for a question mark.

These symbols are used to represent the way the pitch of the talk varies over the turn and are not used in the same way as punctuation which shows the function that an utterance has. For example:

(16) [Car conversation]
```
Nick:                         [ how's it taste man,
Elvis:    it's tastes alri:ght ma:n.
```

In this extract, Nick's turn is a question, but uses a comma to show that there is a slightly rising intonation at the end of the turn, while in (17) Sasha's turn is a question, but has a full stop to indicate a falling intonation.

```
(17) [Car conversation]
     Sasha:    an all- did he tell yuh about his problems
               with his wife an [ that.
```

When the intonation contour becomes more complex, the Jefferson transcription system uses a combination of intonation symbols, lengthening and underlining to represent the intonation. Example (18) shows a rise-fall contour, in which the pitch rises a little before ending as a fall. The underlining of the letter preceding the colon (showing a lengthened sound) indicates the rise, while the fall is indicated by the final full stop.

```
(18) [Keep: 98:6:8]
]
     J:        Hello:.
```

If, however, the colon is underlined this shows a fall-rise intonation where the underlined element is at a slightly lower pitch than the rest of the final part of the contour.

```
(19) [JLK: 98:1:11]
     K:        It's whe:re,
```

These features are used to show the general relatively smooth intonation contour over a segment of talk, however sometimes there may be a sudden shift upwards or downwards in pitch which is very marked within the general intonation contour. To transcribe a rise in pitch, an upwards arrow as in (20) is placed just before the pitch shift.

```
(20) [May and Jo]
     Jo:       What have you got- ↑oh-. more tomatoes,
               ↑lovely. that's ↑grea:t.
```

Here Jo resets her pitch much higher three times in the course of her turn at *oh-*, at *lovely* and at *grea:t*. For a fall in pitch a downwards arrow is placed just before the shift, as in (21).

(21) [Lunch]
```
     Harry:    So I's sorta like ↓euh here we go again.
```

In this case, Harry's groan *euh* is shown to begin at a much lower pitch than the preceding talk.

Sometimes for a very exaggerated intonation a combination of a number of arrows may be used to capture the effect, as in

(22) [(Liddicoat, 1997)]
```
     M:          and did you learn English in: (.) ↑Po↓la↑nd?
```

In this extract M is speaking with a learner of English and the arrows are an attempt to capture a very marked sing-song intonation on the word *Poland*.

The volume of talk is very important to conveying aspects of meaning and import. Talk which is markedly louder than the other talk is shown by capital letters, as in extract (23), where Sasha's *ten dollars a da:y* is said very loudly.

(23) [Car conversation]
```
     Nick:    [We've] been budgeting big time we're
              [like  li ] vin' on ten dollars a day=
     ?:       [ ((cough))]
     Nick:    = sorta shit,
     Elvis:   Yea:[:h
     Sasha:        [TEN DOLLARS A DA:[Y.
     Nick:                           [Yea:h.=
```

Quiet talk is shown by degree signs (°) before and after the segment of talk which is quieter or whispered. For example, extract (24) shows that May's *I think this is it¿* is said more quietly than the talk which precedes and follows it.

(24) [May and Jo]
```
     May:     uh (1.2) °I think this is it¿° she's going
              (.5) (wa-) see where that dark (.) is¿
     Jo:      right¿
```

Where the talk is very soft, two (or even more) degree signs may be used. In extract (25), the transcript shows the talk becoming quieter over series of turns.

(25) [JSK:11:8ii]
```
     Dora:    We'll i's a pity.
```

```
Helen:    °Yeah°
Dora:     °°yyhhh .h°°
          (0.3)
```

Talk may also be noticeably faster or slower than the surrounding talk. Talk which is noticeably faster than surrounding talk is transcribed as >words<, as in (26).

(26) [May and Jo]
```
    May:       and then h uh I think h uh >I don' t know how
               they get from Sydney to the other place,
               [ but then it' ll be a bus.<
    Jo:        [ °right.°
```

Talk which is noticeably slower is transcribed as <words>, as in (27).

(27) [Lunch]
```
    Joy:       ' n then I could' n help myself. I' d told her
               o:ver and o::ver and <she just didn' t [ get
               it.>
```

In addition to these features of talk aspects of voice quality may also be relevant for the transcript, in particular breathiness and creak. Breathy speech is transcribed by inserting an *h* in the transcription of the word which is spoken with breathy voice, as in the word *say* in extract (28).

(28) [Lunch]
```
    Joy:       An' then wha' did sa:hy.
```

Creaky voice is marked with an asterisk before and after the words pronounced with creak, as in Elvis' turn in (29).

(29) [Car conversation]
```
    Sasha:    I was [ gu[nna say yuh poor thing hh.=
    Nick:          [ ye[s::
    Elvis:             [*ohh yeah*
    Sasha:    =I mean Ron' s a ni[ce-
```

Transcribing other speech sounds

Not all of the sounds a speaker uses are necessarily recognized as normal speech sounds in the language being transcribed or may not be considered as 'words' in the language. These sounds include a range of vocalizations as well as the sounds of breathing and laughter, which all play a role in the talk being produced and need to be included in the transcript. These vocalizations include sounds that are made by listeners to indicate they are listening such as *mhm* or *mm*, sounds used for word searches such as *uhm* or *uh* or clicking sounds, which are found as phonemes in some languages, but are not used in words in others. When representing these sounds there is usually no standard orthography and the transcriber needs to represent these sounds in a way which conveys the sound being depicted as accurately as possible for a reader. It is particularly important to show the approximate sound and the syllable-like parts which make up the vocalization. For example, the form *mhm* represents a sound that has two beats/syllables while the form *mm* represents a long *m* sound. These two sounds can have quite different meanings in conversation (Gardner, 2001). Similarly it is important to be able to distinguish between *uh huh* which has a yes-like meaning and *uh-uh* which has a no-like meaning.

For click sounds, forms such as *t!* or *tch* are used for dental clicks while *pt* or *p!* can be used for bilabial clicks.

(30) [Ma:11 (Rendle-Short, 2003)]
```
    Ma:     t! and that' ll be helpful of course, as a
            computer scientist,
```

Audible breathing can be interactionally very important and needs to be included in transcription along with speech sounds. Out-breathing is indicated by *h*'s, with the number of *h*'s indicating the duration of the breathing.

(31) [Car conversation]
```
    Elvis:  I know the:: di:lemma hh. (1.0) ged up an
            scrub concrete huh [ heh
```

In-breathing is shown by a dot before the *h* as in

(32) [May and Jo]
```
    Jo:     .hh see you later then.
    May:    °yeah. (tha[nks.)°
    Jo:                [bye.
```

Another feature that is interactionally important is incomplete speech. Where a sound is cut off abruptly this is indicated by a dash.

(33) [Car conversation]
```
Sasha:    o:h. we saw some briyant ones recently, like
          um (1.0) oh what was that one about- (0.4)
          like Double In- (.) Indemnity= n like lots
          of movies from the thirties that ha- had
          amazing plot lines?
```

Here Sasha abruptly cuts off her talk on *about-*, at *Double In-* and again at *ha-*. The dash can also be used to indicate a glottal stop.

Sometimes a sound may be difficult to represent in orthography and may need to be described in the transcript. The common way to indicate a described sound is to place the description in double brackets, as in the cough in extract (34).

(34) [Car conversation]
```
Nick:     shoulda done that ages a[go.
Elvis:                            [ah that w' s cool
Sasha:    ((cough))
```

The use of the double brackets here shows that the cough is described, not transcribed. Such descriptions have also been used for other aspects of interaction, such as ((laughter)), ((crying)) or ((applause)), however in many cases descriptions can be shown to lack adequate information for understanding the phenomenon they are trying to capture. The transcription of laughter, for example, is quite complex (Jefferson, 1985). When transcribing laughter, transcribers try to approximate the sound of the laugh using *h* to indicate the breathiness and also through their choice of an appropriate vowel. For example, a laugh could be transcribed as *hih* or *hah*. Laughter also comes in pulses and a transcription needs to capture the number of pulses in the laughter.

(35) [Car conversation]
```
Nick:     I musta given away about a hundred bucks in
          free drinks tonigh(h)t huh huh
```

(36) [Car conversation]
```
Nick:     [ an I was goin oh yeah that' s really cool
          ma:n, yep, (.) no worr(h)[ie(h)s
Elvis:                             [heh huh huh
```

In extract (35), there are two pulses of laughter, both of which are produced with the same vowel quality, while in (36) there are three laugh pulses in Elvis' turn, the first of which has a different sound from the others. Laughter can also occur within talk and this is shown by the symbol *(h)* inserted in the talk at the point the laugh pulse occurs. This can bee seen in Nick's <u>no</u> *worr(h)[ie(h)s* which contains two laugh pulses during the talk.

In addition to laughter, speakers can talk with a hearable 'smile voice'; that is, talk produced while smiling. This is shown in transcription by placing £ before and after the words articulated with smile voice, as in (37).

```
(37) [Tel8:1:2]
     Sue:      u-hi:,
     Sal:      Wha's up £don' you recognize me, £
```

Hepburn (2004) uses aspiration marking similar to laughter to transcribe crying using combinations of *hs*, often with vowels. She also uses preceding full stops to mark inhalation and >hhuh< to mark a sharpness of exhalation or inhalation. In addition, she transcribes sniffs as *.shih* (wet sniff) or *.skuh* (snorty sniff) and, by analogy with 'smile voice' uses tildes (~) to enclose 'wobbly' voice or a break in the voice heard during crying. These conventions can be seen in extract (38).

```
(38) [HC boy in attic (Hepburn, 2004)]
     Caller:   Hhuyuhh .shih [ ~it's the] cru̲elles' pl:a̲ce
     CPO:                    [ °N n::.° ]
     Caller:   th' ah' ve e̲ver be-en to, ~↑ .hhuhh
```

Transcribing contiguous or simultaneous talk

When one unit of talk follows another with no discernible interval between the two, this is shown by an equals sign.

```
(39) [Car conversation]
     Elvis:         [ .hh an you jus scre̲a:med an I just
                    sto̲pped.=
     Sasha:    =sl̲ammed on the brakes. in the middle of th[e
               intersection.
```

This shows that Sasha's talk begins immediately Elvis' talk stops. The equals sign can also be used to mark where two parts of the same speaker's talk run together without a discernable break as in (40).

(40) [Car conversation]
```
Elvis:    hey er like I broke one las night=I
          we[nt out see this ba:n' ,
Nick:        [what the coopers
```

Alternatively, the same thing can be shown by using a < mark as in (40').

(40') [Car conversation]
```
Elvis:    hey er like I broke one las night<I
          we[nt out see this ba:n' ,
Nick:        [what the coopers
```

The main difference between what is transcribed in (40) and (40') is that the first shows that there is less than the usual beat of silence between the words *night* and *I*, while the second implies that the sounds are pushed together in a way that obscures the boundaries between the two sections of talk.

Talk may also happen simultaneously. Where one person starts to talk while another person is still talking, the start of the overlapping talk is indicated by [and the beginning of the overlap is aligned in the transcript. Extract (41) shows particularly frequent overlapping talk between a number of participants.

(41) [Car conversation]
```
Elvis:    I know the:: di:lemma hh. (1.0) ged up an
          scrub concrete huh [ heh
Sasha:                        [ poor Ni[ck
Nick:                                  [no    man    I've
          gotta ged up an fo̲ld ju̲mpers
          (0.2)
Nick:     huh huh huh
Elvis:    >an be extreme[ly poli:te,<
Sasha:                  [an-
Sasha:    an look really- [ really together,
Nick:                     [ hey man you take these
          [ ma:n.
Elvis:    [ oh no [ thanks
Nick:            [ an I'll:: see yuh on Tuesda(h):(h)y
          huh huh huh
```

In older transcripts overlap is sometimes shown with two backslashes (//) which indicate where overlap occurs in each relevant turn, as in

(41') [Car conversation]
```
Elvis:    I know the:: di:lemma hh. (1.0) ged up an
          scrub concrete huh //heh
Sasha:    //poor Ni//ck
Nick:     //no man I've gotta ged up an fold jumpers
          (0.2) huh huh huh
```

The layout of this system is less clear when more than one overlap is present and the use of [and alignment makes the transcript much easier to read.

The end of a stretch of overlapping talk is shown by].

(42) [Car conversation]
```
Sasha:    I always think of those days as yihknow all
          fun, an' musicals, but
          [ some of] the movies were really heavy.
Nick:     [ yea:h.]
```

Where two speakers begin to speak at the same time this is shown by a square bracket at the beginning of the turns as with Elvis' and Sasha's talk in (43).

(43) [Car conversation]
```
Nick:     okay ma :n¿
Elvis:    [ alright ma:n. ]
Sasha:    [ alright so-  ]
Nick:     good tuh s[ee yuh ma:n ]
Elvis:             [I' ll see yuh soo] :n mate.
Nick:     uh huh huh
Elvis:    thanks a lot.
```

In cases where there is overlapping talk, it is often necessary to interrupt the transcription of a turn at talk at a point where the talk of one speaker is incomplete because of the limitations of space on the page. Where a turn at talk has been broken up in order to insert overlapping talk, an equals sign is used at the end of the line of talk which has been interrupted and again at the beginning of the continuations to show that there is no discontinuation of the talk being produced and that the break is purely for purposes of layout.

(44) [Car conversation]
```
Nick:     .hhh like Montezuma's pays all her bills,
          all her amex, Rick' s amex.
          (0.2)
```

```
        Nick:     all that sorta shit.<all the electricity,
   →              .h[h she  ]' s got a s:even hundred dollar =
        Elvis:       [*o::h*]
   → Nick:     = a month electricity bill. huhuh
        Sasha:    WHA[T. AT HOME?]
```

Here Nick's talk continues without interruption from *s:even hundred dollar* to *a month electricity bill,* however, in order to transcribe Elvis' overlapping **o::h** the line has had to be broken.

Transcribing pauses

When there is a break in the stream of talk this is transcribed in a number of ways. Where the pause is very short it is transcribed as (.), while longer pauses, usually those lasting for more than two tenths of a second are timed and the timing is shown between brackets.

```
(45) [May and Jo]
     May:     uh (1.2) °I think this is it¿° she's going
              (0.5) (wa-) see where that dark (.) is¿
     Jo:      right¿
```

Here, there is a very short break in May's turn between *dark* and *is*, with a half second pause (0.5) after *going* and a pause of just over a second (1.2 seconds) after *uh* at the beginning of the turn.

There are a number of ways in which a pause may be timed and different ways of timing have different consequences. Jefferson (1989) explains the initial approach to timing pauses as:

> ... I have been timing pauses in tenths of seconds. While I try to be accurate, I have not given particular attention to the phenomenon of silences *per se*, and have been content with rough timings. For example, I started out using a stopwatch, but in 1968 it broke and instead of replacing it I switched over to the method favoured by amateur photographers, simply mumbling 'no one thousand, one one thousand, two one thousand...
>
> (Jefferson, 1989: 168)

Jefferson's counting method is based on the assumption that each utterance is approximately one second long and that, by reciting this formula during a pause, a rough timing in fractions of a second can be arrived at as follows:

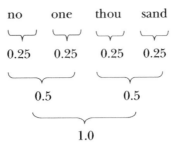

Jefferson (1989) later describes retranscribing pauses using both the rough counting method and stopwatch timing and states that the result is roughly consistent. Psathas and Anderson (1990) argue that what is most important in timing pauses is not the standardized accuracy of the timing, but rather that the timing is internally consistent within the transcript. The advantage of the counted timing is that it is sensitive to the rhythm of the talk and is timed relative to what is happening in the conversation, such as speaking speed. Psathas and Anderson argue in fact that counting is a 'self-standardized' measurement device. However, the counting method means that timings in transcriptions made by different transcribers will not always be the same. Using a stopwatch allows for the possibility of more consistent timing across transcribers. Ten Have (1999), however, notes that using a stopwatch is problematic in that it can be difficult to catch the exact starting and finishing points of the pause and recommends repeated attempts at timing as a way of gaining accuracy. Ten Have (1999) also notes that computer software can be used for measuring pauses. Computer observation of pauses is likely to be very accurate as a measure of elapsed time, but it is not sensitive to the rhythm of particular speakers and to the context in which a pause occurs and so may be less useful as a way of capturing the timing of talk as opposed to elapsed time.

When representing pauses there is an additional issue which needs to be considered in how to place the pause in the text of the transcript. This means considering whether a pause should be transcribed as belonging to a particular speaker or to no particular speaker, or whether it is a pause within a turn or between turns. These issues are essentially analytic and depend on the context in which the silence occurs. For example, the pauses in Nick's turn in (46) is best transcribed within his turn at talk because they come as part of an ongoing and incomplete bit of talk – they are turn internal pauses – and so are hearable as Nick's pausing.

(46) [Car conversation]
     Nick: an it's like (0.2) of this (.) great big (.)
             pheasant or something like that¿

The pause in extract (47) is quite different. In this extract Harry asks
Joy a question and the pause comes after Harry's turn is completed and
is potentially describable as Joy not having begun to talk yet.

```
(47) [Lunch]
     Harry:    Who gave you that one,
     Joy:      (0.4) Y' know I don' remember.
```

The transcript here shows that the pause belongs to Joy by including
it as a part of her turn. In extract (48), the long two-second pause
occurs between turns and so is placed on its own line in the transcript;
as it is not attributable to any one of the participants in the conversation, it does not have a name against it on the left-hand side. This is a
way of showing that no one was speaking at this time.

```
(48) [Car conversation]
     Nick:       [ hey Saf go straight throu[gh man.
     Sasha:                                 [yeah. okay.
                 (2.0)
     Nick:       ah fuckin cool huh huh I got away from Ron
```

While these three examples are quite clear, other examples require a
judgement from the transcriber. This is the case in Sasha's turn at (49).

```
(49) [Car conversation]
     Sasha:    reminds me of this guy I used to go out with
               (when I was in school).
               (2.2)
     Sasha:    he was real nut case [ as well.
```

Here Sasha completes a bit of talk and there is a silence of just over
two seconds before she takes up the talk again on the same subject.
The transcription above shows the talk as an interturn silence
belonging to no one in particular, rather than as a break in Sasha's
ongoing production. If this talk had been transcribed as (49'), the
analysis would have been quite different.

```
(49') [Car conversation]
     Sasha:    reminds me of this guy I used to go out with
               (when I was in school). (2.2) he was real nut
               case [ as well.
```

Here the transcript claims that Sasha held the speakership for the
entire duration of the segment transcribed and that she and she alone

produced the silence in the middle of a turn at talk. The length of the pause and the fact that the talk is produced in two complete units (sentences) suggests that (49') is a less accurate way to represent this bit of talk. Other cases may be harder to decide on. For example, in (50) the pause is shown as a pause between two turns by Joy in which no one was speaking, while in (50') it is shown as part of Joy's ongoing talk.

```
(50) [Lunch]
     Joy:     So we couldn' t rea:lly decide in th' end what
              tuh do.
              (0.3)
     Joy:     Coz i' was gonna be h:ard either way.

(50') [Lunch]
     Joy:     So we couldn' t rea:lly decide in th' end what
              tuh do. (0.3) coz i' was gonna be h:ard
              either way.
```

In this case, the transcriber's sense of what is happening is involved in deciding between the two representations. These examples demonstrate clearly the analytic nature of decisions about transcription and reveal that transcribing is not a neutral objective activity, but rather the theorized construction of a representation of talk (Ochs, 1979).

Dealing with problems of hearing or comprehension

Sometimes it is difficult or even impossible to hear something on the tape. Problems in hearing often happen because naturally occurring conversations are not recorded under ideal acoustic conditions. This means that background noises, interference or low volume can all affect the audibility of the tape. Where the transcriber has difficulty hearing the talk, this is indicated in the transcript by using single brackets around the words being transcribed.

```
(51) [Car conversation]
     Sasha:    reminds me of this guy I used to go out with
               (when I was in school).
```

In this extract the words *when I was in school* are shown as the transcriber's best hearing of the talk, with the brackets showing that there is some doubt about how accurate the hearing is. Sometimes, a transcriber may be unable to decide on more than one possible hearing of the talk and this is indicated by placing both possibilities in the transcript, as with the case of the quiet talk in (52).

```
(52) [TG (Schegloff, 1979b)]
    Bee:      °(I' unno)/(so anyway)° .hh hey do you see v-
              (0.3) fat ol' Vivian anymore.
```

Extract (52) shows a transcriber's best guess between two alternative hearings, both of which are possible, but neither of which is definitive. Where it is impossible to hear enough to transcribe anything, the space between parentheses is left blank, as in extract (53).

```
(53) [Car conversation]
    Sasha:    [ yeah] apparently she' s really she' s- not-=
    Nick:     [ (  )]
    Sasha:    =(0.6) well from it¿
```

Here Nick's talk is overlapped with Sasha's and the words themselves are inaudible.

Transcribing non-verbal elements of talk

Jefferson's original transcription system did not include much information about non-verbal elements of language, especially visual information, largely because the system was developed to transcribe audiotaped data. However, as conversation analysis has evolved, other researchers have developed the system to include additional features designed to capture other elements of interest in discussing language as it is used in a range of types of interaction. In many cases these transcription systems have been developed in order to deal with the particular phenomenon a researcher has been investigating and this is probably the least 'standardized' aspect of transcription among researchers in conversation analysis.

The first systematic treatment of non-verbal information is found in the work of Charles Goodwin (for example C. Goodwin, 1979, 1980, 1981), who developed a transcription system to deal with eye gaze. In Goodwin's transcripts, eye gaze is marked by a line above or below the relevant stretch of talk. The lack of notation indicates a lack of eye gaze. A series of dots indicates the movement from a state of non-gazing to state of gazing, with an X used to mark where the gaze reaches the other. Square brackets are used on the gaze line and the talk line to show how gaze and talk are synchronized. The features can be seen in extract (54).

```
(54) [(C. Goodwin, 1981)]
     Beth:      . . . . [ X _____
                Terry-[ Jerry' s fas[cinated with elephants
     Don:               . . . . . . . .[ X _____
```

In this transcript, Beth is talking to Don and her eye gaze is indicated above the talk. As she begins to talk her gaze travels to Don and reaches him as she restarts her talk with *Jerry* and continues to gaze at Don for the rest of the talk. Don is the addressed recipient of the talk and his eye gaze is noted below the talk. At the beginning of the talk Don is not gazing towards the speaker, but he begins to move his gaze to her at the restart and his gaze reaches Beth just after the start of *fascinated,* after which he continues to gaze at Beth.

In transcribing gaze, Goodwin has developed a different way to transcribe pauses in order to show more clearly what is happening during a pause. Where Goodwin is coordinating gazing and pausing he uses dashes in brackets rather than numbers, and each dash indicates a tenth of a second, as in extract (55).

```
(55) [(C. Goodwin, 1981)]
     Michael: Who kno:ws, .hh (-[ - - -) nu:mbers and letters
     Don:      . . . . . . . . . .[ X _____
```

Here Don's eye movement reaches Michael after a one tenth of a second of a pause which lasts for four tenths of a second.

Goodwin uses commas to indicate movement of gaze away from the recipient of the talk, as in extract (56).

```
(56) [(C. Goodwin, 1984)]
     Ann:      _____
               Karen has this new hou:se. en it' s got all=
               this
     Beth:     _____ , , ,   ((Nod))
     Ann:      _____
               =like- (0.2) ssilvery:: g-go:ld wwa[llpaper.
     Beth:         ((Nod))              ******  . .[X _____
```

Here Beth is gazing at Ann at the beginning of the talk, but after *this* she begins to move her eye gaze away and is no longer gazing at Ann by the end of *hou:se.* Goodwin's early transcriptions also involved some noting of actions, as in the nods in extract (56). In this transcript the row of asterisks are used to indicate where Beth puts food in her mouth. The nods here are described rather than transcribed and Goodwin also uses descriptions in other ways in his early transcriptions of non-verbal elements, for example:

(57) [(C. Goodwin, 1984)]

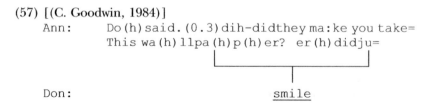

In this extract, the duration of Don's smile is described by a graphic device which shows where it begins and ends. He also uses lengthier descriptions in similar ways:

(58) [(C. Goodwin, 1984)]

This extract shows a point at which an action was relevant, whereas in extract (59), the transcript shows the duration of a similar action.

(59) [(C. Goodwin, 1984)]

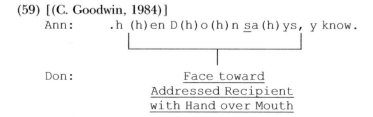

Heath (1984) takes a similar descriptive approach to eye gaze and body movement and produces transcripts such as (60).

In this transcript Heath uses Goodwin's conventions with an eye gaze line, commas to indicate gaze movement and dashes to indicate time. In addition he uses annotations marked against the transcript to give additional descriptive detail.

(60) [(Heath, 1984)]

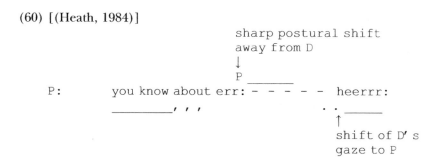

```
                                 sharp postural shift
                                 away from D
                                 ↓
                                 P  _____
    P:          you know about err: - - - - - -  heerrr:
                _____, , ,                   . .  _____
                                                    ↑
                                                   shift of D' s
                                                   gaze to P
```

Schegloff (1984) has developed a more elaborated transcription system for dealing with gesture using letters as coding devices as follows:

o	onset of movement that ends up as a gesture
a	acme of gesture or point of maximum extension
c	body part 'cocked' or 'poised' for release of gesture
h	previously noted occurrence held
t	thrust or peak energy animating gesture
r	beginning or retraction of limb involved in gesture
hm	limb involved reaches 'home position' or position from which it departed
p	point
...	extension of time of previously marked action
(−)	elapsed time in seconds

(Schegloff, 1984)

These conventions show features of gestures rather than coding gestures themselves. They are accompanied by a description of the gesture itself which is combined with the transcript to develop an overall representation of the gesture as it maps onto speech, as in (61).

(61) [MO Chicken Dinner (Schegloff, 1984)]
Gesture has both fingers pointing to speaker's temples.
Lexical affiliate is 'thinks'

```
                                     o. . . . .
    F:          Jus' like a cl(h)a:ssic story,  .HHH An'
                a . . . . . . . . . . . . . . . . .r
                now when I go out to a job, yihknow an'
                                     o . . . . . . .
                . HH before we run the cable ev' rybody
                . . . . . . . . . . . . . . . . . . . .
                thinks, .hh ``fuck the tru:ck.''
```

This transcript shows that the gesture begins towards the end of the word *story* and reaches its point of maximum extension at *now* and then is released during *yihknow*. The gesture is then repeated beginning at *cable* moving quickly to maximum extension at *ev'rybody* and remaining in place for the rest of the talk. The advantage of this transcription system is that it shows the close coordination of a gesture with talk, but the transcript cannot show much about the act of gesturing itself and the coding for extract (61) is very like that for extract (62), although the gesture is not similar.

(62) [Auto Disc: 14:05 (Schegloff, 1984)]
Gesture is a point to the right with the left forefinger.
Lexical affiliate is 't' Florida.'
```
              o . . .  a r . . .  hm
     Gary:    But eez takin it]  t' Florida so, . . .
```

Here Gary's gesture begins at *but*, reaches its maximum extension at *takin*, is quickly released and returns to its starting position at *t'Florida*. The distinctiveness between the gestures is contained in the preliminary description only. This then is a transcript which is very suitable for showing how a gesture coordinates with talk, but not for showing the nature of the gesture, for which an initial description is required.

In addition, Schegloff adds descriptions of special actions which are coded against the talk by number references, as in extract (63).

(63) [MO Chicken Dinner (Schegloff, 1984)]
Several gestures are involved. F is holding a business card in his left hand and gesturing with right hand. He first releases a prior gesture, then repositions the business card with his left hand. He then points at (something on) the business card and animates the point for a few moments. He then stops that gesture and points at a part of one of the listeners' garment at 'this colour'.
```
                                1 . . .
     F:          . . . y' know like three times lo:nger the
                 . . . 2 . . . . .  o . . . . 3 . . . . . . . .
                 bird. .HHH and then: u-thi:s stripe is in a .
                 . .  4  o . . . 5 . . . . . . . . . . .
                 li:ght (.) w' ll it' s in this colour.
     1 =         release of prior gesture toward business
                 card
     2 =         repositioning of business card
     3 =         point reaches its acme and moves back and
                 forth over business card
```

```
4 =        stop back and forth motion
5 =        arrival at target of next point
```

This extract involves a very large amount of descriptive detail in an attempt to represent the gesture involved adequately to support the analysis. The descriptive detail here, however, continues to focus on the coordinating points of the gesture and the talk rather than on the description of the gesture itself. The effect is to reveal the complexity of the action involved rather than the action itself.

A more elaborate transcription system has been developed by Rendle-Short (2002) in her work on non-verbal elements in computer science seminar presentations. Rendle-Short's system is similar to those developed by Goodwin and Schegloff, but has action lines for gaze, hand movement, and body movement, each of which has its own distinctive set of transcription symbols, as shown in Table 2.1.

In a transcription, these action lines are combined with descriptive comments and additional actions lines where relevant, as in extract (64):

(64) [Mi:17 (Rendle-Short, 2002)]

```
    Gaze:    ▣ ▣ ▣ ▣ ▣ ▣ ▣ ▣ ▣ ▣ ▣ ▣ ▣ ▣ ▣ ▣
1.  Pres:    (1.0) °but we [ won' t worry about that.°
    Hands:                 [ LH assessment wave
    Body:    at ▣

    Gaze:    ▣ ▣
2.  Pres:    (1.5)
    Hands:   ↓ ↓ ↓
    Body:    at ▣

    Gaze:    ▣ ▣ ▣ ▣ ▣ ▣ ▣ ▣ ▣ ▣ ▣ ▣ ▣ ▣ ▣ ▣
3.  Pres:    ↑so how do we apply this to [ the rocket? ↓
             (1.0)
    Hands:   BH ↓↓↓↓↓↓↓↓↓↓↓↓↓↓↓↓↓↓ [ LH ▣
    Screen:                              [ new image
    Body:    at ▣

    Gaze:    [ → → → → → → → → → → → → →
3.  Pres:    [ ↑well in the [ the rocket¿
    Hands:   [ hands in pockets
    Body:    [ steps to L of ▣
```

This transcript maps a number of non-verbal elements onto talk in a way which shows the clear interrelationships between talk and body. In

Table 2.1:   Transcription symbols for non-verbal communication
(*source Rendle-Short, 2002*)

Gaze direction	
_____	directs gaze towards audience, straight ahead
→ → →	directs gaze towards right
← ← ←	directs gaze towards left
↓ ↓ ↓	directs gaze downward
🖥 🖥 🖥	directs gaze at computer
↘ ↘ ↘	directs gaze towards right middle distance
↙ ↙ ↙	directs gaze towards left middle distance

Hand movements	
LH	left hand
RH	right hand
BH	both hands
cccc	hands are clasped in front of body
oooo	hands are 'open', i.e. not clasped and moving in some way
LH →	moves left hand to right
← RH	moves right hand to left
LH ↑	raises left hand into air
BH ↑	raises both hands into air
RH 🖥	interacts with computer with right hand

Body alignment	
_ _ _	body is facing audience
/ / / / /	body is partially facing audience
| | | |	body is turned away from audience
→ → →	moves to right
← ← ←	moves to left
bbbb	backward position
ffff	forward position
at 🖥	presenter stands at computer

this extract, the presenter is standing at the computer while speaking. He begins by gazing at the computer, during this he gestures at the word *won't*, lowers his hand, then lowers both hands and moves his left hand to the computer, at which point a new image appears on the screen. He then looks to his right, places his hands in his pockets, and moves to the left of the computer while continuing his talk. This provides a complex transcript with much information about the coordination of talk, gaze, gesture and movement, but again provides little information about the appearance of gestures, posture, etc. The resulting transcript is very detailed, but the amount of information coded here makes the transcript more difficult to read, while at the same time still being only a partial representation of what is happening.

In order to overcome some of the limitations that a transcription system, even one using detailed descriptions or multiple layers of information, has in representing non-verbal elements of interaction, many researchers have begun to add images to their transcripts in order to better portray the non-verbal. This is either done by producing line drawings based on the video image, which has the advantage of preserving the anonymity of the participants in the interaction, or by using frame grabs from the video source, which enables much more information to be included. A multilayered approach to using visual information in the transcript can be seen in the following transcript from Goodwin (2003).

(65) [(C. Goodwin, 2003)]

Here Goodwin combines transcription, video capture, line drawing and other markers such as arrows to capture the action of eye gaze and body movement in static form. The various stances of the participants and the direction of eye gaze are shown by the images, which are then mapped onto the points in talk where the image is relevant. The line drawing shows detail not available in the video capture and arrows signal gaze direction. In this combination, Goodwin tries to capture all the salient information a reader needs in order to understand the transcript for his analysis.

All of these transcription systems are limited by the difficulties of representing dynamic action in the static form of print. Electronic publication, however, has made it possible to include sound and video in the publication itself, alongside the transcripts (cf. ten Have, 1999). In this case, the primary data used by the transcriber is made available to the reader in its full richness, alongside a transcript which helps in directing the reader's use of the data set for the purposes of the particular analysis being done on the data.

The transcription systems discussed so far are all trying to represent the details of individuals' gestures, gaze and body movements, but there are also elements of non-verbal behaviour which are relevant to certain types of interaction. One of these is audience applause, which is especially relevant in the context of speeches and other forms of monologue. A transcription system for dealing with applause has been developed by Atkinson (1983, 1984a, 1984b, 1985). In Atkinson's approach, applause is marked by a series of *x*s, with upper case *X* indicating loud applause and lower case *x* indicating quieter applause, as in:

```
(66) [GE:79:4B (J. M. Atkinson, 1984b)]
     Audience:  xxXXXXXXXXXXXXxx
```

Extract (66) shows applause in which the volume increases and then decreases as the applause starts and finishes. The transcription system used here, therefore, allows the dynamics of applause to be captured in ways which a description, such as ((applause)), would not. Atkinson's transcription system has other features which build the dynamism of applause further. A single isolated clap is indicated by the symbol -*x*-.

```
(67) [GE:79:4B (J. M. Atkinson, 1984b)]
     Audience:  -x- (0.2)
```

This symbol may also be used in transcribing longer stretches of applause in which the applause begins and/or ends hesitantly or raggedly:

```
(68) [GE:79:3B (J. M. Atkinson, 1984b)]
     Audience:  -x-xx-xxxxxxxxxxxxxxxxxxxxxx-x
```

In transcribing applause, the number of *x*s is not used to show the duration of applause. Instead Atkinson times clapping in a similar way to the way pauses are timed, placing the duration of the clapping on a line indicating the span of the timed applause, so in extract (69), the applause is shown as lasting for five seconds.

```
(69) [GE:79:3B (J. M. Atkinson, 1984b)]
     Pardoe:     >THAT' S THE ↑FIrst ↓thing to guaran↓tee<
                 |————————— (5.0) —————————|
     Audience:   -x-xx-xxxxxxxxxxxxxxxxxxxxxxxx-x
```

Adding transcriber's information

In addition to capturing the features of the talk and its non-verbal accompaniment, the transcriber may also wish to add comments to the transcript in order to explain contextual information or to encode events which are difficult to transcribe. This is done by placing the information in double brackets at the appropriate point in the transcript, as in extracts (70) and (71).

```
(70) [Car conversation]
     Sasha:    I always think of those days as yihknow all
               fun, an' musicals, but [ some of] the movies=
     Nick:                            [ yea:h.]
     Sasha:    = were really heavy.
               (4.0) ((car turns a corner))
     Nick:     jus' go like follow this roa[d almost all the
               way . . .
```

```
(71) [Car conversation]
     Elvis:    see yuh soon.
     Nick:     yeah.
               ((Car door slams))
```

These additions are in effect descriptions which add to the contextual information in the transcript which may be relevant to the way in which talk is shaped and produced.

In addition to such descriptions, a transcriber may also wish to highlight features of the transcript for attention. For example, when preparing a transcript for publication the researcher may wish to signal which element of the text is the salient element for analysis. This is done by placing an arrow on the left margin of the transcript.

(72) [Mary and Jo]
```
     Jo:               [ ↑No. that's ↑lovely. ↑No, ↑no. ↑I can
                       see::, gorgeous.
                       So she hiring a car.
  →  Mary:            No::, she's gone on a (0.3) tour.
     Jo:               Right.
```

Where there are multiple points to be considered in the analysis the arrows may be marked with a letter for clarity.

(73) [Labov:T.A.:4r (Jefferson, 1978)]
```
a→ Marge:   Very- It's terrific I
            bec[ause I'm telling yih-]
b→ Rita:        [En  she   couldn'  ev] en fini-sh
            [::i(h)t,]=
   Marge:   [There's ]
   Marge:   =E:vrybody's e[couraging[ her there.]
c→ Rita:                   [enna cupp[a ca:wfee.]
```

In addition, for clarity of presentation, it may be desirable to omit some parts of a transcription in a published analysis. Where material has been left out of a transcript, this is represented by a series of dots. The dots are put horizontally to show that material is deleted within a turn, as in the last line of extract (74) and vertically to show where a series of turns have been deleted, as in extract (75).

(74) [Car conversation]
```
     Sasha:   I always think of those days as yihknow all
              fun, an' musicals, but [ some of] the movies=
     Nick:                           [ yea:h.]
     Sasha:   = were really heavy.
              (4.0) ((car turns a corner))
     Nick:    jus' go like follow this roa[d almost all the
              way . . .
```

(75) [Car conversation]
```
     Nick:    but I didn' see a fuckin' ca:r? and like the
              pedestri[an didn']
     Elvis:           [this w' z] th-
     Nick:    ye[ah.
```

```
Nick:        [ this- th] is pedestrian didn' have right
             of way but I thought (.) okay I' ll be polite
             an stop,
```

Translation

Translating data is an issue where an analysis is to be published in a language which is different from that in which the data was collected. This means that the reader of the analysis cannot be assumed to have access to the data in its original form. Where the reader of an analysis may not necessarily be able to read the data directly, it becomes important to provide some form of translation to make the data accessible.

The issue of translation in transcription has not been widely discussed in the literature on discourse analysis, although ten Have (1999) and Duranti (1997) are notable exceptions. The key problem for a transcriber is how to deal with the different structures of the languages being transcribed so that the translation does not distort the original interaction. Consider extract (76) in French:

```
(76) [(Crozet and Liddicoat, 1998)]
     Monique:  oui ça- oui ici j' trouve que c' est ↑plus
               difficile d' êt' végétarien [ moi j' étais =
     Suzanne:                              [ ouais c' est
               c' que Michelle dit
     Monique:  =dans zun environnement' y avait des maga-
               sins [ biologiques
     Suzanne:       [ ah oui
```

Here the transcript shows two overlaps, one at Monique's *moi* and the other at Monique's *biologiques*. These both represent problems for translation in a transcript. Monique's turn at talk here would be translated as *Yes that- yes here I find that it's more difficult to be vegetarian I was in an environment where there were health food shops.* Expressed as a translated transcript, this would look like:

```
(76')
     Monique:  yes that- yes here I find that it' s more
               difficult to be vegetarian [ I was=
     Suzanne:                             [ yes that' s what
               Michelle says
     Monique:  = an environment where there were health
               food [ shops
     Suzanne:       [ ah yes
```

The first problem here is that Monique's *moi*, which serves to make the *I* emphatic would not be translated in English, where the same function is normally done through stress and so there is no accurate point at which to indicate the overlap in a translated transcript. The second problem is that the adjective *biologiques* follows the noun in the French, but *health food* has to precede the noun in English. This means that in (76') the marking of the overlap in the translation has a choice between showing the overlap with the last word of the turn (as it does), and therefore short; alternatively, it could be faithful to the meaning of the French and show the overlap at the beginning of health, as in (76''):

(76'')
```
    Monique:  = an environment where there were [ health=
    Suzanne:                                    [ ah yes
    Monique:  =food shops
```

Here the overlap is represented as starting well before the ending of the turn. As will be shown later, the differences between an overlap in the middle of a turn and one at the end of a turn are interactionally important. The problem becomes even greater where the languages involved are substantially different. For example, consider the overlap in the following translation of data from Japanese:

(77) [8.10 (P:#3-B:2) Translation (Hanamura, 1998)]
```
    R:         They were [ good flowers. They were fine.
    I:                   [ Thank you very much
```

The original version is:

(77') [8.10 (P:#3-B:2) Translation (Hanamura, 1998)]
```
    R:         ii ohana de[shita kara. Daijyoobu desu kara.
    I:                    [arigatoo gozaimashita.
```

In this extract, R has received flowers from I and has called to thank him for them. Her first line is an appreciation of the flowers she has received and I thanks R for her appreciation. Each of the transcripts shows that R produces a turn made up of two elements, each with falling intonation and that there is an overlap in the middle of the first sentence. There is a slight difference between the two in that Hanamura's English translation shows the overlap at the beginning of a word while the Japanese shows it in the middle of the word. This is a minor issue in this transcript. The more important issue is that, because of grammatical differences between English and Japanese, this overlap occurs in very different points in the TCU in each version. In the English the overlap occurs after the subject and verb; these contribute very little information to the developing talk and in particular there is not enough information so far to project the action under way in R's talk. In the translation I seems to predict the trajectory of the talk and I begins his thanks quite early. In the Japanese version, however, the overlap occurs after *ii ohana* 'good flowers' and in the middle of the verb *deshita* 'were'. In the Japanese version the appreciation of the flowers is already clear and I's turn cannot be heard as predicting anything but rather responding to an appreciation. Moreover, the honorific particle *o* at the beginning of the word *hana* 'flowers' also signals that the flowers to which R is referring are the flowers that I had sent. If this data were presented in English only, it would be a misleading account of the talk. Reporting only the translated data, therefore, is a serious difficulty for accurate understanding of what is going on in the talk and is to be discouraged.

In order to overcome the problems of using only a translated version of the text, it is common to include both the original and the translation in a published version of a transcript. Here too there are important decisions to be made about how this is to be done.

Some studies use the translated version of the data in the text and place the original version in a footnote or appendix. This does give the reader access to the original, but has the effect of subordinating the original version to the translation. This solution ignores the fact that the original is the primary data and the translation is a construct which is in many ways different from the data on which the analysis is based. A preferable practice is for both the original and the translation to be included in the body of the text as separate text items.

(78) [(So'o and Liddicoat, 2000)]

A	halou?	hello?
L	Tiva	Tiva
A:	oe	yes
L:	o a tou mea o faiga.	what are you doing.
A:	e leai ni mea o lea	I'm not doing anything
	e fai a' u mea:' oga,	I'm studying,
	a o lea e matamata le	but the boys are
	tivi a le 'auli' i ia.	watching television.

In this extract, the translation is presented alongside the original and this is possible because the lines in the transcript are quite short and there is no overlapping talk. More often the translation is given after the original version, although in some cases the translation may be placed first. It is better that the translations come after the original to emphasize the fact that the original is the primary data and the translation is a secondary artefact to make the data more intelligible to some readers.

Separate translations would appear to be most suitable where the emphasis is on higher level features of the data, like the sequencing of actions, as is the case in the So'o and Liddicoat (2000) study from which extract (78) is taken. Where more micro-level features are important, as for example in the case of examining turn construction and overlapping talk, the use of separate transcriptions can make for difficulty for readers in mapping the translation onto the original.

Some studies overcome the problem of mapping the translation onto the original by giving a line-by-line translation inside the transcript, as in:

(79) [(ten Have, 1999)]
```
    O:        Schrama
    B:        dag met Paul
    B:        hi Paul speaking.
    O:        ja Paul
    O:        yes Paul
    B:        ik kom even melden dat ik eh geslaagd ben
    B:        I just called to tell you I uh succeeded
    B:        in het kopen van een telefoonspoel
    B:        in buying a telephone coil
```

This translation shows better the relationship between elements within the turn, but here the grammars of the language involved (Dutch and English) are quite similar and ten Have (1999) argues that such interlinear translations are in fact best suited where languages are similar. However, it should be noted that even in this extract, there are some elements which have quite different grammatical structures between the two. For example, while *hi Paul speaking* is an idiomatic translation of *dag met Paul*, the two phrases are in fact quite different as *met* translates literally as *with* not *speaking*. In ten Have's example, this is not an important difference, but in some analyses similar distinctions may be important.

The most accurate way to provide a translation, especially where micro-level features are important, is to provide an interlinear gloss of each element in the sentence as well as a translation. This is especially important in cases where the grammars of the languages are different (ten Have, 1999), but also where the analysis gives attention to detail in the production of talk.

(80) [Taxes: 5–6 (Sorjonen, 1996)]
```
    S:    ö Nyt kyllä nyt valehtele-t [ jotta vipa:t] taa.
          now surely now lie-2         so that swings
          uh Now surely now you' re lying in your throa:t.
                                      [                  ]
    E:                                [ ↑No ei::.        ]
                                      [ PRT NEG3         ]
                                      [ ↑Well no::.      ]
```

Here the transcript has three lines, the Finnish original, a word-by-word gloss and an idiomatic translation. The first presents the original data on which the analysis is based. The interlinear gloss provides an explication of the Finnish structure and enables the reader to know what is happening word by word in the Finnish original. There are, however, a number of grammatical conventions in the gloss, which themselves need defining in the key to the transcript (2 = second person, 3 = third person, PRT = particle, NEG = negation). Finally, the translation gives a version of the meaning which is no longer dependent on the structures of the original in order to convey the meaning, together with some indication of where elements marked in the transcript map on to the translation.

Transcribing conversation: some final comments

It is clear from the discussion so far that transcription is a detailed endeavour and because of the detail transcription is quite time-consuming. Moreover, transcription is rarely 'finished', as each new hearing can reveal something new in the data that the transcriber did not hear or notice on earlier hearings. For this reason, transcribers usually make repeated transcripts of their data, building an increasingly detailed representation of the talk they are studying. In fact, it is usually easier when beginning a transcript to concentrate on one aspect of the talk at a time as a way of dealing with the complexity and richness of the data. For example, a first pass through transcription might concentrate on trying to capture the words being spoken, while noting other aspects of the data as they occur. Next, it may be useful to concentrate on features such as intonation, loudness, lengthening, etc., as a way of building towards a more complete version of the data.

In many cases, transcribers note features in the talk that cannot be transcribed using the conventions listed in this chapter and they may need to make up their own ways of representing sounds or behaviours that they observe. This is in fact how the conventions for transcribing have developed over time, as people have needed to note new phenomena in their transcripts in order to be able to study them. Symbols that are developed for the transcription system should, therefore, be listed whenever they are included in material that others will read.

By way of summary, it is important always to remember that a transcript is a created artefact, not an objective account, and that it will always be a selective representation of the data itself. Therefore it is important to use the transcript alongside the original video or audio-tape so that the transcript can be checked, revised and supplemented as needed. There is then no final version of a transcript, but rather transcripts continue to evolve as they are used in response to greater familiarity with the data, developing analysis of the interaction being studied, different analytic aims and different intended audiences. While conversation analysis cannot be done without a transcript, it nonetheless remains an analysis of an instance of conversation, not of the transcript itself.

3 Turn-taking in Conversation

Introduction

One of the most noticeable features of conversation is that speakers change. In fact, in most cases, only one person speaks at a time and transition from speaker to speaker occurs fluidly with few gaps and little overlap. This is of course not to say that gaps and overlaps do not occur. However, where gaps or overlaps occur, they can be seen as doing something of interactional significance, as will be seen below. Moments in which one speaker speaks at a time can be considered as a default setting. It does not indicate that something other than simply changing speakers is going on at this point in the conversation. Gaps and overlaps, however, are likely to be interpreted by participants as indicating that something additional is happening.

Speaker change is a normative process which must be achieved by participants in the conversation. That is to say, turn-taking behaviour is socially constructed behaviour, not the result of an inevitable process. For example, the fact that overwhelmingly one person talks at a time is not the result of any physical or psycholinguistic constraint on human beings and there are also some activities, such as laughter or responses to greetings addressed to a group, which can overlap regularly and unproblematically, and where one person speaking at a time would be very unusual. Moreover, it is not even the case that more than one speaker speaking at a time inevitably causes problems for under-standing, as (1) shows.

```
(1) [Car Conversation]
        Elvis:   Like there was a bus right the:re man, in that
                 fuckin' bli:nd spot, [ an' I ] looked =
        Nick:                         [ Yeah,]
a→ Elvis:   =th[rough an I didn' t see   ] =
a→ Sasha:      [An he' s drivin' through] =
a→ Elvis:   =[anything so I wen' through]
```

```
a→ Sasha:    =[an' I' m jus screamin'      ] my lung[s out
b→ Elvis:                                           [.hh An
             you jus screa:med an I just stopped.=
   Sasha:    =slammed on the brakes. in the middle of
             th[e intersection.
   Nick:       [Didjou have the right of way?
```

At the arrowed turns marked 'a', Elvis and Sasha produce talk as part of the same story at the same time. However, this does not prevent Elvis from being able to paraphrase Sasha's *an' I'm jus screamin'* in the turn marked 'b'. Clearly, Elvis must have been able to process the over-lapping talk in order to be able to do this, even though he was speaking at the same time. He shows very clearly that he can understand someone else's talk while talking himself.

Some possible models of turn-taking

In seeking to establish some rules for turn-taking it is important to understand that these rules are enacted interactionally by participants in a conversation. They are not a set of pre-allocated rules for speaker change, although such a set of pre-allocated rules is often posited for speaker change. For example, if people are asked how they know when it is their turn to speak, their intuitive responses often suggest that there is such a set of rules. They will often say that they know they can start speaking because the previous speaker has paused to show s/he has stopped speaking. However, in looking at actual conversation, it becomes clear that pausing is not very useful in determining speaker change. Most speaker changes occur without an appreciable pause after the prior speaker's turn and, in fact, an appreciable pause after a turn may be interpreted as an interactional difficulty or problem of some sort as in extract (2).

```
(2) [Lunch]
    Harry:    Didjih speak tuh Mary today?
→             (0.2)
    Harry     Did yih speak tuh Mary?
    Joy       Oh, yea:h I saw her at lunch.
```

In this interaction, an appreciable pause occurs after Harry's turn. This pause is treated as Joy's not responding and Harry repeats the question. This example shows that an appreciable pause after a speaker finishes is treated not as space for the next speaker to come in, but as a failure of the next speaker to speak. The silence in (2) can be inter-preted by participants as a problem because of the context in which it occurs. The previous speaker has asked a question and a question obliges the next speaker to produce an answer as an immediately next action. In this context, the pause is not seen as a space to show that the prior speaker has finished, but that the next speaker has not yet begun, and Harry's repetition of the question shows that this is how he sees the silence. The appreciable space in this extract requires an explanation: in other words, it is *accountable*. The explanation here is treated by Harry as a problem of hearing, although in other contexts different interpretations of silences can also be possible. Silences between turns are, then, not simply spaces where a next speaker hears that a prior speaker has finished.

Silences in talk are also not simply opportunities for a next speaker to begin, and it is possible to find cases in talk where silences occur but where speaker change would be inappropriate, as in extract (3).

```
(3) [Mary and Jo]
      Jo:              [ ↑No. that's ↑lovely. ↑No, ↑no. ↑I can
                       see::, gorgeous. So she hiring a car.
  → Mary:      No::, she's gone on a (0.3) tour.
      Jo:              Right.
  → Mary:      and .h uh (0.3) they go by plane from here to
                       Sydney¿
      Jo:              Right¿
      Mary:      and then h uh I think h uh >I don't know how
                       they get from Sydney to the other place,
                       [ but then it'll be a bus.<
      Jo:              [ °Right.°
```

In (3), appreciable pauses of about a third of a second (0.3) appear at each of the arrows; however, these pauses could not be considered as even potential sites for legitimate speaker change as they occur within Mary's ongoing and demonstrably incomplete talk. Any attempt by Jo to become a speaker at this point would be accountable. From these examples, it is clear that pauses themselves do not function as signals for speaker change but have other interactional significances.

It is also clear that no other possible set of pre-allocated rules for organizing speaker change are in operation. Turn length is not fixed, but varies. Sometimes a turn can be a single word, at other times it may be quite a long sentence. A recipient cannot tell simply on the basis of length of utterance when a turn will end. It is also not true that the content of turns is fixed in advance. What speakers say varies. The sorts of turn-taking systems discussed above are used in some forms of human behaviour – such as fixed turn length in debates or pre-specified content in rituals – but they are not the case for everyday conversation generally (Sacks, 2004; Sacks *et al.*, 1974).

A model of turn-taking can only account for the facts of turn-taking if it deals with the 'randomness' of turn-taking in terms of what is said, for how long and by whom. In order to achieve this, a model of turn-taking needs to be sensitive to each 'next bit' of talk, rather than trying to describe or prescribe behaviour over a whole conversation. Turn-taking works at the level of each next bit, not at the level of the whole conversation because speakers in a conversation only have access to the conversation as it unfolds. Moreover, the action of turn-taking is not imposed externally on a conversation but is run internally by the participants themselves; it is locally organized (that is, it is organized at the moment it happens by the participants themselves) and interactionally managed (that is, it is accomplished within the process of interaction between the participants).

There is a model of turn-taking which is sensitive to the unfolding nature of talk in the work of Sacks, Schegloff and Jefferson (1974), who have proposed such a model of the turn-taking system based on study of a corpus of spontaneously occurring interactions. In order to account for the ways in which speaker change occurs, Sacks *et al.* propose that two separate, but interrelated components are involved: a turn constructional component and a turn allocation component. These two components are related by a set of rules. This proposal maintains, therefore, that turn-taking in conversation is an orderly, rule-governed process. Each of these aspects of this turn-taking model will be discussed in detail in the next sections.

The turn constructional component

A first step towards understanding how turn-taking works in conversation involves understanding what turns at talk actually look like. Turns at talk are made up of stretches of language, but, as has already been seen, these stretches of language can vary a lot in terms of their structure. Sacks *et al.* (1974) state that turns are made up of units which they call turn constructional units (TCU) and that the composition of TCUs is highly context dependent.

Turn constructional units

A variety of grammatical units may function as TCUs: words, phrases, clauses and sentences. In fact, any linguistic constituent can potentially function as a TCU. Although TCUs are made up of structural elements, TCUs themselves are not structurally defined units, such as those typically used in grammatical accounts of language, including word, clause and sentence. While these more traditional units of linguistic analysis are defined in structural terms in ways which are context-free, TCUs are context-sensitive and a decision about what constitutes a TCU can only be made in context. Importantly, it must be acknowledged that people do not just talk in sentences, but can use a range of different structures to construct their talk. This can be seen in the following extract.

(4) [Lunch]
```
     Joy:      hh. so we decided tuh go to that place th's
               jus' opened up.
     Harry:    where's that
  →  Joy       over near dee jays.
     Harry:    oh I haven' seen 't.
```

Extract (4) contains TCUs which are also sentences: for example *so we decided tuh go to that place th's jus' opened up.* and *where's that* and also a TCU, indicated by the arrow, which is a prepositional phrase. This phrasal TCU is nonetheless adequately complete at the point at which it occurs and counts as a whole and an appropriate contribution to the conversation at this point. In context, even linguistic forms which are not usually considered to be able to stand alone can be found as TCUs, as in (5).

(5) [Jones and Beach (1995) -FAM:A2, simplified]
```
     Ther:     What kind of work do you do?
     Mother:   Food service
  →  Ther:     At?
     Mother:   (A)/(uh) post office cafeteria downtown main
               post office on Redwood
     Ther:     °Okay°
```

In (5) the arrowed turn contains the word *At?*, and in this case it functions as a complete TCU. That is, this single word in and of itself functions as a full unit in this conversation at this point in the conversation. Moreover it is recognized as a sufficient unit by Mother, who produces a response. This response in turn is recognized as appropriate and sufficient by the Therapist, who accepts it with *°Okay°*. Schegloff (1996b: 78) argues that *At?* in this turn is grammatically continuous with the previous talk and that it provides an opportunity for the recipient to produce a unit of talk. This further unit of talk is grammatically continuous with the *At?* and the *At?* implements the action of 'prompting' at this point in this conversation. It is clear that *At?* here must be considered to be a complete unit in its own right.

Schegloff (1996b: 63) posits the possibility that phrasal and lexical TCUs may be sequence-specific and occur in positions which are symbiotic with the preceding constituent. This is certainly the case with the TCUs in (4) and (5), both of which gain their interactional status by being second elements after the turns which precede them. This is particularly the case in (5), where the word level TCU *At?* and the noun phrase TCU *(A)/(uh) post office cafeteria downtown main post office on Redwood* are both interpretable as complete and meaningful contributions because of the prior talk.

The contextual nature of TCUs becomes clear from examples like those above and it can be argued, as does Schegloff (1996b), that the grammar of TCUs is a positionally sensitive one. It is clearly the case that the word *at* is not always a TCU, nor is it likely that it will often be a TCU and in most contexts it will clearly not be a TCU. *Within its context, a TCU is a TCU because it is recognizably possibly complete.* If a piece of talk is not recognized as possibly complete at a particular point in the ongoing talk, then it is not a TCU.

Together with this notion of possible completion, TCUs are also projectable: that is, a recipient can know roughly what it will take to complete the unit of talk currently under way. This means that speakers are able to project where a TCU under way will be possibly complete and this projection is important for the organization of turn-taking (Liddicoat, 2004). It is possible to see the ways in which recipients make projections about the trajectory of talk in their spoken language behaviour. In example (6), the recipient projects forward to a possible conclusion and produces the same piece of talk at the same time as the speaker.

```
(6) [Jefferson (1983)]
      Joe:      B' t he wannid the] dawg dih bite iz wife.
                (0.5)
      ():       [ ] °ehhh°
      Joe:      [ ] So ↑he come[s ho:me one] night ] =
      Carol:                    [ heh heh heh] heh he] h =
  →   Joe:      =the sonofa] bitch [ bit hi:m.]
  →   Carol:    = heh heh   ]        [ bit hi:m,]
```

In order to be able to do this, the recipient is clearly able to tell what it will take to complete the unit under way. The context in which the talk is produced, in particular the line of the transcript, *he wannid the] dawg dih bite iz wife.*, and the sentence structure of the turn so far provide information which aids in projecting the trajectory and assists in the precision timing of Carol's talk. In example (7), there is a different realization of TCU projection.

(7) [Lerner (1991) C124A/C244A]

```
    D:          They haftuh run programs for them to re-
                habilitate them tuh- to deal with the new
→               materials. and if they ca:n' t,
→   A:          They' re out.
                ( . )
    D:          Mm hm,
```

In this case, A completes D's utterance by providing the *then* component of an *if . . . then* construction. In this case a single TCU is spread over two turns at talk and, in order to be able to do this, A needs to be able to tell roughly what it would take to complete the TCU under way using the *if . . . then* syntactic frame to aid the projectability of the talk (Lerner, 1991). TCUs are, then, characterized by the projectability of a possible completion point at some time in the future. The argument is then that TCUs end at places of possible completion. These points of possible completion are called transition relevance places (TRP).

Possible completion and turn construction

So far the term 'possible completion' has been used a number of times in the discussion without considering exactly what the term means and it is now necessary to consider this idea in a more focused way. Possible completion itself requires more development, and there has been a large amount of discussion in conversation analysis about what it actually means to say that some stretch of talk is possibly complete.

Sacks *et al.* (1974) discuss a number of levels of possible completion which are relevant to TCUs. In this discussion, an utterance can be seen as possibly complete in three main ways. First, it may be grammatically complete: that is, it may be a syntactically complete unit. Secondly, it may be intonationally complete: it may occur with an intonation contour which indicates that the unit is now ended. For example, *what* with rising intonation can be hearable in context as a complete question TCU, while *what* with level intonation may not be hearable as a complete question in the same context. Thirdly, and most importantly, the TCU needs to be complete as an action: it must count as having done what needs to have been done at this point in the conversation, for example having asked a question, provided an answer, issued an invitation, etc. Early discussions of TCUs (see, for example, Jefferson, 1973; Sacks, 2004; Sacks *et al.*, 1974; Schegloff, 1982) have a strong tendency to privilege the role of syntax in determining completion, although in all such discussion the nature of the TCU as action has been important. The idea of a TCU as action has become increasingly important in later discussions. Schegloff (1996b) sees turns as 'interactional habitats' in which language (TCUs) are deposited, and as such places the notion of action at the centre of the nature of TCUs.

Ford and Thompson (1996) posit three levels of completion: syntactic completion, intonational completion and pragmatic completion, and argue that intonational completion is more important than it may have appeared in earlier work. They argue that intonational completion may be more important than syntactic completion as almost all instances of intonational completion in their data coincide with syntactic completion, while instances of syntactic completion only correspond with intonational completion about half the time. Moreover, they maintain that speaker change occurs usually where all three types of completion co-occur. The concept of pragmatic completion in this study is, however, problematic. While they argue the aim of pragmatic completion is to capture the 'notion of conversational action' (Ford and Thompson, 1996: 148), a definition which corresponds to the importance of action accorded to TCUs by authors such as Sacks *et al.*, they found pragmatic completion as action difficult to operationalize and defined it as follows:

> an utterance was required to have a final intonation contour and has to be interpretable as a complete conversational action within its specific sequential context.
>
> (Ford and Thompson, 1996: 150)

The inclusion of intonation in the definition of pragmatic completion seems to be problematic, as it makes it difficult to interpret the significance of their claim that speaker change occurred usually where all three types of completion co-occurred; pragmatic completion must by definition co-occur with intonational completion. The inclusion of intonation in pragmatic completion would seem to blur the distinction between action and intonation, and also to a lesser extent between syntax and action, and it appears that this analysis privileges the linguistic features of TCUs over the action being performed. Nonetheless, it remains true that completion based on the notion of action is difficult to operationalize because such completions are highly sensitive to their context.

Selting (1998) further extends the argument about the relative importance of syntax and intonation in delimiting TCUs and for effecting speaker change. She argues that points of possible syntactic completion are potential completion points for TCUs, but that it is the prosodic features of the talk which signal whether or not the syntactic unit is designed for possible speaker change. This means that a continuing intonation contour effectively overrides a syntactic possible completion, leaving the talk to be heard as incomplete. Selting's proposal is, however, a purely linguistic one which considers only the role of syntax and intonation and the role of linguistic action is not considered in her study. While she does acknowledge the possibility of utterances being 'syntactically, semantically and discourse pragmatically' complete (Selting, 1998: 37), she argues that the role of prosody is more important in determining whether a turn is completed or not.

In addition to the elements of syntactic, intonational and pragmatic completion, some non-verbal behaviours may also be implicated in turn-taking. Goodwin (1981) has demonstrated that turn completion may be linked to a combination of gaze and syntax in face-to-face interaction. In particular the coordination of gaze is important for helping to determine whether the end of the talk so far has reached a possible completion point and whether speaker change would be relevant at this point. Goodwin argues that towards the end of talk speakers direct their gaze towards an interlocutor and withholding gaze from an interlocutor displays that the turn-so-far is incomplete and that securing a recipient's gaze is implicated in passing a turn to a next speaker. Gaze, however, must of necessity play a more minor role than other features of completion because participants are still able to project completion and organize turn-taking when visual clues are absent, such as in telephone conversations.

The various studies of aspects of completion reveal that the definition of TCUs is problematic in conversation analysis and in part the definition problem stems from an attempt to find a decontextualized set of linguistic forms which account for occurrences of speaker change. The discussion turns on the relative importance of types of completion: syntactic, intonational and pragmatic. This is problematic because a TCU is fundamentally a context-sensitive phenomenon which is not so readily identified in formal terms. The central issue for defining TCUs would, therefore, appear to be the notion of conversational action. If a unit is not potentially complete as a relevant conversational action in its context, it cannot usefully be considered as a constituent unit of a turn, which is itself a site for pursuing some action within conversation and through language.

The discussion above has turned around the notion of *possible* completion and the word 'possible' here is central to the turn constructional component of the turn-taking model. Participants in conversation project *possible* completion not *actual* completion. Actual completion can never be predicted as speakers can and do prolong their talk beyond what is needed to complete a particular action under way. Participants cannot know in advance where a turn will end, only when it *could* end (Liddicoat, 2004). Actual completion is in a sense an irrelevant issue for conversation, as participants need to orient to moments when talk may be complete rather than moments when talk is known to be complete. This can be seen in the behaviour of participants in actual conversation, as in examples (8), (9) and (10).

(8) [Trio:II Sacks *et al.* (1974)]
```
    Penny:   An' the fact is I- is- I jus' thought it was so
             kind of stupid [ I didn' even say anything[ when=
    Janet:                  [ Y-                        [ Eh-
    Penny:   =I came ho:me.
             (0.3)
    Janet:   Well Estelle jus' called'n . . .
```

(9) [Sacks *et al.* (1974)]
```
 →  A:          Uh you been down here before [ havenche.
 →  B:                                       [ Yeh.
```

(10) [Jefferson (1973)]
```
    Penny:   O:kay. I' ll see yuh.
 →  Agnes:   A::l? right [ Dear,
 →  Penny:               [ Bye bye,
    Agnes:   Bye bye,
```

In these examples, next speakers begin to talk during the ongoing turn of the current speaker. What is of interest here is the placement of these attempts to effect speaker change. In each case, the next speaker begins at a place where the action under way is possibly complete and where the syntactic units being produced are possibly complete, although not at points of intonational completion. In each case, the possible completion is not an actual completion, but rather a projected point at which the talk could relevantly be ended. The issue here is, then, that speakers are waiting to get to a point where the prior speaker's turn is possibly complete so that they can become next speakers. They do not wait to hear actual completeness. This orientation to possible completion allows for a smooth transition with no gap between turns, which could be hearable in some contexts as a delayed or absent response.

Transition relevance places

The notion of possible completion is linked fundamentally to the idea of transition relevance places (TRPs). It has been argued above that there are points where a speaker's talk is possibly complete and that at points of possible completion, speaker change is a possible next action. Such points are transition relevance places, places at which speaker change could be appropriate. This means that TRPs are not places where speaker change has to occur, but rather places where speaker change could occur. In fact, TRPs are the sites in conversation in which speaker change can be a 'legitimate next action'. That is, speaker change which occurs at a TRP will not normally be heard as interruptive and therefore will not be an accountable action. That is, speaker change is not an appropriate action except at the possible completion of a TCU and attempts at speaker change other than at a TRP are accountable. Once a speaker has begun to speak, s/he has the right to produce one potentially complete bit of talk and only one such bit of talk. At completion of this TCU, the right to produce the next TCU must be gained interactionally. Because possible completion is transition relevant, current speakers have rights to produce a single TCU and to complete a whole TCU. There are, however, some cases in conversation where speakers do work to gain a right to produce an extended turn at talk which is made up of more than one TCU, for example telling a story. In these cases, the current speaker can be seen as having some rights to produce each next TCU until the extended turn is 'complete'. While such extended turns look quite different from other instances of conversation, the right to an extended turn is still gained interactionally and participants do this by orienting to a turn-taking system which guarantees rights to only a single TCU.

Extending turn constructional units

In conversation, speakers can and do continue to talk beyond the completion of a single TCU and how this occurs will be discussed below. Where talk proceeds beyond a first TRP, this additional talk may involve a new TCU or it may be designed as an increment to a preceding TCU. An increment is a further bit of talk which builds onto the TCU so far, without creating a distinctly new unit (Ford, Fox and Thompson, 2001). This is what happens in Penny's talk in (11).

```
(11) [Sacks, et al. (1974)]
     Penny:   An' the fact is I- is- I jus' thought it was so
              kind of stupid [ I didn' even say anything[ when=
     Janet:                  [ Y-                        [ Eh-
     Penny:   =I came ho:me.
              (0.3)
     Janet:   Well Estelle jus' called 'n ...
```

Penny produces a complex sentence, which is itself a single TCU: and *the fact is I just thought it was so kind of stupid I didn' even say anything when I came home.* This TCU is possibly complete syntactically, intonationally and as an action at the point of its actual completion. However, it is also possibly complete at other points in its trajectory as can be seen from Janet's attempts at speaker change. Penny's talk is possibly complete in both its syntax and as an action at *stupid,* and her next talk is not designed to be a new TCU, but rather as an extension of the previous one. The same is true at *anything,* which is again a possible completion, and which is followed by a further increment to the TCU under way. This means that this turn at talk has been designed in such a way that continuations beyond possible completions are constructed so that at the end only a single TCU has been produced. While Penny's talk at the possible completions at *stupid* and *anything* are not intonationally complete (the transcript shows a continuation in the intonation contour), TCU extensions can also occur where the turn so far is not intonationally complete, as can be seen in (12).

```
(12) [Joyce and Stan 2:01–09]
  → Joyce:   Yeah t[hey give it back to you. Later. =
     Stan:         [ (Yeah the)
     Joyce:   =[ (See an' )
     Stan:     [ THE WAY I BEAT MINE it was a pa:rking
              ticket. Yihknow, so I was able ta go ta night
              court (wu) then beat the ten dollar ticket.
     Joyce:   Oh:,
```

In Joyce's turn the TCU *they give it back to you* is possibly complete with completed (that is, falling) intonation. Joyce then adds an increment *later* again with a completed intonation contour. What she has effectively done here is cancel the prior possible completion and deferred the possible completion to the end of the increment. In fact, she appears to be beginning a further increment with *see and,* although this TCU remains uncompleted. TCUs are to some extent quite fluid units in the sense that they can be made up of any linguistic constituent and they can be interactionally reshaped during their production (C. Goodwin, 1979; Streeck and Hartge, 1992). Nonetheless, they are always characterized by their status as possibly complete in their context and that speaker change is a possible next action after the completion of a TCU and in some cases a required next action.

The discussion so far has established where speaker change can occur but not how it occurs. The latter is handled by the turn allocation component and the rules which link turn construction to turn allocation.

Turn allocation

At any TRP, there are two basic ways in which a next speaker can come to have a turn at talk: either the current speaker can select the next speaker or a next speaker may self-select. These two possibilities, however, are not equally present at the end of every TCU and at any TRP only one of these may be the appropriate way for speaker change to occur.

Current speaker can select the next speaker

If a current speaker is to select the next speaker, the talk must be designed to achieve this. Only some forms of talk can select the next speaker: for example, questions can, but answers do not. If a current speaker produces a question, s/he produces some talk which makes a particular type of action a relevant next action (i.e. an answer) and at the same time may make some recipient the relevant participant to perform that action. Questions, however, do not inherently select a next speaker. A question for example may be addressed to a group, any one of whom could be an appropriate next speaker. Nonetheless, questions do make speaker change a highly relevant next action and at the same time constrain what can be considered appropriate talk from the new speaker. A current speaker who selects a next speaker must design the talk in a way which selects this speaker and can do this in a number of ways (Lerner, 2003).

An address term, such as a name or the pronoun *you*, can be used to select a next speaker. However, addressing by itself does not select a next speaker, rather it is the combination of the type of talk in which the address term is embedded and the address term which does this, as can be seen in extracts (13) and (14).

```
(13) [Lunch]
     Joy:     Have yuh got the papers for the meeting ye'
              Carol¿
     Carol:   Yeah=they came in th' s morning.


(14) [Lunch]
     Joy:     how' s things
     Harry:   not ba:d Joy.
```

In (13), Joy selects Carol as the next speaker by a combination of both the question form and the name. Essentially, the question makes speaker change a relevant next action and the naming works to select Carol as the new speaker. If someone other than Carol speaks in this position it would be accountable because the next turn has been allocated to Carol and it is Carol, as the recipient of the question, who is required to provide the answer. A silence after this question would be hearable to participants as Carol's silence and this could be formulated by participants as 'Carol didn't answer'. In (14), however, the naming does not work to select a next speaker. Here, Harry's turn is an answer and does not require or constrain future talk. If someone other than Joy talks next it would not be accountable and a silence would not be heard specifically as Joy not doing something.

The use of *you* as an address term creates further complexities in multi-party talk because of the potential vagueness of the reference (Lerner, 1996b), and indicates some other techniques that can be used by current speakers to select next speakers, including context, turn design and non-verbal cues such as gaze direction.

Lerner (1996b) has shown that the use of *you* to identify an addressee functions through features of context and recipient design to uniquely identify referents. Identifying *you* in a multi-party conversation depends on features such as the sequential positioning of the turn which contains the address, visible actions, associations with material objects and speaker gaze.

(15) [Chicken Dinner (Lerner, 1996b)]
```
Shane:   I can' t get this thing mashed
Nancy:   You do that too to your potatoes?
Shane:   Yeah
```

In (15), Nancy's turn is explicitly tied to Shane's prior turn and the use of *you* and *your* tie the two turns grammatically. At the same time, Nancy initiates an action, in this case a question, which makes further talk relevant as a next action, that is, an answer. In this context, the *you* can be seen as selecting Shane as the relevant next speaker as the result of the sequential position of the turn containing the reference.

(16) [Chicken Dinner (Lerner, 1996b)]
```
         (2.8)
Vivian: C' n you pass the butter,
         (3.1)
```

In (16), Vivian's talk cannot rely on sequential positioning to identify the addressee, but rather relies on environmental cues such as the positioning of the butter in relation to other participants. In Lerner's (1996b) analysis, the participants use their location in relation to the butter as a resource for determining who the addressed recipient is, and who should perform the required next action.

In addition, gaze may also be deployed in indicating to whom turn at talk is addressed and so select a next speaker. A recipient who has established eye contact with a speaker can as such be designated as a next speaker where a turn requires some next speaker. However, gaze direction, like naming, is not enough to select the next speaker. Speaker selection depends on where in the turn this happens. At the beginning of a turn, gaze can select the primary recipient of talk and over the course of a turn the primary recipient of the talk can change (C. Goodwin, 1979, 1981).

(17) [Car conversation]
```
Sasha:   an all- did he tell yuh about his problems
         with his wife an [ that
Nick:                     [ yuh. oh I knew all about
         that anyway.
         (0.2)
```

In this extract, Sasha's *you* addresses Nick primarily as her interlocutor. For a number of lines prior to this extract, Nick has been talking about his experiences with a mutual acquaintance. Sasha's talk in this context is designed to find out if Nick, the previous teller, knows what she does about this acquaintance, and in this context *you* is construable as Nick and not the other potential recipient in this conversation, Elvis, who so far has participated little in this stretch of conversation.

Next speaker self-selects

Self-selection occurs when a participant becomes next speaker, but nothing in the previous talk has selected this person to be next speaker, as in extract (18).

```
(18) [SF:ST:4]
                (0.2)
     Sue:       Ggo:d whadda Day.
     Trish:     hh whadda wee[:k.
     Mary:                    [yeh than' g(h)od i's
                Fr(h)[iday
     Sue:            [hh. Huh
```

Here, Sue self-selects as next speaker following a brief silence, but her talk does not select any next speaker. Trish then self-selects immediately as next speaker providing an upgraded version of Sue's prior turn and likewise does not select a next speaker. Mary then self-selects aligning with the prior talk.

Self-selection can also occur where the prior talk is designed to require that someone speak next, but does not constrain who that person should be.

```
(19) [SF:ST:4]
     Sue:      Hi.
     Trish:    Hi[: Sue
     Mary:       [Hello:,
```

In this extract, Sue's greeting requires a greeting response; however, it is addressed to both Trish and Mary. As such, it cannot select either of them as next speaker even though it does make it relevant for them to produce greetings. The turn type is constrained by Sue's talk, but not the identity of the next speaker. Trish, therefore, self-selects as next speaker, as does Mary.

However, not all possible verbalization functions as self-selecting as next speaker. For example, laughter does not claim the floor and is commonly done as a choral action in which no one participant could be considered the current speaker. Other forms of talk are designed specifically to show that a participant is not taking the floor. Continuers, such as *yes, mm hm, uh huh*, etc., produced during an extended turn, indicate to the current speaker that the recipient of the extended turn is orienting to the talk as continuing past the current moment and that s/he is not taking up speakership at this point (Schegloff, 1982).

In some cases where a next speaker self-selects, this speaker may be the person who produced the immediately prior turn, as in (20):

```
(20) [Car conversation]
     Sasha:   reminds me of this guy I used to go out with
              (when I was in school)
              (2.2)
     Sasha:   he was real nut case [ as well.
```

Here, Sasha's first turn is possibly complete and does not select a next speaker. No other participant speaks after her turn and there is quite a long silence, which ends when Sasha again becomes the speaker. In so doing, she self-selects as next speaker.

Sacks *et al.* (1974) have indicated that there is a bias in talk so that the last speaker but one often becomes the next speaker. This is, however, simply a bias in the system, not an inherent feature of the system itself. Turn allocation cannot be ensured beyond the immediately next turn and at the end of each turn speaker allocation strategies apply equally to all participants: that is, any recipient may be selected as a next speaker by the current speaker or any participant may self-select. The observable fact that the last speaker but one becomes next speaker in a particular conversation is not therefore evidence for the application of a rule to that effect, but rather the locally managed outcome of a set of rules which allocates speakership at the end of each emerging turn.

These options for speaker change can now be mapped onto the turn constructional component by a set of rules in order to provide an account of how and when speaker change happens in conversation.

Rules linking turn construction and turn allocation

Sacks *et al.* (1974: 704) have outlined a small set of rules for relating turn allocation to turn construction which coordinate speaker change. These rules link turn allocation explicitly to the idea that the possible completion of a TCU is transition relevant, and also provide for an ordering of the two possible options for speaker selection discussed above.

(1) At any transition relevance place of an initial turn constructional unit:
   (a) if the turn so far uses a 'current speaker selects next' technique, then the selected person has the right and obligation to take the next turn to speak, no other speaker has such rights or obligations;
   (b) if the turn so far is not constructed to select a next speaker, then self-selection may, but need not occur. The first participant to begin speaking acquires the right to a turn;
   (c) if the turn so far is not constructed to select a next speaker, the current speaker may, but need not continue if no other speaker self-selects.
(2) If the current speaker continues after the initial TCU, these rules apply again at the next transition relevance place, and at each subsequent transition relevance place until speaker change occurs.

Rules 1(a)–(c) are ordered: that is, rule 1(b) applies if rule 1(a) has not been applied, and rule 1(c) applies if rules 1(a) and 1(b) have not been applied. Self-selection can only legitimately apply if a 'current speaker selects next' strategy has not been employed, and the current speaker can continue as next speaker only if another speaker does not self-select. These rules, therefore, constrain each other and this constraining effect applies to each of the rules, not just to the lower ordered rules. Thus, if a speaker is going to apply rule 1(a), then s/he has to construct the turn in such a way that rule 1(a) has been invoked before the first TRP of the initial unit. If s/he does not do so, rule 1(b) would apply at that TRP. In the same way, the presence of rule 1(c) necessitates that an application of rule 1(b) can only be assured if it occurs at the first TRP of the initial unit. These rules constrain each other therefore in that each lower order rule can only apply in the absence of a higher order rule, and also in that each higher level rule must be enacted before the first TRP of the initial unit of talk in order to assure its operation.

The ordering of the rules also works to prevent instances of more than one speaker at a time. If the rules were not ordered, a 'current speaker selects next' strategy and a 'current speaker self-selects' strategy could both be legitimately employed at the same time; however, the ordering of these rules means that if a current speaker selects next strategy is deployed, then this pre-empts self-selection. This not only blocks an application of self-selection, but also provides for such self-selection to be seen as an accountable action, that is, as misplaced in this context.

These rules provide, as an inherent feature of the system, for a limit of turn size to a single TCU – a single possibly complete unit of talk. Speakers gain the right to a single TCU and at the completion of that TCU, the right to speak lapses. The end of each TCU, therefore, becomes an important strategic point in conversation, as it is at this point that the current speaker's speakership is vulnerable and a current recipient's speakership becomes possible. This means that current non-speakers need to monitor the talk in progress for possible completion, because possible completion can allow or require talk. At the same time, speakers need to design their turns in order to get things said by the end of the first TCU.

The existence of rules which constrain the talk in such ways does not inevitably lead to situations in which a speaker produces only a single possibly complete unit or where speaker change occurs at the end of such a unit. Speaker change is a social phenomenon which is worked out by participants throughout the interaction TCU by TCU. The system is locally managed by the participants and is interactionally sensitive. At each point in the talk participants respond to what has just happened and this reaction is used to demonstrate how what has just happened has been understood. Speakers' behaviour differs according to understanding and the next action has the capacity to display the understanding achieved so far. Participants also have to analyse what is going on as it is produced, monitoring for possible completion. This provides a powerful motivation for listening as the end of each TCU may make a display of understanding possible or even necessary because if such a display of understanding is not made when required it is seen as lacking. Participants have to respond directly on completion because the first to respond has rights to the turn. This provides a need, especially in multi-party conversations, for self-selecting next speakers to begin as soon as possible.

Features of turn-taking in conversation

Sacks *et al.* (1974: 700–1) outline a set of 'grossly apparent facts' observed in their data which need to be accounted for by the turn-taking model, and they indicate how these facts are addressed by the model they propose.

Speaker change recurs, or at least occurs

The power of the Sacks *et al.* (1974) model lies in the fact that it accounts for turn-taking, but does not make it an inevitable consequence of the system. The model does not prevent one participant from dominating the conversation nor does it require all those present to participate at all points in the conversation. The model provides a set of rules which are equally relevant for all participants, but which does not imply or impose equality of participation because the conversation is interactionally created by the participants themselves (Schegloff, 1999). At the same time, speaker change is built in as a recurrent part of interaction, which operates as a possibility at each possible completion of each turn, because any talk produced must reach a TRP.

One person talks at a time and occurrences of more than one speaker at a time are common but brief

The system allocates to any one speaker the exclusive right to speak until s/he reaches the first possible completion. The exclusivity of this right allows for a standard case where a participant who has become current speaker will get to produce one TCU, and attempts at speaker change prior to possible completion will be accountable.

The focus of speaker change at moments of possible completion regularly localizes competition for talk at TCU boundaries. At these boundaries, the inclusion in rule 1(b) of the provision that the first to start has the right to become the current speaker provides a mechanism to deal with simultaneous starts. The model makes simultaneous starts a possibility, but also provides a way to deal with them. The turn-taking system also provides for the possibility of overlap between current speaker and next speaker at a TRP. Because speakers rely on projections of possible completion rather than actual completion, variation in the form or delivery of final components can lead to overlapping talk between the end of one turn and the beginning of the next. As these are places where speaker change could or should occur, the model provides for resolution of such overlaps in the shortest possible time. Thus, the features of the model which lead to the possibility of overlap also provide for the possibility of resolving overlapping talk quickly.

Transitions with no gap and no overlap are common

This is again related to the locus of speaker change being places of possible completion. The projectability of such completions allows for speaker change to occur without a noticeable gap between the prior talk and the current talk in ways which could not be assured by orientations to actual completion. Additionally, projectability allows for the possibility of talk beginning after another speaker has completed an utterance.

Turn order varies and the relative distribution of turns is not specified in advance

The system provides that only the immediately next turn is allocated at any time and that speaker change applies at every possible TRP, with the same series of ordered options for speaker change occurring at each point. The order of speakers is therefore locally managed by participants. The rule set allows for the possibility of the bias towards the last speaker but one becoming the next speaker mentioned above, but also allows for other possibilities. The bias towards last speaker but one becoming next speaker is therefore locally managed by participants rather than being invoked by the system.

The system does not provide for an equal distribution of turns, nor for a particular concentration of turns. The distribution of turns is locally managed for each conversation. Rule 1(b) in particular allows for any participant to self-select as next speaker and this maximizes the set of potential next speakers at this point, but does not predetermine which member of this set will be next speaker, except that the first starter gains rights to a turn.

Turn size is not fixed, but varies

Two elements of the system allow for turn size to vary. First, the constituent elements of turns are variable in size, ranging from words to complex sentences. The system requires that a turn contains a possibly complete unit, but does not specify in a context-free way what such a unit will look like. Speakers have a free selection among possible unit types. Secondly, the possibility of current speaker continuing as next speaker allows for the possibility that a turn can contain more than one TCU, or an extension of an existing TCU beyond the first possible completion. The recurrent nature of this rule means that the system does not provide for a maximum turn size, although it does provide for a normal minimum turn size of one TCU.

Number of parties can vary

The turn-taking system is not dependent on a specified number of participants and applies equally to conversations between two people or between much larger groups. In two person conversations, the application of rule 1(b) is less problematic because of the reduced size of the pool of potential next speakers, but the rule set applies equally to these sorts of conversations as well as to larger groups.

At the same time, the nature of the turn-taking system favours interactions within small groups. The rule set refers to only two participants, current speaker and next speaker, and this, coupled with the bias towards last speaker but one becoming next speaker, allows for the possibility of some participants being left out where there are three or more potential participants. In many cases in conversations between four or more people, where turns at talk are concentrated among only a small number of participants, the conversation may schism into two or more parallel conversations (Egbert, 1997). Within each of these conversations the turn-taking system will apply only to that particular conversation as long as the schism lasts.

Talk can be continuous or discontinuous
The turn-taking model explicates how talk can continue to occur in a conversation, but also provides for the possibility that talk may cease for a time during a conversation. Rules 1(b) and 1(c) provide for the possibility of some participant becoming next speaker, but they do not oblige any participant to become next speaker. This means that when a current speaker stops and has not selected a next speaker, it is possible that no speaker will self-select to start or continue to speak and a lapse in the talk results. At the same time, if a current speaker selects a next speaker, a silence would be problematic, because rule 1(a) both confers a right to speak and an obligation to speak. The system, therefore, provides for situations in which silences will be heard differently. In some sequential positions a silence will be hearable as a particular participant's silence and will be accountable as a lack of talk from that participant. In other sequential positions, a silence will not be hearable as anyone's particular silence, but as a lapse in the conversation – as a discontinuity in the talk. Once a conversation has become discontinuous, it can be revived by any participant self-selecting as next speaker.

Repairing turn-taking errors and violations

The model proposed by Sacks *et al.* (1974) is, as has been seen, susceptible to troubles in its organization, such as overlapping talk or silences, and because the system is interactionally accomplished by participants in conversation, violations of the system must inevitably occur. If the turn-taking system is to function, there must be some mechanisms by which the normal functioning of the system can be restored.

In English, there are a number of explicit devices designed specifically for repairing problems of turn-taking. These include devices like *Who me?* for repairing problems relating to 'current speaker selects next' or *Excuse me* for repairing speaker change at points in the talk where such change is accountable. In addition, there are a range of less explicit interactional practices relating to dealing with problematic instances of overlapping talk (see Chapter 4). For example, practices such as false starts, repeating or recycling speech which has occurred in overlap, and various hitches and perturbations in the delivery of talk in overlap can be deployed by speakers to repair turn-taking problems, as can stopping talk before possible completion. Some of these devices (*who me?*, *excuse me*, etc.) are external to the turn-taking system itself, while others (stopping, continuing, recycling, etc.) are internal to it. Stopping before possible completion as a device for repairing 'more than one speaker at a time' is based on the turn constructional module which provides for speaking to possible completion of a TCU. Sacks *et al.* (1974) also argue that the application of the 'current speaker continues' strategy can also be seen as a repair device in its own right in that it serves to repair an absence of speaker change after a TRP. At the same time, Sacks *et al.* (1974) argue that the turn-taking system itself provides constraints on other types of repair behaviour. As such, repairs of problems of hearing and understanding are not done until a turn has been completed: that is, at the TRP after the repairable has occurred. Repair is initiated by recipients at the moment it occurs, but is integrated into the turn-taking system relevant to conversation.

Turns and TCUs

The argument so far has been that speakers gain rights to produce a single TCU when they gain the floor and that this right expires at the first possible completion point unless the right is re-established. This gives the impression that a turn at talk consists of only a single TCU, and to some extent this is normally the case. However, in conversation other possibilities are also found. A turn at talk may sometimes consist of more than one TCU, and sometimes a single TCU may be constructed over a series of turns and by more than one participant.

Multi-TCU turns

The possibility of a turn including more that one TCU has already been raised above as an operation of rule 1(c), current speaker continues, which allows for current speakers continuing speaking and producing a new TCU, leading to a multi-TCU turn at talk. There are, however, other ways in which speakers may be able to produce more than one TCU in a turn. In all cases, however, being able to produce more than one TCU in a turn is the result of interactional work, not the result of a right to produce more than one TCU. In other words, there is no guarantee that a speaker will be able to produce more than one TCU before speaker change occurs and longer turns are created jointly as the work of the speaker and of the recipient. Speakers can carry out a project of gaining a multi-unit turn at one of three points in a turn: at its beginning, at its middle and at its end (Schegloff, 1982).

At the beginning of a TCU, the speaker may produce a device which indicates that there is a longer than usual piece of talk to come. One such device is producing a list beginner such as 'first of all'. List beginners make a claim for a certain type of structure as the proposed action under way. Lists are themselves multi-part activities, typically but not universally, being made up of two or three parts (Jefferson, 1990). A list beginner can, therefore, indicate that what is to come will be completed when it is hearable as a list and in so doing foreshadows a more complex turn at talk. A second common but less overt device found at TCU beginnings is audible breathing. Like a list beginner, a large audible in-breath can indicate that there is a longer than usual bit of talk to come and more breath will be needed to get through it.

In the middle of a TCU, devices can be employed which project more talk to come. These devices include markedly first verbs which indicate more to come. For example, the verb *tried* in English presupposes the idea of failure, as is shown in (21).

```
(21) [Lunch]
     Harry:   so did- did you ask him if he w' d do the ses-
              sion next week
  →  Joy:     I tri:ed. He' s sorta got a lot on ' t the
              moment
     Harry:   hhhh well we' ll jus haftuh think of some-
              thin' else 'f' e can' do it.
```

Joy's answer in extract (21) contains two TCUs: *I tri:ed* and *He's sorta got a lot on 't the moment*. The first TCU implies more to come and this is produced as the next TCU. In this extract, Joy achieves a second TCU, but it also needs to be considered as an application of rule 1(c): Joy continues as speaker because Harry does not become next speaker at the end of the first TCU. Speaker change could still legitimately have occurred after Joy's *I tri:ed*.

In a similar way, speakers may deploy a prospective indexical (C. Goodwin, 1996), that is an element which makes cataphoric reference to some, as yet to be produced, unit of talk, and which requires the use of further talk to elaborate or resolve the reference. This can be seen in extract (22).

```
(22) [Complaint]
        Andy:     I jus' can get anythin' through.
        Bert:     i's a bugger when tha' happens.
    →   Andy:     so this is what I did. I went do:wn to the shop
                  and I took the antenna . . .
```

Here, Andy produces an initial TCU in which the word *this* points forward to a future telling, which then unfolds as a multi-unit turn. The indexical projects beyond the first possible completion to something coming up next and, in the absence of talk from Bert, Andy proceeds in the same turn to produce additional units of talk. Andy's *this* is a cataphor which works to indicate further talk because it requires additional information to interpret the reference of this in the talk (Gernsbacher and Jesceniak, 2002). In order to resolve the reference of *this*, Bert needs to monitor future talk for something which will count as the projected *this* (C. Goodwin, 2002).

Current speakers may also do work near the end of a TCU to secure more talk within the current turn. The typical device found in this position is a 'rush through', as in (23).

```
(23) [Schegloff (1996b) TG]
        Bee:      yeh I bet they got rid of all the one::well
                  one I had, t!. hhh in the firs' term there,
                  fer the firs' term of English, she die::d
                  hhuh-uhh [ .hhh
        Ava:               [ oh:.
```

A 'rush through' (Schegloff, 1982) involves a decrease in the transition space between two TCUs as the result of speeding up delivery, withholding falling intonation and bridging the juncture between the two TCUs. In this case, Bee bridges the junction between the two TCUs by stretching the sound in *one::* and not producing the final *s* of *ones*, the appropriate word here. Instead she immediately moves into *well* at the beginning of a next unit, establishes this unit and then pauses (*t!. hhh*) at a place of maximal incompleteness of the unit she has just launched. By producing the rush through she has become the next speaker and having ensured her speakership through the early start can pause without the possibility of transition relevance occurring.

In the discussion above, the multi-unit turns were launched by work done by the current speaker; multi-unit turns do not only result from the behaviour of the current speaker within a current turn, but can be launched by a prior speaker. Devices which do this include:

1. current speaker producing a single TCU which counts as a story preface, and which solicits an extended turn for the speaker in the next turn but one (see chapter 8);
2. prior speaker soliciting something which by its nature is a multi-unit turn, such as a story in response to a question;
3. current speaker producing a preliminary to a preliminary, such as *Can I ask you a question? Can I ask you a favour?* (Schegloff, 1980), which solicits an extended turn in the next turn but one (see chapter 6).

The common element in all of these devices is that they are inter-actionally accomplished between the participants to the talk. None of the devices ensures a multi-unit turn, but rather provides an indication that a multi-unit turn is a possible action for a particular participant. Whether or not the participant produces a multi-unit turn depends as much on a recipient allowing the turn as it does on the speaker pro-ducing it.

Multi-turn TCUs

It is possible in some cases that a TCU can be distributed over more than one turn at talk. Lerner (1991, 1996a) has identified compound TCUs with two-part formats where this may be possible. Lerner iden-tifies units such as *if ... then* and *when ... then* construction as typical examples of these compound TCUs, as in (24).

        (24) [Lerner (1996) Smith: Thanksgiving]
            Lynn: When you don't get any appreciation back
                     from teachers, well its like ferget it.

These TCUs are made up of two components, a preliminary com-ponent which has its own projectable possible completion and which also projects a possible form for the final component of the TCU and the TCU as a whole. It is, however, only in the final component that the possible completion of the TCU as a whole becomes roughly predictable. These units, Lerner argues, provide both recognizable possible completion and also projectable possible completion, which provide resources for recipients to provide an anticipatory completion, as in (25).

(25) [Lerner (1996) GTS]
```
Dan:     When the group reconvenes in two weeks=
Roger:   =they' re gunna issue straitjackets
```

In this extract, the *when ... then* structure provides both a place for anticipatory completion – the end of the preliminary component – and also a form – the projected final component. The next speaker is able to predict roughly where the turn at talk will be complete and provides a candidate version of that completion (Liddicoat, 2004). The result is that a single TCU is spread over two turns at talk by two speakers. Lerner (1996a) characterizes what is happening here as conditional access to the turn space, because the speaker change here is highly constrained. The next speaker must provide talk which completes the prior TCU and talk which is not hearable as completing the TCU would be accountable. As such, the result is a collaboratively completed TCU.

Sacks (1992: Fall 1965, Lecture 3) has identified another device which leads to the development of a single TCU across multiple turns at talk. In this case, however, rather than being based on a two-part format, it is achieved by adding increments to the talk of a prior speaker so that the talk produced becomes effectively part of a single grammatical unit.

(26) [Sacks (1992: 144)]
```
Joe:     We were in an automobile discussion.
Henry:   Discussing the psychological motives for
Mel:     Drag racing in the streets.
```

In each of the turns at talk by Henry and Mel, the current speaker adds an increment to the prior talk, and the talk over the turns has the form of a single sentential unit. Mel provides a collaborative completion for Henry's talk, but in this case it is based on the predictability of Henry's TCU so far. Henry does something different from the cases we have considered so far: he produces a further increment to Joe's already possibly complete utterance. In this case, the access to the turn space is not conditional and the talk in this position is not constrained. The talk at this point is possibly complete without projecting more talk. The next speaker, however, produces talk which is designed as second to the prior turn and which is implicated in the action undertaken by the prior turn. Schegloff (1996b) analyses turns such as those in (26) as TCUs which are designed not to have TCU beginnings: that is, they are designed not to start at a new point but to continue or augment prior talk.

These examples show that, while it is a feature of turn-taking that a speaker has the right to produce a single TCU and only a single TCU, this feature is not a deterministic rule. Instead, it provides a resource to which participants orient in creating their talk and which can be deployed in talk to achieve social effects. Phenomena such as multi-TCU turns and multi-turn TCUs do not, therefore, provide evidence against a basic organizational pattern of 'one TCU and only one TCU', instead they provide evidence for participants' orientation to this pattern and demonstrate that this orientation is a resource for constructing participation in talk.

Conclusion

The turn-taking system proposed by Sacks *et al.* (1974) is a system which is both context-free and context-sensitive. It is context-free in the sense that it is not dependent on characteristics of the talk, of the topic or of the participants. As such, it applies in any conversation. At the same time, it is context-sensitive in that what counts as possible completion determining speaker change varies according to what has gone before in the interaction and that mechanisms for turn allocation can be sensitive to the talk preceding the TRP. The turn-taking system provides a basis for the nature and organization of conversation. It very strongly links the construction of talk and the allocation of talk so that these two facets of talk can be integrated into a single set of procedures. The turn-constructional and the turn-allocational components of the Sacks *et al.* model are themselves resources which speakers can draw upon in order to construct talk. The components, and the rules which relate them, are not static invariable constructs for organizing talk, but rather are deployable resources which can be used to claim or demonstrate understanding and to organize participation.

4 Gaps and Overlaps in Turn-taking

Introduction

The preceding chapter examined speaker change as it relates to transition relevance places: points at which speaker change becomes a possible next action. It was argued that speaker change is a relevant next action at such a place and that speaker change typically occurs at such a place with neither a gap nor an overlap. However, both gaps and overlaps do occur in talk and they have an effect on the interaction. That is, gaps and overlaps are interpretable as doing something interactionally. Sometimes gaps and overlaps are problematic for turn-taking in conversation; however, this is not always the case. In order to develop a fuller understanding of how turn-taking works and when gaps or overlaps become interactionally problematic, the idea of a transition relevance place needs to be considered in relation to the idea of a *transition space* (Sacks, Schegloff and Jefferson, 1974; Jefferson, 1986; Schegloff, 1996). The transition space can be thought of as that part of a stretch of talk in which transition may occur and it can be characterized as commencing just prior to a TRP and finishing just after the end of a TRP. The idea of a transition space gives a sense of duration to the locus of speaker change and it is possible to identify a normal transition space, in which there is no gap and no overlap and deviations from this norm. The normal value for the transition space, a beat of silence, indicates that nothing special is being done in the transition between speakers. However, it is possible that the transition space may be longer than normal, for example as a gap, or shorter than normal, as in the case of overlap. Both of these possibilities have an interactional importance above and beyond speaker change itself.

Increased transition space

A lengthened transition space results in a silence in the talk. Silences work in different ways in different contexts and have different

interpretations in these contexts. When a silence occurs at the end of a
completed action in the talk, such as after the answer to a question, the
silence is not attributable to any particular speaker, as is the case in
extract (1).

(1) [HG:II:15 (Button and Casey, 1984)]
```
    N:          =You'll come abou:t (.) eight. Right?=
    H:          =Yea::h,=
    N:          =Okay.
                (0.2)
    N:          Anything else to report,
```

In this extract the action being undertaken is completed and it is
possible either of the speakers could legitimately speak in the place
occupied by the 0.2-second silence and the possible contribution that
could be made to the talk here is relatively unconstrained. Moreover,
the silence here is not attributable to a particular participant not
speaking; that is, N's silence is no more and no less relevant to the
interaction than H's. In this extract, neither party is talking and neither
is required to talk. This is not the case, however, in extract (2).

(2) [Lunch]
```
    Harry:      Didjih speak tuh Mary today?
      →         (0.2)
    Harry       Did yih speak tuh Mary?
    Joy         Oh, yea:h I saw her at lunch.
```

In this extract, the silence is hearable as belonging to one of the
participants (that is, Joy). Harry has produced a turn at talk which
requires further talk from Joy – an answer to the question. Harry has
selected next speaker in his turn and this next speaker has an obligation to speak on completion of this turn, as was seen in Chapter 3. The
silence here is therefore attributable to Joy and is interpretable as Joy
not speaking. Here, Joy's silence is interactionally relevant: she is not
speaking in a place where she is required to speak. Thus, while it is true
that neither party is speaking during the silence, this is not a complete
description of the pause, as talk is accountably absent for only one of
the participants.

When they occur, silences are treated in different ways in each of the two contexts. Where a silence does not belong to any particular speaker, it may become quite prolonged, and may result in a lapse in the talk. These lapses may be quite long and in some cases, such as where participants are travelling together, may be measurable in minutes or even hours. However, where a silence is attributable to an individual participant, it is likely to be repaired if it becomes too long, as in extract (2). Joy's silence is accountably absent and is therefore interpretable – it does something or indicates something about the interaction at this point. The presence of such a silence is usually interpretable as an indicator of some problem; in this case as a problem of hearing, and Harry repeats his original turn at talk as an attempt to repair the problem. Silences after a possible completion can also be repaired by the current speaker continuing with further talk as in (3):

(3) [OH: Anne and Beth 15]
```
Anne:     so are yih gonna be free on the weekend,
          (0.4)
Anne:     say on Saturday
Beth:     yeah
```

In Anne's first turn she produces a question and in so doing she produces talk which requires a response from Beth. As such, the 0.4-second silence is attributable to Beth, who is not providing an answer to the question. As with extract (2), the silence in extract (3) is interpretable as an indicator of some problem, however, in this case, Anne does not treat the turn as not having been heard, but rather a problem with the form of the turn itself. Anne's second turn adds an increment to her previous turn, giving additional precision about her prior *on the weekend*. This increment has the impact of repositioning the silence from being an inter-turn silence during which Beth is not speaking, to being an intra-turn silence during which Anne is not speaking. The increment here in a sense undoes the fact that Beth is not speaking and recharacterizes the silence as an instance of Anne not speaking. The effect of this is to undo the interactional problem occasioned by the prior talk.

In the above extracts it is clear that where a speaker expands the transition space by not providing talk which has been projected by prior talk, this expansion is interpretable as indicating some problem for the talk. The nature of the problem, however, is not specified by the expanded transition space itself, but rather by the context in which the silence is heard.

Reduced transition space

One way to reduce the transition space is for the next speaker to *latch* his/her talk to the talk of the prior speaker. When a speaker latches talk to the prior turn, there is no beat of silence between the turns, but there is also no overlap.

```
(4) [NB:II:3:R:1 (Jefferson, 1986)]
    Emma:    G' morning Letitia=
    Lottie:  =u-hHow' r YOU:.=
    Emma:    =FI:NE
```

In extract (4), the transition between turns at talk is done with what Jefferson (1986) calls 'absolute adjacency'; immediately after Emma finishes, Lottie starts and immediately after Lottie finishes Emma starts. The beat of silence which is the normal value of the transition space is not present.

The transition space may be further reduced to create a small amount of overlapping talk between the current speaker and the next speaker. Overlapping talk is often thought of as interruption, but the term *interruption* really conflates a number of different interactional features of overlapping talk. Overlapping talk can be either problematic or unproblematic. Small amounts of overlap do not usually seem to be problematic, as they are not treated as such by participants. Longer overlaps, however, may be problematic and speakers may do things through their talk to deal with the problem. The term *interruption* is best reserved for these problematic overlaps.

It is also important not to consider overlap simply as something that the speaker entering the talk does to the speaker who currently has the floor. Overlapping talk is an interactional phenomenon which is produced by speakers together. In some cases, overlap may be occasioned by a speaker continuing past a possible completion, as in extracts (5) and (6), which we discussed in the previous chapter.

```
(5) [Sacks, Schegloff and Jefferson (1974)]
    → A:        Uh you been down here before [ havenche.
    → B:                                     [ Yeh.
```

```
(6) [Jefferson (1973)]
    Penny:   O:kay. I' ll see yuh.
```

```
→ Agnes:    A::1? right [ Dear,
→ Penny:                [ Bye bye,
  Agnes:    Bye bye,
```

In these examples, the overlap can be seen as the result of the current speaker continuing beyond a TRP, rather than the next speaker unambiguously reducing the transition space by beginning to speak just before possible completion. The resulting overlap is short and is not treated by the participants as a problematic instance of two people speaking at the same time: there is no attempt to repair the overlap, or to undertake any other actions relating to the overlap.

Not all unproblematic overlap is produced by a speaker speaking beyond a TRP. Jefferson (1986) has identified cases in which a next speaker does not wait for possible completion but starts speaking just before a possible completion, as in extracts (7) and (8).

(7) [Crandall:2–15–68:93 (Sacks *et al.*, 1974)]
```
    A:      Well if you knew my argument why did you
            bother to a:[sk.
    B:                  [Because I'd like to defend my
            argument.
```

(8) [Her:01:2:2 (Jefferson, 1986)]
```
    Jean:    So well they won't be here Boxing [ Day¿
    Doreen:                                    [ Oh ↓well
             that doesn' mattuh
```

In these extracts, the next speaker begins to talk slightly before possible completion. In extract (7), the overlap begins mid-word, only two phones before possible completion, while in extract (8), Doreen's talk begins one word (or alternatively one syllable) before possible completion. The overlaps do not appear problematic – the possible completion is projectable, speaker change is effected and 'one speaker speaks at a time' is restored quickly at the possible completion itself. In these cases, the speakers have reduced the transition space through the timing of their own talk.

The construction of a reduced transition space may also be the result of the current speaker modifying talk in such a way that a reduced transition space results, especially by modifying the rhythm of their talk.

(9) [Schegloff (1986) 263]
```
    Hyla:    Hwaryuhh=
    Nancy:   =Fine how'r you.
```

```
Hyla:    Okay:[ y
Nancy:         [ Goo:d.
         (0.4)
```

In extract (9), Hyla's *okay:y* with its very lengthened final glide produces a turn at talk which is longer than what would have been projected from the beginning of the turn at talk. As such, Nancy's *goo:d* which begins just before completion has the effect of an early entry into her turn, but the early entry is in part due to the change in the rhythm of Hyla's talk.

In some cases, overlap is brought about by the first speaker producing more talk, where such talk is not usually expected, as in extract (10).

(10) [Her:OII:2:7:5:R (Jefferson, 1986)]
```
Doreen:  Yes well pop in on th' way back' n pick it up
Katie:   °Thhank you ve' y much° eh ha-how are you
         ↓ all.
         [ Yer a l [ittle ti:red] °nah°
Doreen:  [ Oh wir [ all fi:ne,   ] Yes I' m jus: sohrta
         clearing up
```

In this extract, Katie produces a complete question selecting a next speaker and requiring her to talk. At this point she should normally stop to allow the answer to be produced. Doreen's talk orients to the production of the question and she begins as next speaker. However, Katie also produces a candidate answer at the same time.

These examples reveal that overlapping talk is an interactional achievement rather than being simply the case of mistiming of the next speaker's entry into the talk or an interruption of the current talk. In fact, in extract (9) in particular, the overlap appears to have been engineered by the current speaker. As an interaction achievement, interruption is an interpretable action in talk, and the reduction of the transition space is meaningful in context. A reduced transition space may be deployed by next speakers to achieve certain interactional ends. It can, for example, be used where there is possible competition for the floor between possible next speakers. In Chapter 3 it was argued that where more than one speaker starts at about the same time, the first speaker to start usually gets the turn. This means that there is a motivation for starting early and a reduced turn space allows the possibility of pushing the onset of talk to an earlier point than a normal transition space, and in so doing increasing the possibility of becoming the first speaker to start. In extract (11), Carol uses a reduced

transition space to gain early entry to her turn at talk, and proceeds to
tell a second story in response to Joy's earlier telling.

```
(11) [Lunch]
      Joy:       that w' z r:eally a:weful b' d in thuh end we
                 sorta had a good t[i:me
  →   Carol:                       [yeh=th[a' w' z like what=
  →   Harry:                              [i-
      Carol:    = happen' tuh us when we wen' up the coas' we
                 had . . .
```

Carol's strategy seems to have been quite successful as it pre-empts
Harry's becoming next speaker when he begins to talk after possible
completion. Had Carol waited until the TRP, both she and Harry
would have started to talk simultaneously and Harry may even have
emerged as next speaker. However, by the time Harry begins speaking,
Carol has already begun her talk and Harry drops out immediately.

If gaining speakership through an early start were the only outcome
which can be achieved by a reduced transition space, however, many
cases of reduced transition spaces in conversations with only two participants where competition for the floor is less of an issue would be
unexpected, as the rules relating to speaker change at TRPs would
seem to preclude such a motivation. Early entry into a turn is not only
deployable as a way to gain speakership, it also creates interactional
effects. These effects vary a lot with context. In extract (12), the
overlapping talk serves to show understanding.

```
(12) [Jefferson (1983)]
      Joe:       B' t he wannid the] dawg dih bite iz wife.
                 (0.5)
      ():        [ ] °ehhh°
      Joe:       [ ] So ↑he come[s ho:me one ] night ] the sonofa] =
      Carol:                    [heh heh heh] heh he] h heh  heh]
  →   Joe:      =bitch [ bit hi:m.]
  →   Carol:           [ bit hi:m,]
```

In this example, Carol's overlap is a demonstration that she understands the trajectory that Joe's talk has projected – that she is 'tuned in'
to the story. It is a much stronger display of understanding than a
repetition after a normal transition space would have been and is also a
stronger indication of Carol's involvement as a recipient for the story.
Carol uses the context and the unfolding talk as a resource for collaboratively completing Joe's turn at talk and in so doing asserts her

understanding and displays understanding of the humour involved in the telling (Liddicoat, 2004).

A reduced transition space is also common in cases of disagreement or rejection of prior talk, as in extract (13).

```
(13) [Debbie and Shelley 3:12]
     Debbie:   I mean at a:ll.
     Shelley: alright, [ well don get ma:[ d at me.
   → Debbie:             [ .hh               [ .HH I' M NOT MA:D
              but it jus seems like its like you can' t do
              anything unl;ess there' s a gu:y involved an
              it jus pisses me o-<I' m jus bein rea:l
              ho:nest ya cuz it' s like¿ . hh[h   [ why=
     Shelley:                                [whe [ n
     Debbie:   wouldn:t- why wouldn' t you g,b' cuz >I mean<
              that' s what Jay Tee told me you told hi:m¿
```

In the arrowed turn, Shelley begins her turn in overlap with Debbie's talk, beginning her in-breath before Debbie's first possible completion (ma:d) and continues to overlap with the emerging talk. The effect this overlap gives is of strong disagreement, beginning at the first place at which disagreement is possible.

Similarly, overlapping talk can also be used to display enthusiasm, as in extract (14).

```
(14) [SJ: 11]
     Sally:   wull y-I met this really cu::te [ guy,
     Jean:                                    [ OH   WO::W
              REally?
```

In this extract, Jean's early entry in the turn produces an effect of strong interest through quick uptake of the topic. In her talk the loudness and the *wow* both indicate a strong interest and this is further reinforced by the early entry Jean makes into her response to Sally's talk. Extracts (12), (13) and (14) all exploit early entry into the turn to show quick uptake of the trajectory of the prior speaker's talk and uses this quick uptake to emphatically display understanding of the talk, thereby strengthening the effect of the talk produced. The effect or enthusiasm, disagreement, etc., however, is contextual: it is achieved by particular talk produced in relation to the talk it follows rather than being signalled by the early entry itself.

Problematic overlap

In the cases discussed above, overlapping talk occurs in places which are just prior to possible completion, that is, within the transition space, and produces very short overlaps. The overlapping talk registers some interactional goal is being undertaken in the talk and is not treated by participants as problematic. Cases of reduced transition space are not, however, the only instances of overlapping talk found in conversation. Some overlap occurs at a point in the talk which is prior to the beginning of the transition space – that is, it does not orient to the upcoming completion of talk. Where this happens, the overlap is not quickly resolved by one speaker reaching possible completion and so longer overlap is a possibility in these contexts.

In some cases of overlap, the entry of the next speaker during another's talk can be seen as a miscue in the turn-taking system, as was seen in the discussion in the last chapter of the talk repeated in extract (8).

```
(15) [Trio:II Sacks, Schegloff and Jefferson (1974)]
     Penny:     An' the fact is I- is- I jus' thought it was
  →             so kind of stupid [ I didn' even say anything=
  → Janet:                        [ Y-
     Penny:     =[when I came ho:me.
  → Janet:      [Eh-
                (0.3)
     Janet:     Well Estelle jus' called'n . . .
```

Here, Janet produces overlapping talk at possible completion places in Penny's talk; that is, at places where speaker change is possible. However, Penny's turn is not actually complete at these possible completions and Janet and Penny are speaking in overlap. In these cases, extended overlap is a possibility where two speakers are beginning TCUs at the same time. In this extract, the problem does not persist, as it is resolved by Janet discontinuing her talk.

Another possible source of overlapping talk is a simultaneous start by two self-selecting speakers. This can happen when the prior speaker does not select a next speaker and two (or more) next speakers begin at the same time (16). It can also happen where, in the absence of some other speaker starting a turn at talk, the prior speaker self-selects as next speaker at the same time as some other speaker self-selects (17).

```
(16) [Frankel: 67 (Sacks et al., 1974)]
     Mike:     I know who d' guy is.=
     Vic:      =[He' s ba::d.
     James:     [ You know the gu:y?
```

(17) [UTCL J66.3 (Drummond, 1989)]
```
X:        Is that who we use to do those dividers
Y:        Yeah.
          (0.9)
Y:        [ and she] said it took- they didn' t do- (.)
X:        [ Well   ]
Y:        very good proof reading or anything
```

In both these extracts, two speakers begin a TCU at the same time. Sacks *et al.* (1974) have noted that where two speakers self-select as next speaker, the first to begin gets the turn. However, this is of no help in the present cases, as there is no speaker who begins first. In such cases, the overlapping is a problematic instance of more than one speaker at a time.

In some cases, overlapping talk begins just after a prior speaker has begun to speak, as in extracts (18) and (19).

(18) [NB:IV:3:R:5 (Jefferson, 1986)]
```
Lottie:   becuz they would really be the Spri:ng.
          Let' [s see tha] t' s twunny fi:' dollars . . .
Emma:          [ Y e a h. ]
```

(19) [JG:I:24:8–9 (Jefferson, 1986)]
```
Laura:    But I know thet Joe did say he had a letter
          from im.
          (1.2)
Marge:    Eh di[d he tell you- .hh
Laura:         [That' s all he said.
Marge:    Well did he tell you that when you phoned im
          . . .
```

Jefferson (1986) argues that cases of overlapping talk such as those found in these extracts can be explained by the result of an application of the turn-taking system rather than simple cases of a speaker starting in interruption. In these extracts, it appears that the second speaker's talk has been designed to be produced after an expanded transition space; that is, after a pause, but the prior speaker self-selects as next speaker during this transition space. Jefferson sees in these examples cases of simultaneous starts in which one speaker begins the turn with a brief pause. She presents these overlaps as:

(18') [NB:IV:3:R:5 (Jefferson, 1986)]
```
Lottie:   becuz they would really be the Spri:ng.
```

```
              (Let') [s see tha] t's twunny fi:' dollars . . .
Emma:         (___) [ Ye a h.]
```

(19') [JG:I:24:8-9 (Jefferson, 1986)]
```
Laura:    But I know thet Joe did say he had a letter
          from im.
          (1.2)
Marge:    (Eh di)[d he tell you- .hh
Laura:    (____ )[ That's all he said.
Marge:    Well did he tell you that when you phoned im
          . . .
```

In the transcriptions here the underlined space represents the preceding pause in overlap with simultaneous talk. In these cases, both speakers are in speakership and not listening for or hearing a bit of talk by the other. Such overlap is an instance of problematic overlap, in which one speaker at a time needs to be restored. Jefferson (1986) further argues that these cases demonstrate the interactional achievement of not having heard the other speaker rather than simply reflecting a situation in which one speaker cannot hear what the other is doing. They do this by showing that the speaker is not attending to bits of talk to which it would be possible to react.

In the cases discussed so far, overlapping talk, even where it is a problematic instance of more than one speaker speaking at a time, is oriented to features of the turn-taking system. In some cases, however, overlap occurs without such clear reference to features of the turn-taking system, as in extract (20).

(20) [UTCL J66 (Drummond, 1989)]
```
Gloria:   .hhhh that's what I s(h)aid I said well
          [ you can send em to me now huh ]
Pam:      [  you probably wouldn't say ] bring em in
          person or something
```

In this extract, the overlap does not begin either just before or just after a possible completion. Instead it begins at a point of incompletion. Gloria's *I said* projects in the form of a quotation what had been said in the recalled conversation. In cases such as these, the overlapping talk again represents a problem for turn-taking which is not easily resolved by a speaker soon reaching possible completion. This extract shows clearly interrupting talk; that is, talk which is specifically designed to enter into another's talk at a point where speaker change is not a relevant activity.

The nature of overlapping talk

In conversation, it appears that when more than one person is speaking at a time, it is most commonly the case that there are two people talking at a time, regardless of the number of participants in the conversation (Schegloff, 2000b). In fact, Schegloff argues that instances of talk by more than two people at a time are usually instances of two speakers beginning simultaneously in overlap with a third (current) speaker and quickly resolved to instances of two people speaking at a time when the third speaker reaches a completion. Instances of more than two speakers beginning at a time are also possible, but are less easily resolved than in the case of two simultaneous speakers beginning in overlap. Schegloff cites the following extract as a case in point:

```
(21) [Post-party, 7 (Schegloff, 2000b)]
     Marty:    Ih w′ z a liddle well done.
     Fred:     Uhm,
  →  Anne:     Oh[: I      s] aw]   a] l:lot′ v ra:re pieces.
  →  Fred:       [I[t w   z ]   fi] :ne] .
  →  Marty:        [Ih w′ za-] Ih-]  Ih] w′ z a fanta:stic
               piece a′ meat.
```

In extract (21), three speakers (Marty, Fred and Anne) begin to talk at about the same time. Marty is producing an assessment with which the others disagree. This incipient disagreement is indicated by Fred's *uhm,* and Anne's *oh* and these intimations of disagreement prompt a back down by Marty as a pre-emptive response to the projected disagreements from his interlocutors. At this point three turns come to be launched almost simultaneously, with the prospect of sustained overlap by more than two speakers.

Situations in which two people speak at a time fall into three possible configurations (Schegloff, 2000b), which can be represented as:

(22)   (a)   (b)   (c)

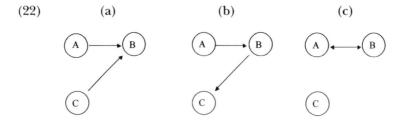

The configuration presented in (22(a)) shows that one possible source of problematic overlap occurs when two speakers address the same recipient. This means that two participants are competing for the attention of another participant and where this occurs the address participant has an important role in resolving the overlap: the eye gaze of the recipient is very important in determining what will happen. In this case, two speakers are competing for a single recipient and securing eye gaze is important in securing a recipient (Goodwin, 1979, 1981). The speaker who does not secure the recipient's eye gaze commonly drops out, although this speaker may also compete more vigorously for the recipient's attention. The configuration in (22(b)) involves each speaker addressing a different recipient and here the roles of both speaker and recipient are problematic. The overlapping talk here can be resolved either by B ceasing to speak and becoming the recipient for A's talk, or by A ceasing to speak and becoming a non-participant in the exchange. The configuration in (22(c)) involves two speakers addressing each other and so the roles of both speaker and recipient are problematic, with each speaker having each of the roles. This configuration is also possible in conversations with only two participants and in which all overlap will necessarily be of this type.

Resolving overlapping talk

The discussion so far has raised the idea of a potential for competition between speakers in relation to overlap. More than one person speaking at a time can be an interactional problem, and this problem can only be resolved by a return to one person speaking at a time. The solution involves one speaker emerging as the only speaker and the other speaker losing speakership. As there is no 'rule' which determines who should emerge as the sole speaker, speakership becomes something for which participants compete interactionally, at moments of overlap, with a view to becoming *the* speaker at this point in the conversation.

Schegloff (2000b) has outlined an overlap resolution device which is employed by conversationalists to deal with problematic instances of overlap. This device is composed of three elements:

1. a set of resources which can be used in the production of a turn;
2. a set of places in a turn at talk in which these devices can be deployed;
3. an interactional logic which relates the resources and places.

Resources for resolving overlap

Overlapping talk is characterized by the deployment of two types of resources within turns: resources which interrupt the continuity of the talk and resources which depart from the prosody of the turn so far. Schegloff (2000b) calls the former 'hitches' and the latter 'perturbations'. Commonly occurring hitches include:

1.   cutting off the talk so far, usually in conjunction with an oral stop, such as a glottal or velar stop;
2.   prolonging a segment of talk;
3.   repeating a just prior element.

Common perturbations found in overlap are:

1.   increased volume;
2.   higher pitch;
3.   faster or slower pace of talk.

These resources are found in other places in talk, but they are very frequent in overlap and are deployed strategically in overlap to achieve relevant interactional goals. This deployment can be seen in extract (23).

```
(23) [Car conversation]
     Sasha:  [ oh yea:h, an there' s a tree: as well] so it
             is a [ bad  ] spot
     Nick:        [ yeah.]
     Elvis:  yea[h, it is] .
 →   Nick:       [this- th] is pedestrian didn' have right
             of way but I thought (.) okay I' ll be polite
             an stop,
```

In extract (23), Nick recycles the beginning of his turn *[this-th]is*, a device which is found in other contexts, such as repair, but which here serves to allow his talk to emerge from the overlap with Elvis' prior talk. The timing of Nick's talk is such that he enters into the talk just prior to a possible completion of Elvis' turn, which is, however, not an actual completion. The recycling helps to overcome the resulting 'mistiming' of his start.

(24) [TG14:36–43 (Schegloff, 2000b)]

```
    Bee:      t! We:ll, uhd-yihknow I-I don' wanna make
              any-thing definite because I- yihknow
              I jis::t thinkin:g tihday all day riding
              around on th' trai:ns hhuh-uh
              hh[h!
    Ava:         [Well there's nothing else t' do<I  wz
              thingin[g of taking the car anyway.       ] .hh
    Bee:             [That I would go into the ss-uh-] =I
              would go into the city but I don' t know,
```

In extract (24), Bee begins deploying hitches and perturbations just prior to Ava's possible completion. As in the previous extract, her talk serves to extend her current talk just to the moment when Ava's turn is coming to a possible completion. Examples such as these show that these hitches and perturbations and not randomly distributed into the talk, but rather are deployed in ways which show a strong orientation to the turn-taking system itself. In each case, the disfluencies in the talk are positioned in such a way as to continue talk past a possible completion and become the sole speaker as the result of the possible relevance of speaker change at such a point.

Places for deploying overlap resolution devices

Overlap resolution devices can be deployed at different places in relation to the beginning of the overlap itself. This means that there is no one canonical position in which overlap resolution devices must be employed, but rather the deployment of these is responsive to the local conditions of talk. Moreover, it is not the case that overlap has to have happened for overlap resolution devices to be deployed. Overlapping talk, like other forms of talk, can be projected by certain speaker behaviours and overlap resolution devices can be deployed where overlap is projectable as a future action, but before overlap actually occurs. Schegloff (2000b) refers to this place as the *pre-onset phase* of overlapping talk.

The sorts of behaviours which can project future overlap include: repositioning of the recipient's body, deploying a gesture, or pre-beginning practices such as audible in-breathing, all of which can indicate that the recipient is about to begin a turn. In the presence of such practices, a current speaker may deploy overlap resolution devices to address the possible overlap even before it has occurred, as in extract (25).

```
(25) [Lunch]
     Joy:      an yih know I didn' wanna do: somethin' like
   → that c' z sh' s my sister an a[ll<I      DI] DN' =
     Harry:                             [ .hhgh yih-]
     Joy:      = wuh- wanna do that tuh her yih know
     Harry:    yeah no yih woudn'
```

Here Joy speeds up her talk by rushing through from *all* to *I* and also upgrades her prosody producing the *I didn'* a little louder than the preceding talk. The 'trigger' for these seems to be Harry's audible breathing (*.hhghn-*) although some non-verbal device may also have preceded this. Joy's talk deploys overlap resolution devices before the onset of the overlap and Harry's overlap does not proceed. By speeding up her talk, Joy seems to be allowing room for the overlapping talk to begin, while the increase in volume competes with any talk which may be produced. Of course, Joy's talk doesn't inevitably head off overlap and overlapping talk can still eventuate even if overlap resolution is attempted in pre-onset position, as extract (26) shows.

```
(26) [Upholstery shop, 43 (Schegloff, 2000b)]
     James:    Alright. Becau:se, it' s insured anyway,
               when I call de office, dey' ll send a man up eh
   → tuh put that glass I:N.
     Vic:      Well,
     James:    But dis [ person thet DID IT, ]
     Vic:              [ If I see the person,]
     James:    -IS GOT TUH BE::. hh taken care of. You know
               what [ I mean,
```

In this extract, James, who is reaching a possible completion, appears to register that Vic is preparing to start a turn, which actually begins just after James' possible completion. James produces much louder talk at the end of his turn, seeking to head off a possible overlap with his next bit of talk; however, Vic goes on to produce talk in overlap.

While it is possible to pre-empt overlap by deploying overlap resolution devices in pre-onset position, most overlap is actually resolved after the overlap has actually begun. Schegloff (2000b) identifies attempts at overlap resolution which begin just after the overlap itself begins as being in the *post-onset phase* of the overlap.

Post-onset overlap resolution typically has the form of slowing down the pace of the talk through such devices as sound stretches and repetitions: marking time until the overlapping speaker reaches completion and talk can emerge in the clear. This shows that overlap resolution is qualitatively different in different places (Schegloff, 2000b): resolution in pre-onset position involves speeding up talk to pre-empt starting, while in post-onset position it involves slowing down talk to delay finishing. As such, the idea of places for overlap resolution is not a convenient way for analysts to categorize the location of a particular type of talk in relation to other talk happening at the same time, rather it is a reflection of the ways in which participants themselves resolve overlap.

Hitches and perturbations can be deployed just before possible completion to hold talk until a projected completion has dealt with the overlap. Schegloff (2000b) refers to this as the *pre-resolution position*. Bee produces overlap resolution devices in pre-resolution position in extract (27).

```
(27) [TG14:36–43 (Schegloff, 2000b)]
     Bee:     t! We:ll, uhd-yihknow I-I don' wanna make
              any-thing definite because I- yihknow I
              jis::t thinkin:g tihday all day riding
              around on th' trai:ns hhuh-uh
              hh[h!
     Ava:       [Well there's nothing else t' do<I wz
              thingin[g of taking the car anyway.      ] .hh
  →  Bee:            [That I would go into the ss-uh-] = I
              would go into the city but I don' t know,
```

Here Bee's talk proceeds normally until her *ss-uh-* which is placed just before Ava's possibly complete TCU comes to its completion point. Through these hitches, Bee holds on to her turn at talk for a little longer and is still speaking when Ava finishes, moving into the clear, becoming a solo speaker and recycling her earlier talk which is no longer in competition.

Overlap resolution devices are also sometimes employed after a speaker's talk has emerged into the clear: that is, after the resolution of the overlap itself. Schegloff (2000b) calls this *post-resolution position*. It does not appear that hitches and perturbations in this position are serving to prevent overlap, but rather they seem to have another function linked to overlap resolution. During overlapping talk, speakers can deploy practices of talking which in other contexts are interpretable as doing something other than speaking normally, for example, loud talk during overlap is competing for the turn space, but when the speaker is speaking alone it may be heard as shouting and consequently as anger or some other condition. Post-resolution position is the place in which adjustments can be made in the way of

speaking once the overlap has been resolved and to return to more
usual ways of solo speaking (Schegloff, 2000b).

```
(28) [Lunch]
     Joy:     an yih know I didn' wanna do: somethin' like
              that c' z sh' s my sister an a[ll<I     DI] DN' =
     Harry:                              [.hhgh yih-]
  →  Joy:     = wuh- wanna do that tuh her yih know
     Harry:   yeah no yih woudn'
```

In extract (28), Joy's talk emerges into the clear after Harry's talk has
stopped, leaving Joy's talk still at a high volume. Almost immediately
after Harry's withdrawal from the overlapping talk, Joy cuts off her talk
(a hitch) and resets her volume to her more 'normal' speaking level
and completes the turn at this level. This means that, while the talk in
this position does not seem to be used to resolve overlap, it is used to
deal with some of the consequences of overlap resolution.

The interactional logic of overlap resolution

Schegloff (2000b) argues that the relevant organizational unit for the
resolution of overlap is the 'beat'. He defines the beat as being roughly
equivalent to a syllable, but acknowledges that the nature of the beat
actually needs further elaboration. What is clear, however, is that the
deployment of hitches and perturbations is oriented to rhythmic
properties of turns as they unfold. Schegloff demonstrates this orientation through examples of a 'fine-tuned fit' between the beats of
overlapping talk, as in extracts (29) and (30).

```
(29) [TG 05:02–05 (Schegloff, 2000b)]
     Bee:     nYeeha. .hh This feller I have- (nn) / (iv-)
              'fellah' ; this ma:n. (0.2) t! .hhh He
              ha:: (s)
              -uff-eh-who-who I have fer Linguistics
              [is] real] ly too much, .hh[ h=]
     Ava:     [Mm]   hm?]
```

```
(30) [TG11:19–23 (Schegloff, 2000b)]
     Bee:              [ Still not gettin married
     Ava:     .hhh Oh no. Definitely not.[mar] ried.]
     Bee:                        [No ] he' s]
              dicided defin[itely?]
```

In these examples, the overlapping talk coincides rhythmically. In extract (29), Ava's *mm hm?* is overlaid on Bee's *is really* in such away that each beat of Ava's talk occurs simultaneously with each beat of Bee's emerging talk. In the same way in extract (30) Bee's *No he's* coincides with the beats of Ava's *married*. These examples show clearly that participants are using a rhythmic structure to organize their talk and give evidence that a unit such as 'beat' is a relevant one for participants.

In examining overlap using the beat as a unit, we can view each bit of overlapping talk as consisting of a series of emerging beats which provide places for sequential and interactional organization. During overlap, what each speaker does at each beat of overlap can be examined as an instance of what speakers do in relation to the immediately preceding beat. Schegloff (2000b) schematizes as in (31).

(31)

	1st beat	2nd beat	3rd beat	4th beat
Les:	[L1 |			
Pat:	[P1 |			

Here, Les and Pat begin to talk simultaneously, producing the first beat of their overlapping talk. As Les begins his talk (L1), he can hear Pat speaking (P1), and Pat, as he is producing talk, can hear Les. The next beat will, therefore, be the place at which they register and react to the overlap which has just occurred. At this point, the speakers have a set of possible alternatives: each speaker could stop at this point and not produce a second beat or he could continue to speak and produce a second beat. These alternatives apply equally to each speaker. If one speaker ceases to speak, the overlap is resolved. The same is true if both speakers cease speaking, although the ensuing result is silence, which, as noted above, is also a turn-taking problem that requires resolution. If both speakers continue, the overlap moves into a second beat as in (31a).

(31a)

	1st beat	2nd beat	3rd beat	4th beat
Les:	[L1 |	L2 |		
Pat:	[P1 |	P2 |		

At the second beat (L2, P2), each participant is able to hear the stance that his interlocutor has taken to the overlap: to stop or persist. Here both speakers persist and the interaction a problem remains.

Again both speakers have available the same alternatives as before: to stop or to produce another (third) beat of talk.

In addition, from the second beat of overlapping talk the speakers also have other resources which can be deployed. They can continue to talk using the usual mode of production employed by a solo speaker or they can shift to competitive production by using the hitches and perturbations discussed above (in this case in post-onset position). This competitive talk projects that the speaker will continue with the turn currently under way, as in (31b), in which Les upgrades his talk to competitive mode.

(31b)

	1st beat	2nd beat	3rd beat	4th beat
Les:	[L1 |	L2 |		
Pat:	[P1 |	P2 |		

At the second beat, Pat can now hear that Les has not only continued talking, but that he has begun to talk in competitive mode. He has made a claim to the turn space and has projected continued talk in the turn. In response to Les' upgraded talk, Pat can now withdraw from the talk, thereby resolving the overlap, he can continue to talk in solo production or he too can upgrade his talk to competitive mode. If Pat continues to talk into the third beat, regardless of the mode of talk he adopts, there will be serious competition for the turn space as neither speaker has displayed a willingness to relinquish the turn to the other.

(31c)

	1st beat	2nd beat	3rd beat	4th beat
Les:	[L1 |	L2 |	L3 |	
Pat:	[P1 |	P2 |	P3 |	

In (31c), Pat has upgraded his talk to competitive mode in the third beat, while Les has continued to talk in this mode. Both have now projected continuing to speak in this turn. In the fourth beat, the speakers can now register their reactions to the talk as it has emerged at the third beat. Both Les and Pat may, for example, further upgrade their talk by deploying further hitches and perturbations and create an extended fight for the floor. Such fights are, however, not common in English (Schegloff, 2000b). Typically at this point, one of the speakers will withdraw from interaction and the overlap will be resolved.

What emerges from this discussion is a model of the interactional nature of overlap resolution. At each next moment in emerging overlapping talk, the participants' stances on the overlap are registered and enacted and at each next moment participants have the possibility of either ceasing to talk, continuing to talk in the same mode or upgrading their talk. The model itself does not require overlap to be short; rather it shows how devices for overlap resolution can be deployed at particular places in emerging talk to deal with the interactional problem posed by overlapping talk. The model does, however, provide for the possibility of overlapping talk being resolved quickly, as a single beat of overlapping talk provides enough opportunity for overlap to be resolved. Much overlap is resolved after a single beat by the withdrawal of one or both parties to the interaction at the first moment at which overlap has been perceived (Schegloff, 2000b), as in extracts (32) and (33).

```
(32) [Lunch]
      Joy:      that w' z r:eally a:weful b' d in thuh end we
                sorta had a good t[i:me
 →  Carol:                        [yeh th[a'] w' z like what=
 →  Harry:                               [i-]
      Carol:    =happen' tuh us when we wen' up the coas' we
                had . . .

(33) [HG, 1 (Schegloff, 2000b)]
 →  Hyla:    [ Bu:t]
 →  Nancy:   [ My ] face hurts
```

In each of these extracts, the speaker drops out after a single beat in the talk. However, in some cases where the rhythmic structures in the talk are not so well aligned, a single beat in one speaker's talk may not coincide with a single beat in the other's talk as in extracts (34) and (35).

```
(34) [Car conversation]
      Nick:    [ yeah.]
 →  Sasha:   i' s [ jus so-]
 →  Nick:          [ we' ve ] been budgeting big time we' re
                 like livin' on ten dollars a day sorta shit,

(35) [HG, 1 (Schegloff, 2000b)]
      Mike:    =y' coudn' t git[ta hol-]
      Vic:                      [m a n ] tell' im.
```

In these extracts, a single beat in one speaker's talk coincides with more than one beat in the other's talk. In each of these cases, the speaker who produces the 'extra' beat stops speaking (although this is not inevitably the case in overlap resolution).

As we have seen, overlapping talk may survive beyond the first beat. Where this happens, the majority of overlaps are resolved one beat after a speaker upgrades to competitive talk (Schegloff, 2000a); that is, immediately after one speaker has heard another project further continuation of talk in this turn space, as in extract (36).

```
(36) [TG, 01:43–44 (Schegloff, 2000b)]
     Ava:    [ °B' t asi] de fr' m that it' s a' right
     Bee:    [ so what-]
```

Here, Bee withdraws from talk immediately after Ava's upgraded talk; however, examples of the rhythmic mismatch we examined above can also been seen with upgraded talk as in extract (37).

```
(37) [Car conversation]
        Elvis:              [ yeah i' w' [z good] you screamed
        Nick:                           [yeah. ]
        Elvis:   =[ heh hah ch(h)ri(h)] st.
        Sasha:   =[ I screamed an-      ]
→ Sasha:   w' ll you' re r- you' re [ luck[y    I-]
→ Elvis:                            [ you [scream] alot of
                the times when I not doin' anything y' kno:w,
                b' t like that time [ heh hah hah]
```

Here, Sasha withdraws from the talk after two beats of her own talk, but immediately after a single beat of Elvis' upgraded _scream_. This extract also exemplifies the very common practice that speakers move to upgraded talk in the second beat of the overlap (Schegloff, 2000b).

Success in overlap management

The system available to speakers for managing overlap provides some resources and places for their deployment, but does not treat the issue of who continues to speak and who ceases to speak. These things must be locally managed by participants and depend on what speakers are doing in the turn and in its sequence.

Schegloff (2000b) argues that cases in which overlap is resolved after a single beat of talk or one beat after a speaker begins talking in competitive mode account for the vast majority of cases of overlapping

talk. Given upgraded talk usually starts on the second beat of overlapping talk, most overlap is usually resolved within three to four beats
of starting. It appears that when overlapping talk is resolved quickly it
reflects a 'lack of interactional investment' in the turn space at issue.
However, where speakers have some interest to pursue which lies
outside the turn-taking system itself, this may lead to extended overlapping talk beyond the three to four beats of a quick resolution in
order to get something said in this particular turn position. Where a
speaker persists in speaking, they are displaying some investment in
holding on to the turn in order to pursue some project in the turn.
The nature of this project may be quite varied, but it may also be
possible for participants in the particular interaction to identify what
this project is.

Success in overlap management is often seen in terms of who
emerges as the solo speaker after overlap. However, such fights for the
floor are comparatively rare and emerging as the solo speaker is not
the only criterion for judging success in overlap resolution. In addition
to winning the floor, Schegloff (2000) proposes three other criteria for
success:

1.   persistence to completion;
2.   persistence to projecting the thrust of the turn;
3.   achievement of sequential implicativeness.

Each of these will be dealt with in more detail below.

Persistence to completion

Some speakers appear to design their talk in overlap in order to bring
their own talk to its projected completion, rather than surviving the
overlap to emerge as a sole speaker. These speakers continue their own
talk in solo production mode, producing no hitches and perturbations.
This means that their talk is produced as if no one else were speaking
at the same time. This orientation can be seen in extract (38).

```
(38) [Car conversation]
     Sasha:    =n' he starts takin' off an the bus is like
               this n [ I' m jus' [ screa:min' ]
  →  Elvis:            [ I  jus'  [ didn'  see ] it. I looked
               there an' I' mustuh been exACTly the:re
               [ yihknow like
```

In extract (38), Elvis' talk is produced in solo mode with no hitches and perturbations throughout the first TCU and remains in solo mode even after Sasha's talk is upgraded. This example shows a speaker doing something other than competing for the floor during overlap and continuing to talk as if there was no overlap at all. Schegloff (2000b) argues that solo talk in overlap may be the strongest possible response to overlapping talk because interactionally it takes a stance of non-recognition of the competing talk.

Persistence to projecting the thrust of the turn

Other speakers seem to orient to bringing their talk to a point at which the thrust of the turn has been projected or is recognizable. Schegloff (2000a) argues that Deb's turn in extract (39) is such a case.

```
(39) [Pre-party, 2–3 (Schegloff, 2000b)]
        Dick:    Y'[know what- y' know[  (   )  ]
        Deb:       [ W h a t  a  w a s [ter you] w e r e          ]
        Anne:                          [ DON' T S] AY that I' m ex]
                   a- just say I' m a liar.
        Dick:    Y' know what, yer [ grandmother-          ]
  →     Deb:                        [ >It' s not a question<] of=
  →              =[<ly:ing' t' s a question of being – >]
        Dick:    [ yer GRANDMOTHER    IS    A    CENTI] PEDE,
```

Here, Deb has to deal with an interactionally sensitive issue: Anne's claim that she is being called a liar. Deb's interactional project in her turn is dealing with replacing this characterization of her mother with some other issue. Completing the project of displacing the talk about lying seems to be Deb's goal at this point and getting this said is interactionally important: more so than competing for the turn or changing the topic, neither of which gets done in Deb's turn.

Achievement of sequential implicativeness

For some speakers during overlap, it appears to be most important that their talk, rather than the talk of the other speaker, is responded to by subsequent speakers. In other words, the speaker works to ensure that his/her talk is sequentially implicative, or at least sequentially con-sequential (Schegloff and Sacks, 1973: 296; Schegloff, 2000b). In order to secure sequential implicativeness, speakers respond to overlap in quite different ways and rather than pursuing talk to gain the floor, may cease to speak in order to achieve their interactional project.

(40) [KC-4, 16:36–17:18 (Schegloff, 2000b)]

```
      Kathy:    So once I'd set up the warp, I' was very
                simple to jus' keep- jus' to weave it.
                (0.8)
      Kathy:    You know
                [ ()
      Dave:     [      (But listen to how long)             ]
      Rubin:    [ In other words, you gotta string up thee] you
                gotta string up thee colours, is that it, =
      Kathy:    =[Right. ]
      Rubin:    =[in thee] in thee [ warp.]
      Kathy:                       [ right] right
      Dave:     (but listen) tuh
                [ how long it took to put in the] =
  →   Kathy:    [A n d    t h e n    e a c h    weft-]
      Dave:     =the the warps [ (though)
  →   Kathy:                   [ and then each weft y' know
                then I did I s- my warp was strung up, so that
                [ I had (each colours.)
      Rubin:    [ (Where's that come from,) 'warp and weft.'
                (0.8)
      Kathy:    ↓I haven't the faintest notion.
```

In this extract, Dave's talk about how long the process took is in overlap with Rubin's talk in response to Kathy's *So once I'd set up the warp, I' was very simple to jus' keep- jus' to weave it.* Once Kathy has confirmed Rubin's understanding of the process involved, Dave relaunches his talk about the length of time. This time Kathy's talk is in overlap with Dave's talk, but Kathy discontinues and Dave emerges as solo speaker. However, at Dave's possible completion, Kathy relaunches her talk repeating the words she began in overlap. The repetition shows that what she is saying here is what she was trying to say earlier (Schegloff, 1996b). In this example, Kathy's discontinuing the talk at her first attempt sacrificed her talk in that particular turn space, but when she relaunches her talk in a different turn space, she makes her talk the relevant talk to which following talk will be addressed. In so doing she has cancelled the sequential implicativeness of Dave's turn at talk, and this talk is never addressed. Dave is also doing something similar in relaunching the turn that he surrendered to Rubin in his first attempt to talk about how long it took to set up the weaving. What Kathy and David are doing here is sacrificing speakership in the short term in order to carry out a longer-term project: lack of success in holding the turn is translated into success in controlling the sequence. David, however, because of Kathy's redoing of her talk, is not successful in securing sequentially implicativeness in this case. This shows that holding a turn is not the only way in which a speaker can exert control over how talk proceeds.

Conclusion

This chapter has discussed deviations from speaker transition with no gap and no overlap. These cases of gaps and overlaps are potentially counter-evidence to the existence of the turn-taking mechanism described by Sacks *et al.* (1974) in that they do affect speaker change at places of possible completion. The discussion here, however, has demonstrated that speakers orient to the relevance of possible completions for speaker change in understanding and responding to cases of gaps and overlaps. Silences after a possible completion are therefore interpretable as a speaker not speaking yet precisely because a contribution is expected at a first possible completion. Similarly overlaps are treated as problematic where entry into talk is not related to a possible completion. In these senses, problems of speaker change are not exceptions to the turn-taking mechanism, but rather instances of it. In turn, the resolution of these problems uses aspects of the turn-taking system in order to repair the talk. For example, an inter-turn pause may be converted to an intra-turn pause by modifying the turn constructional unit by adding an increment, therefore delaying and reproducing a possible completion and the progression of talk in overlap may be delayed by hitches and perturbations which carry talk over until the other speaker reaches a possible completion. In each case, the speaker draws on the turn-taking system itself to repair problems in turn-taking and demonstrate an overall orientation to the system in constructing their talk.

Sequence organization

Chapter 3 included a discussion of the ways in which some turns at talk constrain who can speak next and what a next contribution can be. This indicates that turns at talk are not things which appear independently of each other, but rather are clustered together: they are organized to be coherent and orderly and the relationship between turns is a meaningful one. This clustering of turns at talk is referred to as sequence organization.

The notion of sequence organization is based on the premise that the central consideration for the organization of talk is that talk is a form of social action: that is, turns at talk are places in which the participants in a conversation perform actions through talk. Turns at talk cluster together in order for speakers to develop a course of action. This view maintains that the action being performed is a more important resource for understanding how conversation is organized than is topic. While it does not deny that topic may be an organizational feature of talk (Button and Casey, 1984, 1985; Jefferson, 1984), it does argue that action is more important as an organizational feature than topic (Schegloff, 1991, 1995a). Much talk is problematic if considered solely in terms of topic. For example, in the sentence *Could you open the window?* it is problematic to consider this as primarily an utterance about windows and much more useful to consider it as enacting a request to do something. The legitimacy of seeing such talk in terms of action rather than topic can be seen in the ways in which participants treat such talk in a conversation: further talk on the topic would be considered less appropriate after such a sentence than would the action of opening a window. Opening the window would, in other words, be an expected next action after *Could you open the window?* while further talk would not be expected. Furthermore, if a participant were to report on what had transpired when the sentence was produced, s/he would characterize this as 'X asked me to do something' rather than as 'X said something about windows'. This example also leads to another issue which is important for sequence organization. This is the idea that some actions make other actions relevant as next actions, which are in turn seen as being occasioned by the prior action. This relationship between actions is the basis of *adjacency pairs* (Schegloff, 1991; Schegloff and Sacks, 1973).

Adjacency pairs

In conversation we notice that many turns at talk occur as pairs. A greeting is conventionally followed by another greeting, a farewell by a farewell, a question by an answer. Schegloff and Sacks (1973) called these sorts of paired utterances *adjacency pairs* and these adjacency pairs are the basic unit on which sequences in conversation are built. Adjacency pairs have a number of core features which can be used by way of a preliminary definition. They (1) consist of two turns (2) by different speakers, (3) which are placed next to each other in their basic minimal form, (4) which are ordered and (5) which are differentiated into pair types. The first two features are rather straightforward, but the latter three require more explanation. Firstly, it is normally the case that where an adjacency pair occurs, the two turns occur immediately together with no intervening talk. However, this does not mean that all adjacency pairs are in fact immediately adjacent to each other. In some cases other talk can come between the two turns, although what can legitimately occur in this position is actually quite constrained (these inserted turns will be discussed in Chapter 6). Secondly, the two turns which make up the adjacency pair are ordered so that one of the pair always occurs first and the other always occurs second: for example, a question always precedes its answer. Therefore we can say that some types of talk are designed to initiate next actions, while other types of talk are designed to complete the action initiated. Those forms of talk which initiate actions are called *first pair parts* (FPP), while those that flow from such initiations are called *second pair parts* (SPP). Thirdly, the relationship between FPPs and SPPs is constrained by the type of FPP produced. That is, when an FPP initiates a sequence, not just any SPP can occur in the second position: the SPP must be of the appropriate type for the action initiated by the FPP. Therefore, a question must be followed by an answer to be heard as a completed sequence: it cannot be followed by a greeting or a farewell even though these are also possibly SPPs in other contexts. This latter relationship points to the nature of sequences as coherent actions conducted over a number of turns and which are understood as coherent because they adhere to a programme of action initiated by an FPP. Some examples, by no means exhaustive, of adjacency pairs are:

(1) question–answer
```
John:    What time's it?
Betty:   Three uh clock.
```

(2) greeting–greeting
```
Amy:     Hello.
Jean:    Hi.
```

(3) summons–answer
```
Terry:   hey Paul,
Paul:    uh yeah.
```

(4) telling–accept
```
John:    I've jus' finished my las' exam.
Betty:   that's great.
```

In each of the examples above, the first turn of the pair initiates some action and makes some next action relevant. The second turn responds to the prior turn and completes the action which was initiated in the first turn. These two turns together accomplish an action. The basic sequence, then, is composed of two ordered turns at talk:

A: first pair part
B: second pair part

Participants in conversation orient to this basic sequence structure in developing their talk and adjacency pairs have a normative force in organizing conversation in that adjacency pairs set up expectations about how talk will proceed and if these are not met then the talk is seen as being problematic (Heritage, 1984b).

This basic sequence is closely linked to the turn-taking system itself because it makes speaker change a relevant next action. The practice of producing an adjacency pair requires that once a recognizable FPP has been produced, on the first possible completion, the current speaker should stop and a next speaker should start and produce an SPP of the relevant type. The FPP can be constructed to select a next speaker, but does not have to.

As has been argued then, FPPs, as a primary aspect of their production, make a subsequent action relevant; it projects some second action as a relevant next action. Schegloff and Sacks (1973) discuss this in terms of *relevance rules*: FPPs create a context in which some next action is expected to occur and the talk that is produced after it will be seen as in some way responding in a relevant way to the preceding FPP. This means that if there is no next talk, this talk will be seen as absent, as in (3.2).

```
(5) [Lunch]
      Harry:    Didjih speak tuh Mary today?
  →             (0.2)
      Harry:    Did yih speak tuh Mary?
      Joy:      Oh, yea:h I saw her at lunch.
```

In this case, Harry's question FPP makes it relevant for Joy to produce an answer SPP. The silence indicated by the arrow is hearable here as Joy not producing an answer (as discussed in Chapter 4). That is, in this context, the silence is not heard as no one speaking: it is heard as Joy specifically not producing an answer. The absence of the talk in this position is accountable (Schegloff and Sacks, 1973) and is interpretable; something which was publicly and expectedly relevant to do at that point in the talk has not been done. Harry's recycling of his prior turn is a response to this silence as a lack of an answer and renews the relevance of the answer SPP as a next action.

The force of relevance rules also applies to talk produced after an FPP has been produced, as in (6).

```
(6) [Lunch]
      Joy:      ' N whaddya think ' v Brett,
      Harry:    Brett?
      Joy:      The new guy in accounts.
      Harry:    Oh. He seems oka:y.
```

In this extract, the talk which follows the FPP is not constructed as an SPP. Given that the FPP makes some SPP relevant, the talk in the second turn is interpretable as being constrained by the relevance of the SPP. The SPP is a relevant next action, which has not yet been produced, and the talk can be seen as deferring the SPP while some other relevant work is done. The intervening talk here is constructed with the SPP still 'on record' and the SPP is hearable as 'not having been done yet'. The intervening talk does not cancel the relevance of SPP, which is produced immediately after the inserted talk is completed. Unlike Example (2) in chapter 3, the FPP is not redone and this provides evidence that for these participants the relevance of an answer as second action following the FPP is not in doubt or in need of redoing. Also, the SPP is heard as relevant to a course of action projected by the original FPP and the ongoing relevance of the projected SPP provides a context in which Harry's delayed answer can be interpreted.

Counters

As has been seen above, when an FPP is produced, there are some other elements of talk which can be done immediately after it, but where this happens, the SPP remains a relevant future action. Talk which is not an SPP does not remove the relevancy of an SPP being done in following talk. *Counters*, however, work differently and shape the trajectory of a sequence in a quite different way, as in (7).

```
(7) [Lunch]
    Harry:   so whad' dyuh think of yesterday' s wor' shop.
    Joy:     uh:m (.) wha' dyou think.
    Harry:   well: ' m not tha' sure really,
    Joy:     yeah that' s what I thought, it was like stuff
             we all know anyway.
```

In this extract, Harry produces a question FPP, but without responding Joy provides a reworking of the same FPP and redirects the question back to Harry. Joy's turn here does not defer the SPP, but rather she cancels the relevance of the FPP initially directed to her by replacing it with a new FPP, reversing the flow of the unfolding sequence. In producing a counter, Joy not only reverses the direction of this sequence, but she also reverses the requirement to provide an SPP. The interactional effect of this is that Harry commits himself to a point of view about the workshop before Joy needs to do so. Later in this conversation, Joy does give her opinion about the workshop, but not as a response to Harry's SPP above; instead she is able to express her opinion as an agreement with Harry.

Types of second pair parts

A small number of adjacency pair types have only a single type of SPP. The most common are greeting adjacency pairs (*hello*, *hi*, etc.) *and* terminal adjacency pairs (farewells such as *bye*, *goodbye*, *seeya*, etc.). While greeting and terminal SPPs have a range of possible realizations, all of these possibilities are the same type of SPP; they all perform the same action. Thus, a greeting FPP can only have a greeting SPP and a terminal FPP can only have a terminal SPP (see, for example, Schegloff, 1968; Schegloff, 1979a, 1986; Schegloff and Sacks, 1973). In most cases, these sorts of adjacency pairs have very similar forms for both the FPP and the SPP.

Most adjacency pair types, however, have alternative possibilities for realizing the SPP. Some examples of such possibilities are given below:

> (8) invitation – accept
> Amy: w′ d yuh like tuh come over t′ morrow night
> Jane: yea:h.= that′ d be nice.

> (8′) invitation – decline
> Harry: I don′ have much tuh do on We:nsday.
>   (.)
>   w′ d yuh like tuh get together then.
>   (0.3)
> Joy: huh we::llhh I don′ really know if yuh see
>   i′ s a bit hectic fuh me We:nsday yih know
> Harry: oh wokay

In (8) and (8′), the FPP which launches the sequence is the same – an invitation – but the SPP which responds to the FPP is different – (8) accepts the invitation, while (8′) declines it. In both cases the adjacency pair is completed, but the possibilities for doing this vary and so we can talk about invitation adjacency pairs having two types of SPP. Most types of adjacency pairs have such alternative realizations of the SPP; however, this does not mean that each of these possible SPP types is interactionally equal. In fact, in the examples above, the SPP in (8) is socially and interactionally 'easier' to perform than the SPP in (8′). The differences in these two SPP types are dealt with through preference organization.

Preference organization

In a conversation, a participant may be able to choose among alternatives to design a particular contribution to the talk and, as we have seen above, these choices may have different interactional import. The term *preference* has been developed to characterize these non-equivalent alternatives (Atkinson and Heritage, 1984). The concept of preference deals with the possible ways in which some conversational action may be accomplished. It does not refer to the personal desires of the speakers, but rather to the recurrent patterns of talk in which actions are carried out. The basic distinction made in preference organization is that in a particular context, certain actions may be avoided, or delayed in their production, while other actions are normally performed directly and with little delay.

Returning to extracts (8) and (8'), it can be seen that the acceptance was done without delay, while the declining is delayed in its turn, and, in fact, the invitation is not even explicitly declined. The immediate and direct acceptance of an invitation is usually treated as unremarkable, as nothing unusual being done; however, an equally immediate and direct refusal of an invitation would not normally be treated as unremarkable, but would more likely be interpreted as rude or hostile (C. Goodwin and Heritage, 1990). Actions which are routinely performed immediately, and whose immediate production is unremarkable are termed *preferred* actions, while those which would not normally be performed in this way are called *dispreferred* actions. For example, for invitations we have the following possibilities:

Invitation: Accept – preferred
              Decline – dispreferred

These two concepts – preferred and dispreferred – are essentially social in nature. They express the fact that some responses are problematic for social relationships, while others are not. If a speaker needs to produce a next turn which is dispreferred, then s/he needs to design the turn in different ways in order to do extra conversational work. This extra conversational work orients to the need for the contribution not to be disruptive of the relationship the speaker has with the recipient. As a general statement it may be said that actions such as agreement, acceptances, etc., are preferred, while disagreements, rejections, declinings are dispreferred. This distinction, however, depends on what precedes the turn. For example, next speaker's agreement with a negative self-assessment (*I'm just no good at anything*) would be dispreferred rather than preferred (Pomerantz, 1984).

As a starting point, for considering how preference organization shapes talk, it is necessary to consider two aspects of preference in more detail. These are the *preference for agreement* and the *preference for contiguity* (Sacks, 1987).

Preference for agreement

When some types of talk are considered, it is easy to see that they are designed in such a way as to indicate what the expected next action is likely to be. These types of talk have built into their design an approximate trajectory for the sequence of which they are a part. This can be seen very clearly with questions. The question *That was a great film, wasn't it?* is designed is such a way as to project a *yes* response, while a slightly different design *The film wasn't very good, was it?* projects a *no* response. Sacks (1987) describes these different projected trajectories in terms of preference organization: the former question has a preference for a 'yes-like' response, while the latter has a preference for a 'no-like' response. Answers to either of these questions would be designed with reference to the preferences established by the design of the question turn. Sacks (1987) argues that there is an overwhelming preference for answers to agree with the trajectories of the questions to which they respond. This idea goes beyond a simple understanding of participants in a conversation agreeing with each other, and it is much more useful to think in terms of agreeing with a trajectory. For example, it is not normal to think of people 'agreeing' with an invitation, an offer or other FPPs; however, it can be seen that the construction of invitations, offers, etc., as projecting a trajectory for the sequence they launch and a preference can be observed for SPPs which follow the same trajectory.

Preference for contiguity

A second important organizational pattern identified by Sacks (1987) involves the location of actions within sequences. Sacks notes that, while question or answer turns can contain other pieces of talk, there is a preference for FPPs and SPPs to be contiguous: that is, to occur immediately next to each other. What this means is that people do not usually insert extra material between the end of the question and the start of the answer. For example, questions normally occur at the end of their turns, while answers normally occur at the beginning of the turn. This placement is, of course, not an inevitable feature of talk, but is rather the result of coordination of the actions of the participants: speakers design their talk by orienting to a preference for contiguity. An interesting result of the preference for contiguity is that if there are two questions in a turn, the last question usually gets answered first (Sacks 1987).

(9) [Make-up]
```
Zoe:    When did yuh get in.=Did yuh have a good
        trip?
Joy:    Not bad. I got in last night.
```

In extract (9), Zoe produces two questions in her turn, both of which are answered by Joy. However, Joy answers these questions in the reverse order from the order in which they are asked. She starts with the most contiguous question and then moves to the less contiguous question. This maintains the contiguity as far as is possible in this case.

Preference organization and turn shape

The preferences for agreement and contiguity can be considered to be two basic organizing principles for sequences and there is a relationship between them which plays an important role in how turns at talk are designed. This can be seen in extracts (10) and (11).

(10) [Lunch]
```
    Joy:      Have yuh got the papers for the meeting ye'
              Carol¿
    Carol:    Yeah=they came in th's morning.
```

(11) [Lunch]
```
    Joy:      'N will the report be finished fuh the next
              meeting, dyuh know¿
    Carol:    (0.2) well I dunno: 't seems to be taking
              lon:ger th'n we thought so no, I'd guess not
              until the one after
```

In the extracts above, one SPP is preferred and the other is dispreferred. In extract (10), the SPP is in agreement with the trajectory established by the FPP and the SPP is also immediately contiguous with its FPP. In extract (11), however, the SPP does not agree with the trajectory established by the FPP and the SPP is separated from the FPP by other talk: *(.) well I dunno: 't seems to be taking lon:ger th'n we thought.* These two extracts exemplify a basic principle for the design of turns at talk: preferred SPPs come early in their turns and are contiguous with the FPP, and dispreferred SPPs are delayed in their turns and are thus not contiguous with their FPPs (Pomerantz, 1984; Sacks, 1987).

The fact that disagreements are typically found late in turns indicates that there must be a class of objects which come before the disagreement. These objects can be seen in a way as preparing for the forthcoming disagreement. One member of this class is silence. When a dispreferred FPP is produced, it may be followed by a silence (Pomerantz, 1984). Such silences are breaks in the contiguity of the FPP and the SPP and are, therefore, deployable as devices to delay production of a dispreferred SPP. There is an example of such a silence in extract (11).

The silence may be a short silence before the next speaker's turn begins or it may be filled by the last speaker continuing. Where the previous speaker continues, the next turn may be redesigned with the opposite preference, as in extract (12).

```
(12) [Alice and Betty]
     Alice:   Did yuh have a good time.
              (0.3)
     Alice:   nothing special?
     Betty:   nuh, not so good.
```

In extract (12), Alice asks Betty about her weekend away. Her initial enquiry *Did yuh have a good time.* is designed to project a 'yes-like' response and is followed by a silence. Alice ends the silence with a reformulation of her original question as a candidate answer to her own FPP, this time with a different trajectory projecting a 'no-like' response. Betty then provides her answer with no gap and with the answer *nuh* as the immediately next element after the prior speaker's turn. Here Alice is orienting to the silence as indicating possible disagreement on the basis that a break in contiguity is hearable as problematic for agreement. Her next action repairs this problem by rephrasing her question so that the answer can be produced as an agreement. In this way, Alice's reformulation removes the need for a dispreferred action and makes a preferred action as a possible next action for Betty.

A dispreferred action may also be delayed by talk which is produced before the dispreferred SPP. Some common devices for doing this include tokens such as *uhm, uh, well*, etc., as well as audible breathing. Like silences, the devices are deployable to break the contiguity of the FPP and the SPP. They may also occur in conjunction with silences, and also with other talk which further delays production of the SPP.

```
(13) [Will and Andy]
     Will:    so is Kaye gonna be able to make it?
     Andy:    (.) uh well, she's gotta lotta things tuh do
              just now. I dunno. sh-she prob'ly won't be
              able tuh do it
```

In extract (13), Andy produces a dispreferred SPP preceded by a brief silence, and two 'hesitation' tokens *uh* and *well.* The SPP is also preceded by a warrant, *she's gotta lotta things tuh do just now.* which gives an account of the reason for the dispreferred component having to be articulated. The warrant indicates that the speaker is aware of the dispreferred status of his contribution and is orienting to the accountability of dispreferred responses. Preferred responses do not need to be explained, dispreferred responses do. The placement of the warrant before the dispreferred SPP serves a dual function: it defers the SPP until later in the turn and also provides a context in which the SPP can be heard. The answer is also preceded by a hedge, *I dunno,* which mitigates the 'no-like' answer by claiming a reduced epistemic authority for the SPP (Coates, 1987). This mitigation is also built into the SPP itself through the word *prob'ly.*

Mitigation seems to be an important part of the construction of dispreferreds (Pomerantz, 1984), and dispreferreds are regularly produced as weak disagreements or may be withheld altogether. In cases where a dispreferred is withheld, the SPP is still hearable because of the design of the turn shape. For example, if extract (13) had ended with *I dunno* rather than continuing to the end of the turn as it was produced, it would still be hearable as a 'no-like' response. The silence, the hesitation tokens, the warrant and the hedge all provide information about the likely shape of the answer, but most of all the breaking of contiguity between the FPP and the SPP already strongly indicates a dispreferred SPP is probably being foreshadowed.

Often, turns which are in fact disagreements may be phrased as if they are really agreements (Pomerantz, 1984). These agreements are normally weakened or qualified in some way as in extract (14).

```
(14) [Alice and Betty]
     Alice:   did yuh have good weather?
     Betty:   yeah.=until it started to rain. n' then it
              rained for the WHO:le weekend.
```

Here Alice produces a question which projects a 'yes-like' SPP and Betty produces the projected SPP type. However, she immediately latches onto this answer a dispreferred 'no-like' answer. The overall meaning of her turn is that she did not have good weather: *it rained for the WHO:le weekend.* The agreement token here orients to the preference established by the prior FPP and at the same time provides a device to delay the dispreferred SPP in its turn.

The devices discussed above are all devices that the current speaker can employ in the same turn as the SPP: that is, they are devices for delaying the SPP in its turn. Speakers can also deploy devices (for example, repairs) which delay the SPP in its sequence. While these devices are not specialized for preference, they do serve to break the continuity between an FPP and its SPP and so are useable in the context of a dispreferred SPP.

```
(15) [Schegloff, 1996b) TG1]
     Bee:      Yih sound HA:PPY, hh
     Ava:      I sound ha:p[py?
     Bee:                   [Ye:uh
               (0.3)
     Ava:      No:,
     Bee:      N:o?
     Ava:      No.
               (0.7)
     Bee:      .hh You sound sorta cheerful?
```

In extract (15) Bee makes an assessment *Yih sound HA:PPY*, which like the questions we have seen above, has built into it a trajectory which predicts a 'yes-like' response. Ava initiates a repair through a repeat of Bee's turn (Schegloff, Jefferson and Sacks, 1977). The repair itself is potentially ambiguous: it can be seen as a problem of hearing and understanding or it may be a disagreement premonitory. Ava provides in her turn a redoing of the original assessment, after which there is a pause and a dispreferred SPP. The repair sequence has provided a device for delaying the SPP, and also a possible space for redoing the FPP in ways similar to Alice's redoing in extract (12). The pause is also here a device which is deployed to delay the dispreferred, which is finally produced as a strong disagreement *No:,*.

We have seen that speakers have at their disposal devices for delaying a dispreferred in its turn and also for delaying it in its sequence and that these devices are regularly deployed by speakers in constructing dispreferred SPPs. It is also clear that only certain classes of talk can be deployed in this context and not any talk can be used to delay an SPP; the talk must in some way orient to the upcoming action required to complete the sequence. The prior FPP has established the SPP as the relevant next action and this relevance constrains what can legitimately be used between the conclusion of the FPP and the production of the SPP.

In summary, we can make the following observations about the effect of preference organization on turn shape:

- a preferred action is routinely performed without delay;
- a dispreferred action is routinely delayed in its turn;
- a dispreferred action is routinely prefaced or qualified in its turn;

- a dispreferred action is routinely accomplished in a mitigated or indirect form;
- a dispreferred action is routinely accounted for.

So far we have talked about the preference for agreement mainly in questions, but similar strategies are found in other types of speech events where there are possible preferred and dispreferred responses. Some of these (invitations and assessments) will be discussed below.

Invitations
Invitations, like questions, establish a trajectory. In fact, in English, invitation FPPs are usually realized by questions designed for 'yes-like' answers, as in extracts (16) and (17), which are both constructed around a question with *would you like*...

(16) [Amy and Jane]
```
Amy:    w' d yuh like tuh come over t' morrow night
Jane:   yea:h.= that' d be nice.
```

In extract (16), Jane's acceptance comes immediately after the completion of the FPP and is done with strong agreement. She adds a second, latched, TCU in her turn, but the achievement of acceptance requires only the *yes* token, not the following assessment.

(17) [Lunch]
```
Harry:  I don' have much tuh do on We:nsday.
        (.)
        w' d yuh like tuh get together then.
        (0.3)
Joy:    huh we::llhh I don' really know if yuh see
        i' s a bit hectic fuh me We:nsday yih know
Harry:  oh wokay
```

In extract (17), Joy's declining of the invitation is actually withheld and there is no overt 'no-like' answer; instead her turn is made up of devices routinely used to delay production of a dispreferred: silence, audible out-breathing, *well*, a hedge and a warrant (Davidson, 1984). The SPP is, therefore, made up of elements other than an overt 'no', but these elements all project a possible dispreferred response as the SPP-type under way in this turn.

Responses to invitations may also include elements in the SPP which orient to the nature of invitations, as in (18).

(18) [Tools]
```
    James:    How about going out for a drink tonight
    Graham:   (0.2) tuh- uh sorry b' d I can' make it=c' z
              Jill has invited some' ve her friends over.
              Perhaps some other time
```

In Graham's response, in addition to a pause, a false start and *uh,* he adds an accounting *sorry* to his warrant *I can' make it=c'z Jill has invited some've her friends over.* This *sorry* seems to respond to the nature of invitations as something the issuer does for the recipient of the invitation and the problematic nature that declining the invitation creates – the recipient has done something problematic in declining (Kwon, 2004). In addition, Graham's *perhaps some other time* orients to the invitation as something he would be willing to accept under other circumstances, but that under present circumstances this would be impossible. These projected alternative arrangements are often found with refused invitations. They indicate that while the invitation cannot be accepted at the moment, the speaker is still available for further invitations and is orienting to an ongoing relationship with the speaker who issued the invitation. Again, the actual 'no' response is withheld in this sequence.

Assessments

Assessments are turns which provide an evaluation. This evaluation may be either positive or negative (Heritage, 1985). Pomerantz (1984) has shown that assessments related to participation in an event are routinely followed by second assessments as a way of co-participating in conversation. Because assessments are evaluations, they have built into them a trajectory which establishes possibilities for preference organization. Assessments are interesting, however, in that in some cases, there is more than just a preference for agreement in operation.

When a recipient produces agreement with a prior assessment, s/he can produce one of a range of possible agreements: an upgrade, a same evaluation or a weak agreement. These three possibilities are, however, not all equal (Pomerantz, 1984). An upgraded agreement occurs where the speaker producing the second assessment produces a stronger evaluation than in the first assessment, either by producing a stronger evaluative term, as in (19), or by adding an intensifier to the prior assessment, as in (20).

(19) [Pomerantz (1984) MC:1]
```
      A:        Isn' t he cute
  →   B:        O::h he::s a::DORable
```

(20) [Pomerantz (1984) CH 4.–14]
```
    M:          You must admit it was fun the night we
                we[nt down
→   J:              [It was great fun . . .
```

Upgrades are forms of strong agreement, which never occur in combination with disagreements.

Same evaluations are second assessments in which the speaker asserts that the assessment made by the prior speaker is the same as the current speaker's evaluation. Same evaluations are often marked by the addition of *too* to the first assessment as in (21), or by the use of a pro-term as in (22).

(21) [Pomerantz (1984) J&J]
```
    A:          Yeah I like it [ (        )
    B:                          [ I like it too . . .
```

(22) [Pomerantz (1984) 2.1.8.–5]
```
    B:          I think everyone enjoyed just sitting
                around talking.
    A:          I do too.
```

Pomerantz argues that same evaluations are weaker forms of agreement than upgrades and that this can be seen in the fact that same evaluations can occur both in agreements, but also as prefaces to disagreements.

Downgraded agreements involve a weaker evaluation in the second assessment than that given in the first assessment, as in (23).

(23) [Pomerantz (1984) KC:4:10)]
```
    F:          That's beautiful
    K:          Isn't it pretty
```

Downgraded agreements are very weak forms of agreement, as they may preface disagreements. In addition, they are frequently followed by a disagreement with the downgrade in the next turn, as in (24).

(24) [Pomerantz (1984) AP:1]
```
    G:          That's fantastic
    B:          Isn't it good
    G:          That's marvelous
```

The discussion above demonstrates that for assessments there are a range of possible agreeing responses, which have different properties.

Upgrades are the least problematic and also are the most likely to be performed with a minimization of the gap between the two turns. Same evaluations and downgrades are potentially related to disagreement and so we can see a hierarchy of agreement responses: upgrade > same evaluation > downgrade.

In addition, it is possible to disagree with an assessment. Disagreements regularly show similar turn shapes to the dispreferreds discussed above in that they are often delayed in their turn or in their sequence, as in (25).

```
(25) [Pomerantz (1984) NB:IV:11.–1]
     A:        God izn it dreary.
               (0.6)
     A:        [ Y' know I don' t think-
     B:        [ .hh It' s warm though,
```

Here, B's disagreeing turn, although in overlap is substantially delayed following a 0.6 second pause and audible in-breathing. Weaker agreements can preface disagreements, as in (26).

```
(26) [Lunch]
     Joy:      the new paint job is an improvement isn' t it.
     Harry:    yeh tiz b' d I don' really like the colour
```

So far, assessments have been shown to work a lot like other forms of agreement/disagreement. Agreements are done more immediately than disagreements, which tend to be delayed. However, there are some cases in which assessments do not work the same way. This is most noticeably the case with negative self-assessments, as in (27).

```
(27) [Pomerantz (1984) fn]
     C:        I' m talking nonsense now
     A:        No::
```

In this extract, A's disagreeing response to C's self-deprecating assessment is an immediate on the record *no::*. In this case, and elsewhere where negative self-assessments are made, disagreements are not regularly delayed in their turn or mitigated. Pomerantz (1984: 89) argues that critically assessing one's co-participant is regularly a dispreferred action. Because agreement with a negative self-assessment is tantamount to providing a criticism, agreements are in this context *dispreferred* actions, while disagreements are *preferred* actions. A common turn shape for an agreement with such an assessment can be seen in (28).

(28) [Pomerantz (1984) MC:1.–23]

```
W:          . . . Do you know what I was all that time?
L:          (no).
W:          Pavlov's dog.
            (2.0)
L:          (I suppose)
```

In the extract, L responds to W's negative self-assessment, with a weak agreement after a two second pause: that is, by delaying her agreement and breaking contiguity between the two assessments. Pomerantz (1984: 92) argues that there is a regular pattern for this type of agreement as follows:

```
A:          Negative self-assessment
            Gap
B:          Agreement
```

The gap in this structure is very much the absence of some relevant next activity: a second assessment. At the same time it foreshadows a potential agreement with the assessment.

In sequences involving negative self-assessments, then, we can see a different preference organization from that we have seen in other contexts. It is not the case that agreement is preferred and disagreement is dispreferred; instead it seems that preferences relating to criticism of a co-participant override the preference for agreement. In this case, we can see that the details of preference organization are not a fixed feature of conversations, but rather it is context sensitive. We can also see that in some contexts more than one possible set of preferences may be relevant for the construction of an utterance and these preferences may not be compatible with each other. A speaker may have to disregard one set of preference (such as agreement) in order to realize another (avoiding criticism).

Dispreferred first pair parts

The discussion so far has focused around the ways in which preference affects SPPs; however, preference is also relevant to FPPs and some FPP types are dispreferred. One such dispreferred FPP has already been foreshadowed in the previous discussion: criticisms of co-participants. These criticisms are, in fact, one type of assessment and we can consider these to be cases of negative other-assessments (Pomerantz, 1984). The first thing to notice about these sorts of assessments is that they tend not to be frequent in conversation and frequent production of such assessments may itself be accountable. When a negative other-assessment is produced, it is frequently delayed in its turn and may be prefaced with the sorts of delaying devices we saw above used for SPPs.

```
(29) [Lunch]
     Joy:       . . . now yuh see she won' talk about it.
     Harry:     °Yeah°
                (1.0)
     Harry:     Uh well I don remember much aboud it b' t yuh
                know p' rhaps you w' re a bit hard on her.
     Joy:       puhha::ps
```

In (29) Joy is telling Harry about a problem she is having with a co-worker. After Joy finishes her telling, Harry responds to the telling with a soft °*Yeah*° and then there is a delay of a second before Harry with *uh well* followed by a disclaimer about his ability to comment on the situation and only then does he produce a mitigated criticism of Joy's behaviour in the situation she has been recounting. Joy in response produces a mitigated same evaluation: a weak agreement form. It can be argued on the basis of examples such as (29) that positive other-assessments directed at one's interlocutor are preferred FPPs, while negative other-assessments are dispreferred.

Request FPPs are also routinely designed as dispreferred turns. They are often delayed in their conversation: that is, they may be held back as later topics, even when they are the prime reason for a conversation taking place. Also, requests are regularly accompanied by accounts and mitigations, which occur before the request itself and which delay the request in its turn, as in (30) (cf. Kasper and Faerch, 1989).

```
(30) [Car]
     Jim:       well my car has broken down an they don' know
                if it will be fixed by then an' I w' z wondering
                if I c' d borrow your car.
```

This extract actually occurs after a much longer piece of preparatory talk in which Jim relates how he needs to go to a meeting and the meeting is a long way out of town. After this he produces his request FPP in the turn given above. This turn is prefaced by *well* and a warrant before the request itself is produced.

The preference organization involved with requests is interesting because the preferred version – an offer FPP – is interactionally quite different from its dispreferred, as it is performed by the other participant (Schegloff, 1979a). In fact, many potential requests are actually 'headed off' by their recipients, who convert them into offers, as in (31).

(31) [Lunch]
```
    Harry:    z' there any coffee,
    Joy:      w' d you like one.
    Harry:    yeah thanks that' d be great.
```

In this extract, Harry's first turn is potentially a preliminary to a request for Joy to make him a coffee. This appears to be the interpretation that Joy constructs for the turn and she pre-empts the request with an offer, which is in turn accepted by Harry.

In this case, we have two FPP types which both lead to a similar outcome. In both cases one participant has something or can do something that the other wants. The dispreferred request FPP involves the one participant making an imposition on the other, while the preferred FPP involves a participant undertaking to do something of his/her own accord. The imposition relating to the request is a variable thing. Some requests, such as asking for the time, are for things which are considered 'free goods' (Goffman, 1963), which even strangers can ask for without account and without participants considering much imposition is involved. Other requests, such as asking to borrow a car, are not free goods and a large imposition is seen to be involved. Requests for free goods are, then, much less dispreferred than requests for other goods and we can consider the preference organization here to be scaled from a highly dispreferred request to an only slightly dispreferred request.

Conclusion

Adjacency pairs, together with their preference organizations, provide the basis for sequence organization in conversation. The minimal sequence is composed of an FPP and an SPP. However, sequences can be expanded beyond this basic two turn structure and sequences can potentially become quite lengthy and involve a large number of turns. The ways in which this happens will be discussed in the next chapters. Regardless of how long a sequence may become, it remains based on an FPP and an SPP and the talk in a sequence is relevant to the performance of this base adjacency pair. Adjacency pairs can, therefore, be considered to be the basic building blocks from which sequences in conversation are built up. The ways in which sequences can be expanded will be considered in the next chapter.

Sequence expansion

The preceding chapter discussed the basic features of sequences and proposed the idea that sequences are constructed of two turns at talk: an FPP and an SPP. While the adjacency pair structure is the basis of sequences of talk, it is possible for these sequences to be expanded in various places in their production. Sequence expansion allows talk which is made up of more than a single adjacency pair to be constructed and understood as performing the same basic action and the various additional elements are seen as doing interactional work related to the basic action under way. Sequence expansion is constructed in relation to a base sequence of an FPP and an SPP in which the core action under way is achieved. Expansions may occur prior to the articulation of the base FPP (*pre-expansion*), between the base FPP and the base SPP (*insert expansion*) and following the base SPP (*post-expansion*). Most examples of expansion are also sequences in their own right made up of FPPs and SPPs, and so may also be called *pre-sequences*, *insert sequences* and *post-sequences* in order to focus more on the ways in which the expansions are constructed.

Pre-expansion

Pre-expansions (Sacks, 1992; Schegloff, 1979a, 1988c, 1990) are designed to be preliminary to some projected base sequence and are hearable by participants as preludes to some other action. Pre-sequences come in two basic kinds: generic pre-sequences, which are used with any form of following talk, and type-specific pre-sequences, which are designed to lead to some particular kind of base sequence.

A generic pre-sequence: summons–answer

There is one pre-sequence which is not designed with reference to the nature of the action to which it is prior, but is rather a generic pre-sequence which can be used to launch any sort of next talk. This is the summons–answer sequence. This pre-sequence is designed to gain the attention of a recipient (Liddicoat, Döpke, Brown and Love, 1992; Schegloff, 1968, 2002). This is a basic interactional necessity because interaction can only occur if the participants in the interaction are attending to each other and are available as speakers and recipients. The summons–answer sequence is a two-part sequence composed of an adjacency pair. The FPP has a number of possible realizations: it can be an address term, a politeness term such as *excuse me*, an attention-getting token such as *hey*, or it can be done by touching the intended recipient (cf. Nofsinger, 1975, 1991; Schegloff, 1968, 1979a, 1986, 2002). All of these devices serve a common function of providing an indication that a speaker is seeking a recipient, and where address terms are used, providing an indication of who the desired recipient is.

The SPP also has a variety of forms. The most common SPP following a summons in face-to-face interaction is to redirect eye gaze to the summoner (C. Goodwin, 1980, 1981). The redirection of eye gaze to a prior speaker is enough in itself to show that the gazer has made him/herself available as a recipient for further talk. Other possible SPPs include verbal tokens such as *what* or *yes/yeah*, which likewise signal availability for further talk. In face-to-face interaction, these verbal tokens are frequently connected with redirecting eye gaze and other non-verbal manifestations of attention, such as changing body position to orient to the summoner (C. Goodwin, 1980, 1981).

The production on an SPP regardless of its form makes further talk by the summoner conditionally relevant (Nofsinger, 1975; Schegloff, 1968, 1979a, 1986, 2002). It is the relevance of some sort of talk on completion of the summons–answer sequence which demonstrates how such sequences can be viewed as pre-sequences. The summons–answer does not achieve completion in and of itself, but rather makes a next action relevant as the result of its completion. In other words, it projects some future action as the reason for the summons–answer sequence and it is heard as prior to this action. The summons–answer sequence therefore both pre-shadows and requires some other talk, but does not project what will be done in that talk.

If the intended recipient of a summons does not produce a response to the FPP, further talk is not possible. This lack of an SPP may be the result of the FPP having failed to achieve an effect: if a summons is designed to attract attention, its failure to do so would be manifested as a lack of response. At the same time, it is also possible that the intended recipient of a summons may withhold a response. While it may not be possible to know whether the lack of response is a result of not hearing the summons or is a deliberate withholding of a response by the recipient, in either case the lack of response blocks progression to the next action. Where a response has not been produced, participants may treat this as a problem of hearing and it may be repaired by redoing the FPP, as in (1).

```
(1) [(Nofsinger, 1991)]
      C:          Anne
  → A:          ((Silence))
  → C:          Anne
      A:          What
```

Not all responses to a summons, however, lead immediately to further talk. There are also responses which register that a summons has been produced, but which seek to block or delay the projected next talk. These responses range from indicating availability for further talk after a delay (*just a minute, I'll be right there*, etc.), to providing a warrant for not becoming a recipient for the talk at that time (*I'm busy, I'm on the phone*, etc.), to outright rejection of recipiency of the projected talk (*leave me alone, go away*, etc.). These responses complete the summons–answer sequence, but they also attend to the projection of some next talk and work to block that talk as a next activity, either temporarily or completely. Obviously the degree to which such SPPs are successful as blocks depends on what happens interactionally. The answerer in providing talk has displayed attention to the summoner and is potentially available as a recipient of further talk, even if an unwilling one.

One of the most common locations for summons–answer sequences is in conversational openings; these sequences are frequently the first talk to occur, preceding even greetings (Schegloff, 1968, 1986). Given the function of summons–answer sequences as securing a recipient for talk, it is not surprising to find this sequence at the point where people move from not being engaged in interaction with each other to being engaged in interaction. The first necessity for interaction to occur is to have participants who are available to each other for talk.

Summons–answer sequences are, however, not just specialized for openings (Nofsinger, 1975). They can also be found within ongoing talk, where the availability of an intended recipient may be problematic or may be claimed by a speaker to be problematic. This may be the case, for example, where an intended recipient is currently engaged in some other activity, such as talking to a third participant, where the recipient has temporarily left the room, or where the intended recipient is not currently one's recipient in a multi-party conversation. In extract (2), the three participants are in the middle of a car journey and one of passengers (Nick) needs to give directions to the driver (Sasha).

```
(2) [Car conversation]
    Elvis:        [ three weeks ol=it tastes quite good
    Nick:       better' n the other ↑ stuff, o::r like (.2)
                diff' rent,
    Elvis:      yeah like it' s still young but it tastes good
                alread[y so::
  → Nick:              [hey Sash
                (.)
    Nick:       go straight throu[gh man
    Sasha:                       [yeah. okay.
```

Here Nick is in conversation with Elvis, who is answering a question Nick has asked him. Sasha has not been involved in the talk for several lines. In overlap with Elvis' talk, Nick produces a summons *hey Sash* involving an attention-getting token and an address term, selecting Sasha as next speaker who will provide the answer to the summons and, in so doing, be the recipient of the projected talk. While Sasha does not give a verbal response to the summons, the transcript shows that she does become a recipient for the next talk and responds to Nick's talk as the recipient of the talk.

Type-specific pre-expansions

Most types of pre-expansions project some specific next activity and are designed to be, and are regularly produced as, prior to a particular base sequence. The FPP of type-specific pre-sequences projects a particular next activity as relevant for talk and makes relevant a particular type of SPP response. These pre-sequences are used to project actions such as invitations, requests, offers, etc., and can be considered as pre-invitation sequences, pre-request sequences, pre-offer sequences, etc. Type-specific pre-expansions do not, however, simply project some future activity, but what happens in the pre-expansion influences the way in which the subsequent talk will unfold, and even if the projected base sequence will be done: the production of the projected base FPP is contingent upon the outcome of the pre-sequence and some responses regularly lead to the base sequence being produced while others do not.

Pre-invitations

Invitations are very commonly preceded by pre-expansions, typically of the type *Are you doing anything?* (Atkinson and Drew, 1984; Levinson, 1983). These questions are routinely treated by participants in a conversation not as questions seeking information about what the recipient is doing, but as precursors to invitations (Sacks, 1992: II: 529). The question is designed to check availability for an invitation.

```
(3) [Schegloff (1995a)]
      Clara:    hello
      Nelson:   hi.
      Clara:    hi.
  →   Nelson:   whatcha doin'.
  →   Clara:    not much.
      Nelson:   y' wanna drink?
      Clara:    yeah.
      Nelson:   okay.
```

In extract (3), we can see how such questions function in pre-invitation sequences. Clara gives the answer *not much* to the initial question and this answer can be interpreted, not as a description of activities, but as meaning something like 'nothing which is in competition with an invitation at that time' (cf. Levinson, 1983). In other words, an answer which indicates that one is not doing anything indicates that the invitation is likely to be welcomed. Such responses can be considered to be a 'go ahead' response to the invitation: a response which indicates that the projected invitation can now be done. In extract (3), this is how Nelson interprets the answer and he immediately proceeds to the invitation FPP, which in turn receives a preferred SPP: an acceptance of the invitation.

Conversely, if the recipient of the pre-invitation produces a turn which describes some activity, this indicates the likelihood that an invitation would be declined because of a competing commitment, as in (4).

```
(4) [Fiona and Jill]
      Fiona:    have yuh got any plans for Saddurday?
  →   Jill:     my sister's coming up tuh visit.
  →   Fiona:    o:h that will be nice for yuh.
```

In this extract, Jill's answer turn provides an indication that an invitation would not be likely to be accepted if it were produced following on from this pre-sequence. This answer can be considered to be a blocking response to the invitation: a response which discourages the invitation. In this extract, Fiona does not proceed to the invitation but rather treats Jill's turn as a telling and responds to it on this level. Withholding the projected base FPP is not uncommon in such circumstances. The pre-invitation has done the groundwork to see if an invitation would be likely to be accepted and has shown that if it were produced, it would be declined: a dispreferred SPP. The pre-expansion here allows the speaker to accomplish a different action following on from the pre-sequence and recasts the subsequent talk as undertaking some other action (Fox, 1987).

This recasting, however, raises an analytic problem: how can questions such as that in (4) be seen as *pre*-sequences if the base sequence they are claimed to precede is not actually done? The solution to this problem lies in the behaviour of conversationalists in these sorts of contexts, which demonstrates very clearly that participants are orienting to invitations as relevant activities. One activity which shows clearly that participants do not orient to questions such as 'Are you doing anything?' as questions about activities can be seen in a third possible response to these questions.

```
(5) [S/J 03]
      Sally:   yih doin' anythin' this Friday?
   →  Jean:    why?
      Sally:   well we were thinkin' a goin' to a movie.
      Jean:    which one,
      Sally:   I dunno, perhaps the new Tom Cruise one.
      Jean:    yeah I'd like tuh see that.
```

In this extract, the question does not receive either a go-ahead answer nor a blocking answer; in fact it receives an additional question: *why?* This question is revealing. Jean is not responding to the question itself as the main activity under way here, but rather as an activity which is contingent upon something else. Jean's response here indicates that what she is doing depends on what the projected invitation is. That is, she treats the response slot not as an opportunity to answer a question, but as a locational position in which she is called on to display her willingness to be invited. Her *why?* response indicates that her willingness to be invited is contingent upon the nature of the invitation. This is, therefore, a hedging response to the pre-invitation because it neither gives a go ahead nor does it block the invitation. It is also a clear indication that questions of the type 'What are you doing?' are heard as preliminary to other activities. Sally's response to the *why?* is not, however, produced as an invitation, but rather as a reporting of what the invitation was going to be (Drew, 1984). She does not do an invitation, which may be refused at this point, but recasts her talk to do the invitation in a way which is less on the record. Nonetheless, Sally's turn at this point is treated as an invitation by Jean, who eventually accepts the invitation.

The orientation to invitations as relevant next activities after pre-invitation sequences can also be seen in speakers' turns after blocking responses, as in (6), which continues (4) above.

(6) [Fiona and Jill]
```
        Fiona:   have yuh got any plans for Saddurday?
        Jill:    my sister' s coming up tuh visit.
        Fiona:   o:h that will be nice for yuh.
        Jill:    why::=what' re yih doin'
        Fiona:   oh:: well we jus' thought we might get some
                 friends together and go for a picnic, yih-
                 kno:w nothin' special.
        Jill:    that' s sounds like fu-<I think my sister w' d
                 like tuh do somethin' like that.
        Fiona:   yeah? w' ll we thought we might go out tuh the
   →             river. so whyncha both come.
        Jill:    yeah thadded by nice.
```

Here, Jill's turn has blocked an invitation from Fiona and the pre-invitation sequence has been done as a telling in response to a question. Jill's next turn *why::=what're yih doin'*, however, continues to orient to Fiona's original question as a pre-invitation and asks what the projected invitation was likely to be. Jill's turn, because it orients to inviting as a relevant activity even after the talk has been recast, contains an implication that the recipient might modify her reception of the projected invitation. That is, Jill has revived the possibility of an invitation by remaining in the invitation sequence. Fiona responds to Jill by telling what the invitation would have been. Although Jill is orienting to an invitation sequence, Fiona continues to construct the talk as a telling about an invitation, rather than an invitation as such (Drew, 1984). Jill then indicates that both she and her sister would be willing to participate in the event. After telling some more about the invitation, Fiona then (re)does the invitation as an invitation FPP (at the arrowed turn) and the invitation is now accepted. Throughout the sequence, the participants show that they are orienting to an invitation as a relevant outcome of the initial question turn, even though the invitation is not done until much later. It is only by viewing the initial turn as preliminary to some activity which was withheld that this sequence can be understood and the relevance of Jill's _why::=what're yih doin'_ can be interpreted.

In summary, pre-invitations are typically realized as question–answer sequences in which the question serves to check availability. As such, there are only a limited number of question forms which are hearable as pre-invitations. Availability is a necessary pre-condition for an invitation being accepted and thus availability will determine whether or not a preferred or dispreferred SPP is likely (Levinson, 1983). The pre-invitation, therefore, is work done by a potential inviter to determine before producing the invitation itself, whether or not it is likely to be accepted, and provides a possibility for not doing the invitation in the face of a likely dispreferred response. The sequence also allows for the possibility of the recipient declining an invitation before it is produced, thereby to some extent avoiding having to do a dispreferred action.

Pre-requests
Requests, like invitations, have both preferred and dispreferred SPP types and also often occur with pre-expansion. Here again, the pre-expansion gauges the likelihood of the request being granted before it is performed.

```
(7) [Merritt (1976: 324) from Levinson (1983]
    A:       Hi.  Do  you  have  uh  size  C  flashlight
             batteries?
    B:       Yes sir
    A:       I' ll have four please
    B:       ((Turns to get))
```

Here, A's initial turn launches a sequence to ascertain whether the conditions necessary for the request to work actually exist and once this pre-request has been completed, A produces a request FPP. The pre-request in extract (7) has a go-ahead response, after which the request FPP is done and then receives a preferred SPP. Pre-requests can also receive blocking responses, as in extract (8), and hedging responses, as in extract (9).

```
(8) [Levinson (1983) 170]
    A:        Hullo I was wondering if you were intending
              to go to Popper' s talk this afternoon
```

B:	Not today I'm afraid I can't really make it to this one
A:	Ah okay
B:	You wanted me to record it didn't you heh!
A:	Yeah heheh
B:	Heheh no I'm sorry about that, . . .

In (8), B's turn is a blocking response which indicates that the pre-conditions for the request cannot be met. A orients to B's response as an answer to a question and responds with an acceptance of the telling. The request is not done; however, B's second turn indicates that he is fully orienting to A's first turn as a pre-request and reformulates the thrust of the request.

(9) [Redecorating]

	Andy:	djah have a minute?
→	Chris:	why?
	Andy:	I need a hand with the ladder.
	Chris:	okay'll be there in a moment.

In (9), Chris's *why?* is a hedged response indicating that his availability is conditional upon the projected request.

Pre-requests typically treat two types of pre-conditions for the granting of the request: availability of the requested object or ability of the person to carry out the request. Pre-requests dealing with the availability of an object typically have forms such as 'Do you have an X?', 'Is there any X?', etc., while pre-requests dealing with ability of the person have forms such as 'Have you got a minute?', 'Can you X?', etc. These pre-requests can project a request so strongly that in many cases the pre-sequence itself can achieve the request without the request itself being produced, as in (10).

(10) [Sinclair and Coulthard (1975) from Levinson (1983)]

| S: | Have you got Embassy Gold please? |
| H: | Yes dear ((provides)) |

Here the customer (S) produces a pre-request, asking about the availability of a brand of cigarettes and is then given the cigarettes without any overt request being produced. The pre-request here is functioning in what Searle (1975) calls an indirect request. Levinson (1983) however provides a competing analysis of these forms as pre-requests with an omitted base sequence. He makes this argument because an utterance such as *Have you got Embassy Gold please?* can actually launch more than one possible trajectory. It can launch the sequence in (10) which is made up of the FPP of the pre-sequence and the SPP of the base sequence. It can also launch a sequence involving the full base request sequence, as in (11).

(11) [Merritt (1976: 324) from Levinson (1983)]
```
        A:          Hi. Do you have uh size C flashlight
                    batteries?
        B:          Yes sir
        A:          I'll have four please
        B:          ((Turns to get))
```

Similar arguments about the relationship between pre-sequences and indirect speech acts are made by Herringer (1977) and Schegloff (1988c) and within a conversation analytic perspective indirect speech acts can be best treated as truncated versions of expanded sequences. Levinson (1983), Herringer (1977) and Schegloff (1988c) argue that, if one codes the pre-request FPP as an indirect request, this is a category imposed by the analyst, because it is only possible to know that the talk constitutes an indirect speech act after the sequence has been played out. The same form may launch very different sequences and it is only by understanding utterances such as 'Do you have X?' as presequences that the commonality of all these possible outcomes can be recognized by participants as well as by analysts. This argument also applies to a third trajectory which may follow a pre-request which allows the pre-request to be followed by an offer, as in (12).

(12) [Merrit (1976) in Levinson (1983)]
```
        C:          Do you have a pecan Danish today?
        S:          Yes we do. Would you like one of those?
        C:          Yes please
        S:          Okay ((Turns to get))
```

In this extract, the request pre-sequence provides an opportunity for the recipient of the pre-sequence to convert the sequence from a request to an offer (Sacks, 1992: I: 65). In these cases, a dispreferred request FPP is replaced by a preferred offer FPP and the pre-sequence provides a resource to allow this to happen.

Levinson (1983) argues for a hierarchy of preferences for request sequences, which deal in different ways with the doing of a request FPP, which is a dispreferred FPP type.

(13) (i)	most preferred	pre-request
		response to request
(ii)	next preferred	pre-request
		offer
		acceptance of offer
(iii)	least preferred	pre-request
		go ahead
		request
		compliance

Some forms of pre-requests are designed to achieve the most pre-ferred sequence (Levinson, 1983). This is possible when the pre-request FPP contains all of the information necessary to complete the request. That is, fully specified pre-requests FPPs are designed to enable request-oriented SPPs in immediate next position. Other pre-request FPPs usually occasion some other talk before the request can be granted. Some pre-requests, such as 'Have you got a minute?' are designed in such a way that immediate compliance with the request cannot be done and further talk must occur.

Pre-offers

Participants in conversation may try to assess in advance whether their offer is likely to be accepted before producing the offer. This is done through pre-offer sequences (Raymon, 2003).

```
(14) [S/J 04]
     Sam:    The farm' s a long way outta town yih know bud
             i' s gunna be a great party though
             [ i' s (gunna) ]
     Simon:  [ I' m driv- I' ] m takin' my car
     Sam:    Y' are?
     Simon:  Yih c' d come with me if yih wan.
     Sam:    Okay thanks
```

In this extract, Sam and Simon are discussing a party to which they have both been invited. In the context, Sam's observation about the farm where the party is being held being a long way from town is potentially an indication of a problem in getting there. Simon's observation that he is taking his car is not directly relevant to the preceding discussion of the party; rather the mentioning of the car in this particular position invites understanding of his potential to resolve the problem foreshadowed in Sam's talk. When Sam registers this as news he is registering interest in the action which is projected by the mentioning of taking the car. This expression of interest counts then as a go-ahead response for the offer, which is produced in the next turn by Simon and immediately accepted by Sam. In this extract, the mentioning of taking the car does work to see whether Sam is likely to be interested in the offer of a lift to the party and works as a pre-offer rather than as just a telling, at this point in the conversation. The pre-offer here is highly context-specific and pre-offers in general do not have the formulaic features found in the other pre-expansions discussed so far.

Like other pre-sequences, pre-offers can also be receiving blocking responses as in (15).

```
(15) [NJ]
    Nick:    so:: have yuh got a lift?
    Joan:    yeah. I'm goin' with Jodie.
    Nick:    okay.
```

In extract (15), Nick's question turn deals with the pre-conditions of an offer being accepted by examining if his recipient has a need which his offer could fulfil. Joan's answer indicates that she is not in need of a lift and that the offer is likely to be rejected because of the already arranged lift with Jodie. In this case, Nick does not proceed to an offer and the pre-offer is recast as a simple question–answer sequence. It does not seem that pre-offers are as open to hedging responses as the other pre-sequences discussed above and this seems to be the result of aspects of the ways in which pre-offers are designed. In the case of extract (14), the construction of the pre-offer is so highly contextualized that a hedging response would not appear to be a possible response at any point in the unfolding talk, while in extract (15) the question about a need may not allow the same possibilities for a contingent response.

Pre-tellings

When a speaker wishes to convey news to another, there is a constraint on what is tellable to a particular recipient. Ordinarily one should not tell a recipient something that s/he already knows (C. Goodwin, 1979; Sacks, 1973). Pre-tellings (or pre-announcements) are aimed at gauging whether or not a recipient is an appropriate recipient of some telling (Terasaki, 2004).

Many, but by no means all, pre-tellings are quite formulaic, consisting of the basic components in (16):

(16)

guess	what	
(do) you know	who	± information
remember	when	
	where	

The minimal form of a pre-telling is 'Guess what'. This device indicates that the speaker has something to tell, but gives no additional information about the telling; other pre-tellings may give the recipient more information about what the telling will involve, as in 'Guess who I saw on the weekend', which gives some indication about the topic of the news. Regardless of the amount of information or the degree of formulaicity, the common function of pre-tellings is to alert the recipient that what is to follow is a telling of some news. This enables the recipient to recognize the telling as news when it is delivered, especially if the news is topically discontinuous with previous talk. In addition, pre-tellings may also include an assessment about the news as good or bad, giving the recipient a framework in which to interpret the telling (C. Goodwin, 1984; M. H. Goodwin, 1990; Terasaki, 2004).

As with other pre-sequences, pre-tellings have more than one possible response type. Often, the response to a pre-telling is a go-ahead response. One common design for go-ahead responses is a repetition of the question word in a formulaic pre-telling as in 'guess what/what' (extract (17)) or a 'no' answer to a 'do you know ...?' or 'have you heard ...?' pre-telling (extract (18)).

(17) [Terasaki (1976) in Levinson (1983)]
```
D:      .hh Oh guess what.
R:      What.
D:      Professor Deelies came in, 'n he- put
        another book on ' is order.
```

(18) [Car conversation]
```
Nick:    [djyou] know how much money she takes home a
         week?
Sasha:   nah?
Nick:    three thousand fuckin' dollars.
```

These responses indicate that the news is unknown to the recipient and that a telling would be appropriate. Pre-tellings may also receive blocking responses as in (19).

```
(19) [Car conversation]
        Sasha:    an all- did he tell yuh about his problems
                  with his wife an [ that
    → Nick:                        [ yeah. oh I knew all about
                  that anyway.
                  (0.2)
        Nick      an he's got this tattoo on his ↑che:st
        Elvis:    yeah?
        Nick:     an it's like (0.2) of this (.) great big (.)
                  pheasant or something like that,
```

In this extract, Nick shows that the constraint on newsworthiness has not been met and he is not a candidate recipient for a telling on this topic because he already knows the news. Sasha does not tell her story of 'his problems with his wife', but rather Nick, after a pause, begins another telling of his own.

Pre-tellings can also function to provide a space for making a guess about the news, especially in the case of telling bad news, which can be considered a dispreferred action (Levinson, 1983; Schegloff, 1988b). By prompting a guess through a pre-telling, the need to perform the dispreferred turn may be removed.

```
(20) [Schegloff (1988) DA:2:10]
        Belle:    I I-I had something (.) terrible t' tell
                  you.=
                  =So [ uh:  ]
   a→   Fanny:        [ How t] errible [ is it. ]
        Belle:                          [ .hhhhh]
                  (.)
   b→   Belle:    Uh: ez worse as it could be:.
                  (0.7)
        Fanny:    W' y' mean Ida?
                  (.)
        Belle:    Uh yah.hh=
   c→   Fanny:    =Wud she do die:?
        Belle:    =Mm:hm,
                  (.)
        Fanny:    When did she die,
```

In this extract, Belle produces a pre-telling which characterizes her news as *terrible*, but it is actually Fanny who guesses the news (at arrow c) rather than Belle who tells it. In fact, Belle passes up opportunities to deliver her news at arrow b. Fanny's talk has shown that she is a potential recipient of the news at arrow a, but rather than proceeding to a telling, Belle provides a reformulation of part of her pre-telling and allows a 0.7-second gap. This can be heard as Belle withholding the news, providing a space and a prompt for Fanny to guess the news, which she eventually does, first identifying a person about whom the news could be *as worse as it could be* and then identifying what could be told about this person which could be characterized in this way.

Preliminaries to preliminaries

Schegloff (1980) has described a pre-sequence which is distinctive in a number of respects: the preliminary to preliminaries sequence or the 'pre-pre'. These sequences are type-specific, but there are a range of base sequences which can be projected by them. The form of these pre-sequences is typically *Can I . . . ?* or *Let me . . .* with an indication what the nature of the projected base sequence is: 'Can I ask you a question?', 'Can I make a suggestion?', 'Can I ask a favour?', etc. As such, these pre-sequences look similar to the sorts of type-specific pre-sequences discussed above.

In spite of the similarity, pre-pres work and are understood in very different ways. Pre-pres do not seem to be designed in the first instance to anticipate or avoid rejection of a base sequence and do not typically receive blocking responses. Although pre-pres do not receive blocking responses, the 'go ahead' SPP of the pre-expansion is not immediately followed by the projected base FPP: for example, *Can I ask you a favour?* does not regularly lead to the production of a request in the speaker's next turn. This means that pre-pres do not appear to be designed as immediately prior to a projected base sequence, but as prior to something else. The ways in which pre-pres function can be seen more clearly if we consider extract (21).

```
(21) [J/S 02]
     Jim:      C' n I ask yuh a big favour?
     Sarah:    Sure
     Jim:      Yih know how I have tuh go tuh this meetin'
               out at Cra:nbourne on Wensday¿
     Sarah:    Mm hm.
     Jim:      Well my car has broken down an they don' know
               if it will be fixed by then an'
→              I w' z wondering if I c' d borrow your car.
     Sarah:    U:h so when do yih need it? all day?
     Jim:      No jus' from twelve until abou' three¿
     Sarah:    We:ll I don' need it then so I guess it' ll be
               okay.
```

In this extract, Jim produces the pre-pre *C'n I ask yuh a big favour?* which gets a go-ahead response from Sarah. He then asks a question which indicates that he has a meeting at a place quite distant from his place of work. Jim then produces a brief telling about his car, before producing the projected base FPP at the arrowed line. Jim's pre-pre leads in his next turn to talk which serves as preliminary work which needs to be accomplished before the base FPP is done. The pre-expansion is not immediately a preliminary to the projected base sequence, but rather a preliminary to talk which is itself preliminary to the projected base sequence. These pre-pres seem to establish a trajectory in which what comes after them is not heard as a base FPP, but rather as preparatory talk for a base sequence, while also providing for recognition of the base sequence when it is produced. Thus, in extract (21), Jim's pre-pre foreshadows that his request to borrow the car will be understood as the FPP of the projected base sequence and that the previous talk should be heard as preparatory to this request. The relationship between the pre-pre and what follows it can be seen even more clearly in extract (22).

```
(22) [J/S 05]
  → Carol:    Can I ask y' a question.
    Joe:      Yeah.
    Carol:    Yihknow Sally Smith?
    Joe:      Yeah.
    Carol:    An yih know that she's changed jobs.
    Joe:      yeah.
    Carol:    Well I want tuh get in touch with her but I
              don't know where she is working now.
  →           do you have her phone number¿
    Joe:      I think so. just a moment while I check.
```

Here, Carol produces the pre-pre *Can I ask y' a question*, thereby projecting a question as a relevant base sequence. She then produces two questions, which Joe does not appear to treat as the particular question which Carol has asked permission to produce. Even though Carol's next talk has the form of the projected base sequence, these questions are heard as preliminaries to some other question. A trajectory has been established in which the talk immediately after the pre-pre SPP will not be heard as the projected action but rather as a preliminary to this action and this trajectory is more important for interpreting what is said than the form of the talk which appears. When Carol produces her projected question, *do you have her phone number¿*

(which is a request for a phone number rather than a question), she also precedes it with a warrant for the asking.

Schegloff (1980) argues that there are two main sorts of preliminaries which are produced in the space made available by the pre-pre: pre-mentions, where speakers provide information to their recipients, and pre-conditions, where speakers ensure that the necessary conditions for complying with the base FPP exist. In the extracts above, Jim and Carol produce base FPPs dealing with possible problems of knowledge. In extract (21), Jim's request to borrow a car involves relevant information which his recipient cannot be presumed to know (his car has broken down and will take time to repair) or cannot be presumed to recognize as relevant (he has a distant meeting). He therefore needs to do work to establish this information so that it will be recognized as relevant to the base FPP when it is produced. In extract (22), Carol faces a similar problem. Her recipient can only provide the information she needs if he knows the person involved and knows that she has changed jobs. Her preliminaries follow a sequence from the more general condition (does Joe know Sally Smith) to the less general one (does he know she has changed jobs). Obviously if the first condition for providing the necessary information does not exist (Joe doesn't know Sally Smith), he cannot possibly meet the second condition. If the first condition is fulfilled, he may, however, not be aware of the second condition, in which case he is unlikely to be able to provide the information. Carol, therefore, refines her knowledge about whether or not the conditions exist for her to be able to secure Sally Smith's new phone number. Once the conditions have been established, she also provides a pre-mention of her situation before proceeding to the projected base FPP. In both of these extracts, Jim and Carol do work in the conversational space which the pre-pre creates to provide a context in which their talk can be heard and understood.

Multiple pre-expansions

It is possible in conversation to have several pre-expansions before the relevant base FPP is produced. The multiple pre-expansions may be made up of generic and type-specific sequences, or of a number of type-specific sequences. Where summons–answer sequences occur in multiple pre-expansions, they tend to occur as the initial pre-expansion. Extract (23), a fuller version of extract (21), shows in a very short conversation how such multiple pre-expansion can work.

```
(23) [J/S 05]
a→ Jim:      Sarah?
    Sarah:    Uh-yeah,
b→ Jim:      Yih god a moment,
    Sarah:    Yeah.
c→ Jim:      C' n I ask yuh a big favour?
    Sarah:    Sure
    Jim:      Yih know how I have tuh go tuh this meetin'
              out at Cra:nbourne on Wensday¿
    Sarah:    Mm hm.
    Jim:      Well my car has broken down an they don' know
    →         if it will be fixed by then an' I w' z wondering
              if I c' d borrow your car.
    Sarah:    U:h so when do yih need it? all day?
    Jim:      No jus' from twelve until abou' three¿
    Sarah:    We:ll I don' need it then so I guess it' ll be
              okay.
```

In extract (23), the pre-pre discussed above is preceded by two other pre-sequences. At arrow a, Jim begins with a summons–answer sequence which is preliminary to the next talk he produces and also serves to initiate the conversation by securing Sarah's recipiency for the talk. Sarah gives a 'go ahead' response to this, both positioning herself as a recipient of further talk and making further talk relevant. Jim's next talk is a pre-request which seeks to establish the possibility that Sarah will grant the projected request. Sarah's SPP is again a 'go ahead' response. The request which Jim produces is simultaneously a request and a pre-pre *C'n I ask yuh a big favour?* which again receives a 'go ahead' response. The result is an elaborately constructed stretch of talk in which the three pre-expansions each serve a further purpose in establishing the trajectory of the talk.

This extract shows something else about the nature of pre-expansion: in expanding sequences *any* sequence can be the basis for expansion. As expansion sequences are sequences, they too include points at which further expansion can be made, just like any other sequence type. In the above extract, it is not just the base sequence (the request) which is expanded, as the pre-sequences themselves are also expanded. The summons–answer is a pre-expansion of the pre-request, the pre-request is a pre-expansion of the pre-pre, and the whole is a pre-expansion of the base request. From this we can see that a single base adjacency pair can provide the basis for a substantial amount of talk, even before it is produced. The coherence of the talk in turn derives from the fact that such talk is hearable as prior to some projected next action and this provides a context in which the talk is interpretable for participants.

Conclusion

Pre-expansions, particularly type-specific pre-expansions, have as a primary role avoidance of problems in talk, particularly in dealing with problematic responses to FPPs. Pre-expansion is therefore closely related to preference organization, as it deals with the potential for different types of SPPs in response to a particular FPP. The role of pre-expansions is to gauge the likelihood of a particular FPP receiving a preferred or dispreferred SPP even before it is produced. They provide for the possibility that FPPs which are likely to receive dispreferreds will not be produced and so avoid the problem of rejection before it arises. This means that pre-expansions are not just possible locations for talk relevant to a particular project, but are resources for the organization of that project, and even for determining whether a particular project gets done.

Insert expansion

In the discussion of adjacency pairs, it was claimed that some types of talk can occur between an FPP and an SPP and these types of talk are quite limited. These types of talk are cases of insert expansion: expansion which occurs within the adjacency pair itself and separates the FPP from the SPP. The talk which occurs between an FPP and an SPP, however, does not cancel the relevance of the yet to be produced SPP. Insert expansions interrupt the activity under way, but are still relevant to that action (Jefferson, 1972). Insert expansion allows a possibility for a second speaker, the speaker who must produce the SPP, to do interactional work relevant to the projected SPP.

As with pre-expansion, insert expansion is realized through a sequence of its own, which we can call an insert sequence (Schegloff, 1972, 1990). Typically, insert expansion is launched by an FPP produced by the second speaker which requires an SPP for completion. Once the sequence is completed, the base SPP once again becomes relevant as the next action (Sacks, 1992: II: 529). This allows the insert expansion to delay a base SPP until some preliminary work can be done and completes this work. The type of work being done by the insert is determined by the sequential relationship of the insert itself as insert expansions can relate to either the FPP which has launched the adjacency pair in which they are inserted or they may be addressed to the SPP which needs to be produced because of that FPP. These are called *post-first insert expansions* and *pre-second insert expansions* respectively (Schegloff, 1990).

Post-first insert expansion

Post-first insert expansions are designed to address issues arising from the FPP which precedes them. They are therefore second to that FPP. In any conversation, problems may arise and when they do arise they need to be repaired. Overwhelmingly this repair occurs in the immediate next turn after the problem occurs (Schegloff *et al.*, 1977). This can be seen in extract (24).

(24) [Schegloff *et al.* (1977) CD:SP]
```
        D:        Wul did' e ever get married' r anything?
        C:        Huh?
        D:        Did jee ever get married?
        C:        I have // no idea
```

In this extract, C produces a turn after the production of D's FPP which does not count as an answer to the question. This turn indicates a problem of hearing or understanding relevant to the FPP and in doing so it initiates a repair sequence. This means that C's turn is also an FPP and requires its own SPP for completion. In this case, the SPP produced must count as a repair of the problem indicated by C's turn. In extract (24) the repair is provided by D in his next turn and the inserted repair sequence is completed. This structuring of repair is a case of *other-initiated self-repair* because it is the recipient of the problematic talk who initiates the repair sequence and the producer of the problematic talk who provides the repair (Schegloff *et al.*, 1977, see also chapter 7).

This extract also demonstrates that in this sequence the repair must be completed before the base SPP can be produced. It is impossible for C to provide the relevant SPP until the problem of hearing or understanding can be resolved and this requires that the base SPP be displaced until the repair can be achieved. At the same time, the repair remains relevant to the action currently under way: it is seen as connected to this action and as a component of the action. The participants in producing the insert are still orienting to the course of action which was initiated by the base FPP and are still orienting to the SPP which this required. The structure involved here is then:

A: FPP_{base}
B: FPP_{insert}
A: SPP_{insert}
B: SPP_{base}

In extract (24) the insert sequence involved is addressed to the FPP. It is derived from it and responds to it as a problematic instance of talk, without reference to the SPP which has been invoked. It is thus quite clearly post-first in its design. However, while these repair insert sequences are designed as post-firsts, this does not mean that they may not also orient to aspects of the SPP. Other-initiated repair sequences, because they are inserted within an adjacency pair, break contiguity between an FPP and an SPP. Like other elements which break contiguity, insert sequences can be implicated in the possible production of a dispreferred SPP, as in extract (25).

(25) [Schegloff (1996) TG1]

Bee:	Yih sound HA:PPY, hh	FPP_{base}
Ava:	I sound ha:p[py?	FPP_{insert}
Bee:	[Ye:uh	SPP_{insert}
Ava:	(0.3)	
Bee:	No:,	SPP_{base}

Here, Bee's dispreferred *No:,* is separated from the assessment which launches it by an inserted other-initiated repair and a silence. The repair here is premonitory of an upcoming dispreferred. Inserted repairs, however, are not inherently markers of a pending dispreferred, but rather because of their placement in the sequence they can be deployed as a device to achieve the break in contiguity that is usually associated with dispreferreds. Moreover, regardless of their function as a pre-indication of a dispreferred second, the inserted repair sequence remains, in its design, tied to the FPP, not to the SPP. The problem being repaired here appears to be one of preference: the FPP is designed in such a way as to project a particular answer response (that of yes) and Bee's answer requires a breach of the preference for agreement and the insert expansion allows not only for a break in contiguity but also for the possibility of redoing the problematic FPP (Sacks, 1987). The inserted repair sequence allows an opportunity to modify the preference organization of the FPP which occasioned the repair, as happens in extract (26).

(26) [Lunch]

Harry:	Aren' t you supposed to go up there	FPP_{base}
	with John though?	
Joy:	Wha' ¿	FPP_{insert}
Harry:	Y' aren' t goin' up there with John.	SPP_{insert}
Joy:	Na:h that fell through weeks ago.	SPP_{base}

Here, Harry produces a question FPP which Joy follows with the repair initiator *Huh¿*. Harry's question is designed to predict a 'yes' answer, but he modifies the form of the base FPP in the SPP turn of the repair sequence to change the expected answer to a 'no'. Joy then produces the base SPP, which now aligns with the new preference organization in the reformulated FPP: that is the same base SPP would have been dispreferred given the first formulation of the FPP.

Post-first insert sequences can be repeated through more than one sequence if the first attempt to repair the trouble is not successful.

```
(27) [TG 1:7–14]
      Ava:          [ <I wan]' dih know if yih got
                    a-uh:m wutchimicawllit. A::     FPP_base
                    pah(hh)hking place°th' s mornin'.
                    .hh
      Bee:      A pa:rking place                  1FPP_insert
      Ava:      Mm hm,                            1SPP_insert
                (0.4)
      Bee:      Whe:re.                           2FPP_insert
      Ava:      t! Oh: just anypla(h)ce? I wz jus'  2SPP_insert
                kidding yuh.
      Bee:      Nno?=                      SPP_base
```

In this extract, Bee initiates a repair of Ava's FPP question by providing a candidate hearing of what she considered to be a problematic item in the question. Ava responds with an SPP which indicates that Bee's candidate hearing is correct, without resolving the problem as Bee initiates a further repair on the original base FPP. This repair receives a different response indicating that the question was meant as a joke rather than a true enquiry. The base FPP and SPP are separated here by two repair sequences, both of which orient to the same trouble in the base FPP.

Pre-second insert expansion

Pre-second insert expansion occurs in a similar sequential environment, between the FPP and the SPP of an adjacency pair, but it works in different ways. Most importantly, pre-second insert expansion orients to the SPP which has been made relevant, rather than to the preceding FPP. The insert is projecting forwards in the conversation, rather than referring back to a prior action. In addition, while post-first insert expansion is generic in the sense that it can be used to repair ostensible problems in *any* FPP, pre-second insert expansion is type specific (like most pre-expansions). Pre-second insert expansions are designed to do some work relevant to the upcoming SPP and the work which needs to be done is different for different SPPs.

Pre-second insert expansions are particularly common in direction giving, because, when giving directions, the direction giver may need to know information about such things as the starting point or the mode of travel as these will affect the form of the directions given (Psathas, 1986, 1991). The ways in which these insert expansions work can be seen in extracts (28) and (29).

(28) [Psathas (1986) Insight Workshop]
```
        C:      Right an lets see now Walnut      FPP_base
                Avenue in Burbank where is that?
        A:      Awright. Where- where yu coming
                from Eaglerock?                          FPP_insert
        C:      uh huh The store                    SPP_insert
        A:      Get on the free:way             SPP_base
        C:      Mm hmm,
        A:      An get off at Burbank Boulevard.
        C:      Mm hmm,
        A:      Head towards the mountains,
        C:      Mm hmm,
```

(29) [Psathas (1991) FH]
```
        A:      Do you know the directions?     FPP_base
        B:      uh (.) You driving or walking?        FPP_insert
        A:      Walking (0.2)                        SPP_insert
        B:      Get on the subway . . .         SPP_base
```

In each of these two extracts, the first speaker launches a direction-giving sequence by asking a question. This question makes an answer (the directions) relevant; however, the answerer in each case does not provide directions, but rather asks a question. The questioner does some preparatory work before answering. This question turn is clearly not orienting to some trouble in the base FPP, but rather it is searching for some necessary information the speaker requires in order to be able to produce the SPP. It is orienting to the form which the direction-giving SPP will take and attempts to establish the necessary pre-conditions which will shape the form of the SPP. In each case the answer turn in the insert sequence is relevant for the formulation of the route which is presented to the enquirer (Psathas, 1991). When the insert SPP has been produced, the sequence can then move to providing the base SPP: the directions themselves. This type of pre-second insert expansion can be considered to be a *direction-giving pre-second*, designed specifically to do work related to direction-giving SPPs. The sequential structure of the insert sequence is identical to that for post-first insert expansions:

A: FPP_{base}
B: FPP_{insert}
A: SPP_{insert}
B: SPP_{base}

However, the function of the sequence is quite different. What these extracts show is that the same locational position within a sequence can be used for different purposes: repair or information-getting.

Pre-second insert sequences are very common in service encounters, as in the interaction shown in extract (30).

(30) [Sandwich shop]
```
Customer:   C' d I have a turkey sam' wich
            please.                       FPP_base
Server:     White or wholegrain,              FPP_insert
Customer:   Wholegrain.                       SPP_insert
Server:     Okay.                         SPP_base
```

In this extract, the customer produces a request for a sandwich and the server then asks a question about the type of bread required for the sandwich. As in the direction-giving examples, the server needs this information to be able to produce the SPP (the giving of the sandwich: the *okay* here is not strictly speaking the SPP for the request, but rather a verbal indication of preparedness to grant the request). This insert sequence is a *request pre-second*, designed to facilitate the granting of a request.

It is quite possible for there to be more than one insert sequence in such encounters, as in (31).

(31) [Sandwich shop]
```
Customer:   Uh-I' d like a ham sandwich.  FPP_base
Server:     Whide or wholemeal,             1FPP_insert
Customer:   Wholemeal.                      1SPP_insert
            (15)
Server:     Yih want mustard.               2FPP_insert
Customer:   Yuh- jist a liddle bit          2SPP_insert
            (40)
Server:     Salt ' n pepper?                3FPP_insert
Customer:   Yes please.                     3SPP_insert
            (70)
Server:     Here yih are.               SPP_base
```

In this example, the server asks a number of questions relevant to the making of the sandwich in the course of its making. The server asks about bread types, mustard, salt and pepper and then complies with each answer before moving to the next insert sequence. In each case, the insert sequence is orienting to the SPP, the giving of the sandwich, as the relevant next action. Zimmerman (1984) refers to these repeated insert sequences as interrogative series: a sequence of sequences with the same basic interactional aim.

In the cases above, the insert sequences all function as occasions for gathering information prior to finalizing the request and all assume a preferred SPP: that the sandwich will in fact be given to the customer. However, insert sequences can also be used to determine whether the SPP will be preferred or dispreferred, as in (32).

(32) [GHT]

Joe:	woud' juh like to come over on	
	Friday night,	FPP_{base}
Sam:	what's happenin'.	FPP_{insert}
Joe:	nuthin' special. Jus' to have a	
	few drinks.	SPP_{insert}
Sam:	okay.	SPP_{base}

In this extract, Joe issues an invitation to Sam; making acceptance or declining of the invitation a relevant next action. Sam, however, asks a question about what the invitation is for, orienting to the fact that this is an invitation sequence, but at the same time gaining information about the invitation before accepting or declining. Once this insert sequence is completed, Sam produces an acceptance SPP. This can be considered an *invitation pre-second,* as it appears to be designed to determine which of the possible SPP types that occur in invitations will be produced. Here, the pre-second insert sequence is functioning in a similar way to a pre-invitation sequence. In both cases, the sequence is being used to determining the likely outcome of the sequence. The pre-invitation provides a location for the inviter to gauge whether or not the invitation FPP will receive a preferred or dispreferred SPP. The invitation pre-second allows a structural position for the person being invited to do work to determine whether the SPP will be preferred or dispreferred.

Multiple insert expansions

In the discussion above it was seen that post-first insert expansions could be repeated if repair was not achieved by the first try and that pre-second insert expansions could occur where multiple pieces of information were relevant to the accomplishment of the SPP. It is also possible for both types of insert expansion to occur within the same sequence. This can be seen in extract (33).

```
(33) [Schegloff, 1995]
    Caller:     send'n emergency to fourteen
                forty eight Lillian Lane,     FPP_base
    Dispatch:   fourteen forty eight-[ what sir?       1FPP_insert
    Caller:                          [ yeah.
    Dispatch:   Li[llian Lane?
    Caller:        [fourteen forty eight Lillian       1SPP_insert
    Dispatch:   Lillian,                               2FPP_insert
    Caller;     yeah.                                  2SPP_insert
    Dispatch:   what's th' trouble sir.                3FPP_insert
    Caller:     well, I had the police out here
                once, now my wife's got cut.           3SPP_insert
    Dispatch:   alright sir, we'll have'em out
                there                            SPP_base
    Caller:     right away?
    Dispatch:   alright sir,
```

This extract, from a call to an emergency service, involves a request for assistance *send 'n emergency to fourteen forty eight Lillian Lane*, which is only responded to by the dispatcher after three insert sequences have been accomplished. The first two insert sequences involve problems in hearing and understanding of the street name in the FPP initiated by the dispatcher: that is, they are post-first insert expansions. Once this has been resolved the dispatcher then initiates a question–answer adjacency pair dealing with the reason for the call. This sequence is directed at establishing whether or not the request for assistance warrants granting of the request. If the conditions prompting the request for assistance are appropriate, then a preferred SPP is likely; if not, a dispreferred SPP is likely. This then is a case of pre-second insert expansion.

The ordering of post-first insert expansions and pre-second insert expansions is not random. The sequencing found in extract (33), post-first insert then pre-second insert, is normative. That this is so is unsurprising. Post-first insert expansions deal with problems of hearing and understanding in FPPs and these must be dealt with as soon as possible after they have occurred (Schegloff *et al.*, 1977). Moreover, the

FPP needs to have been heard and understood before the form of the SPP can be considered. This means that work relating to the FPP needs to be done before work relating to the SPP is done.

Conclusion

The discussion of insert expansion has shown that there are sequences which can occur between the two turns of an adjacency pair, breaking the contiguity of these turns. However, these sequences do not challenge the place of the adjacency pair as the basic organizational unit of the sequences to which they belong. Where these insert sequences occur, the relevance of an SPP in response to the FPP is maintained and the SPP is delayed by the insert, not cancelled by it. Participants in conversation understand these inserts as being a part of the sequence which has been launched and interpret them as relevant to that sequence. Insert expansion, whether it is a post-first insert sequence or a pre-second insert sequence, accomplishes necessary work which needs to be done for a base sequence to be accomplished successfully. When a particular speaker produces an FPP, his/her interlocutor may not be in a position to provide an appropriate SPP immediately after the production of the SPP. Insert expansion provides a place where such work can be done and the nature of adjacency pairs as base sequences provides an environment in which talk can be heard as *inserted* into a sequence even though the talk which completes the sequence has not yet been done. That is to say that insert expansions are not analytical categories which are applied to the talk after it has been completed; participants in conversations are able to hear and understand such sequences as inserted into an activity while that activity is under way and before it is completed.

Post-expansion

Introduction

Sequences are also potentially expandable after the completion of the base SPP. Once an SPP has been completed, the sequence is potentially complete: the action launched by the FPP has run its course and a new action could appropriately be begun. However, it is also possible for talk to occur after the SPP which is recognizably associated with the preceding sequence. That is, it is possible for sequences to be expanded after their SPP. This phenomenon is known as *post-expansion* (Schegloff, 1990).

Minimal post-expansion: Sequence-closing thirds

Minimal post-expansion is minimal in several senses. Firstly, these post-expansions consist of the addition of only a single turn after the SPP. Secondly, these turns may be made up of a single item such as *oh* or *okay*, although combinations of these and other longer turns are also possible. Thirdly, these turns do not project any further talk beyond their turn. This means that ending the sequence is a possibility after the completion of such a turn. Minimal post-expansion, unlike the other examples of expansion discussed so far, is not in itself a sequence. Rather, minimal post-expansions are designed to propose closing of a sequence and can be referred to as *sequence-closing thirds* (SCT). The following sections will examine some common SCTs to examine how they function in interaction.

Oh

The token *oh* is used to register that a recipient has received information and that the recipient as a result of this has moved from a state of not knowing to a state of knowing (Heritage, 1984a). Heritage demonstrates that *oh* as a change-of-state token can be found in a range of sequential positions; however, one very common position is following the completion of an adjacency pair (that is as an SCT), especially a question–answer adjacency pair, as in (34).

```
(34) [Heritage (1984) WPC:1:MJ (1):1]
        J:        When d' z Sus' n g[o back.=
        M:                       [.hhhh
        J:        =[ (                 )
        M:        =[u-She: goes back on Satida:y=
   →    J:        =O[h:.
        M:          [A:n' Stev' n w' z here (.) all las' week . . .
```

J's *oh* at this point receives the news of the prior telling and marks that J now knows something that wasn't known before. *Oh* is therefore well suited to question–answer sequences, as questioners are, by asking a question, placing themselves in the place of not knowing information and on receiving answers they move from a state in which they did not know to one in which they do know. Moreover, *oh* is not found where the question was one seeking confirmation of something already known or guessed rather than information, as here there is no change of state to be displayed (Heritage, 1984a). Heritage argues that *oh* itself does not reflect the degree to which the answer was unexpected, but rather that the information is new. Additional features of the production of the *oh*, such as its volume, length or pitch, are important for marking surprise or registering the unexpectedness of the news in addition to registering the talk as newsworthy. In this way *oh* responds to the information as new and unknown, while prosody is linked with the affect of the news.

By registering a change of state from unknowing to knowing, *oh* can propose the possible closing of the sequence. This is most obviously the case where the sequence is made up of a question–answer adjacency pair. In such sequences, getting information is the central project of the sequence and registering that information has been received is a clear signal that the purposes of the sequence have been achieved. Given its change of state value, *oh* is also well designed for closing other-initiated repair sequences, as in (35).

```
(35) [EJ:Park]
      Emma:     then we' re goin' tuh thuh park tuhmorruh
      Jane:     wher:e?
      Emma:     Hyde Park.
  →   Jane:     o:h,
                (.)
      Emma:     an then we' ll go tuh see some of the other
                things an' make a day of it.
```

In repair sequences, the project launched by the repair initiator is linked to information: resolving a problem of hearing or understanding. In the extract above, Jane's *o:h*, proposes that she is now in a state of knowing – of having resolved the problem of reference created by the term *the park* – and that the repair sequence can now be completed and other talk can now be done. In both repair sequences and question–answer sequences, then, *oh* functions as a signal that the purposes of the sequence have been achieved. *Oh* is, however, not limited to sequences in which securing information is the central concern, as in the arrangement in extract (36).

```
(36) [JSK:11:8ii]
      Dora:     An' d' yuh think you' ll still be able tuh come
                up on the weekend¿
      Helen:    Uh. hh well no I don' think we' ll be able tuh
                do it this weeken' .
      Dora:     O↓uh.
```

In arrangements as in questions, an *oh* token can register that information has been received, but registering receipt of information does something very different in this sequence. Because the sequence in (36) is not about information, the *oh* here does not really respond to the SPP as part of the overall project of confirming a prior arrangement: by displaying that she now knows something she did not know earlier, Dora responds to Helen's turn primarily as a telling rather than as a cancelling of a prior arrangement. This means that Dora's *oh* can be seen as a withholding of some other form of talk in this position. We will turn to this issue below when we consider composite SCTs.

Okay

Okay, like *oh*, can occur in a range of different positions (Rendle-Short, 1999; Schiffrin, 1987); however, this discussion considers only its function as an SCT. While *oh* as an SCT claims receipt of information, *okay* usually claims acceptance of an SPP and what the SPP has done in the sequence (Beach, 1993). *Okay* is therefore relevant for sequences such as invitations, requests, offers, etc., where information is not the central concern and where it is possible for the SPP to indicate more than one possible outcome of the sequence (that is a preferred or dispreferred SPP). *Okay* commonly works to propose closure for a sequence which has received a preferred SPP.

```
(37) [Schegloff (1995a) CG,1]
      Clara:    hello
      Nelson:   hi.
      Clara:    hi.
      Nelson:   whatcha doin' .
      Clara:    not much.
      Nelson:   y' wanna drink?
      Clara:    yeah.
  → Nelson:   okay.
```

In this extract, Nelson's *okay* accepts the preferred SPP and proposes that the sequence is, for him, potentially closable at this point. The action of inviting has been completed and Nelson displays his understanding of what has been done in the sequence, ratifying the invitation and its acceptance. Similarly, *okay* can also serve to close a sequence which has received a dispreferred SPP.

```
(38) [AS:Off 2]
      Andrew:   so do yih need any help,
      Sam:      (.) uh I don' think so. it should be quite
                easy an' it won' take long.
  → Andrew:   o:kay.
```

In extract (38), Andrew's offer FPP receives a dispreferred SPP. Here the *okay* both accepts Sam's response and accepts that Sam's response is a rejection of the offer. This acceptance of the stance which Sam has adopted to the FPP in his turn provides for the potential closure of the sequence indicating that no further talk is necessary at this point. However, it needs to be borne in mind that *okay* only proposes closure; it does not ensure it, as extract (39) demonstrates.

```
(39) [Mike and Ben]
        Mike:      an I wannid tuh know if yih c' d give me a hand?
        Ben:       on Saturday? u:h I' m not sure I c' n make it.
                   we were supposed tuh be goin' out with Fran' s
                   mum.
 a→ Mike:          okay.
        Ben:       ' n it' s a while since she' s seen thuh kids
                   yih see.
        Mike:      yeah.
        Ben:       ' n so I don' t see how I c' n get there.
 b→ Mike:          okay.
        Ben:       b' t I' ll see wh' t I can do.
 c→ Mike:          okay. I think I c' n get Dave in any case, so
                   ' ts not a big problem.
```

In this extract, Mike proposes closure at arrow a, indicating that he has accepted the dispreferred SPP that Ben has produced. However, Ben continues with an expansion of his SPP turn, giving additional warrants for his inability to grant the request. Mike again accepts this with *okay* at arrow b, proposing closure but this is again followed by further expansion of the dispreferred SPP, with a further *okay* from Mike at arrow c, in this case followed by further talk proposing an alternative arrangement and mitigating the impact of the rejected invitation.

Assessments

The SCT *oh*, which claims that information has led to a change of state in knowing for the recipient, and *okay*, which registers acceptance of the stance taken by a responsive action, are minimal in form and lexical content; however, SCTs are not restricted to such tokens. Assessments may also be used as SCTs and in this case they display a stance which is taken towards what an SPP speaker has said or done in the prior turn. Assessments are, in this position, evaluations by the next speaker of some aspect of the prior speaker's turn. Such assessments are particularly common in what Sacks (Sacks, 1975) calls 'personal state enquiries', as in (40).

```
(40) [Schegloff (1986) 263]
     Hyla:    Hwaryuhh=
     Nancy:   =Fine how' r you.
     Hyla:    Okay:[y
 →   Nancy:        [Goo:d.
                  (0.4)
     Hyla:    mkhhh[hhh
     Nancy:        [What' s doin.
```

In this extract, the *how are you* sequence launched by Nancy is closed with the receipt of the SPP by an assessment *Goo:d*. The assessment here is an assessment of Nancy's answer turn and displays an affective evaluation of it. By providing an evaluation of the action launched by the question, Nancy proposes that the action is complete – only a completed project can be evaluated in such a way. After the assessment, and a pause, Nancy launches a new sequence. Assessments are not, however, limited to personal state enquiries, but may be used as receipts for other types of sequences. Extract (41), for example, uses an assessment rather than an invitation to close an invitation adjacency pair.

```
(41) [AS:2]
     Annie:   we were wondering if you ' n Fra:nk w' d like
              to come over Sat' day night for a few drinks.
     Sue:     Yeah we c' d do that.
 →   Annie:   Goo:::d.
```

Here Annie's *Goo:::d* also evaluates the action which has been completed and conveys her affective response to the form that the SPP has taken. Assessments can also be found as SCTs after dispreferred SPPs, as in extract (42).

```
(42) [Lunch]
     Joy:     we thought we might have a few drinks after
              work to y' know sortta s-celebra:te, so if
              y' d like to join us thad' d be great.
     Harry:   sounds like fun b' t I dunno:, (.) Friday (.)
              I think we' re- I think it' s the theatre, n
              um,
 →   Joy:     Tha' s a bummer=we' ll just have to celebrate
              with(h)out yo[(h)u.
     Harry:                [heh h.
```

Here, Joy's *Tha's a bummer* displays an affective evaluation of Harry's dispreferred response to her invitation. In evaluating the response, Joy accepts the dispreferred action and proposes a possible closure to the sequence.

Composite SCTs

So far the discussion has examined SCTs as single-token types occurring after an SPP; however, it is possible also for composites made up of combinations of these types to be found in a third position turn. One very common composite is *oh* plus *okay*, as in (43).

```
(43) [Lunch]
     Harry:   I don' have much tuh do on We:nsday.
              (.)
              w' d yuh like tuh get together then.
              (0.3)
     Joy:     huh we::llhh yuh see things a bit hectic fuh
              me We:nsday yih know I don' really know
→    Harry:   oh wokay
```

Joy's SPP turn here is performing a number of actions which are working simultaneously to achieve an effect. At one level, her turn is a telling *things a bit hectic fuh me We:nsday yih know*: it conveys information to Harry, while at another level it is declining an invitation. Tellings such as this are particularly common ways of refusing an invitation (Drew, 1984). Harry's third turn response is composed of two elements which respond to the dual project being done in Joy's turn. The *oh* registers what is said as new information, while the *okay* accepts what Joy has done through the telling (and through other elements of her turn). So in Harry's turn one element of his talk (*oh*) responds to the form of the preceding talk as a telling and the other element (*okay*) responds to action which has been performed. The discussion of extract (43) now provides a resource for understanding the assertion made above (in extract (36), which is reproduced below as (44)), that there was something missing in Dora's SCT.

```
(44) [JSK:11:8ii]
     Dora:    An' d' yuh think you' ll still be able tuh come
              up on the weekend¿
     Helen:   Uh .hh well no I don' think we' ll be able tuh
              do it this weeken' .
→    Dora:    O↓uh.
```

Dora's *O↓uh* here is responding to Helen's talk as a telling: the information is new to her and she now knows something she did not know previously. However, Helen's turn is not being done in this context primarily as an informing, but rather as a cancelling of a prior arrangement. Dora's *O↓uh* does not contain in it an acceptance of what has been done through the telling. She is responding to the form of the turn, but not to the action under way. It is, therefore, possible to see instances such as this as *withholding* acceptance (Heritage, 1984a). Extract (44) shows that, given that composite SCTs are not simply longer versions of SCTs but rather turns in which each element of an SCT responds to something different in the prior talk, it is important to consider single SCTs as potentially 'missing' something. Whether a single SCT is all that is required in a particular sequence depends on the nature of the prior talk: is it talk in which multiple actions are being performed? Where there are multiple actions under way, a single SCT may be doing something which is interactionally quite important and which goes beyond simply proposing closure of a sequence. The sequence we have been discussing goes on as follows:

(45) [JSK:11:8ii]
```
Dora:    O↓uh.
         (0.6)
Helen:   It' s uh:m [ s-
Dora:              [ Y' re dad will be so::
         disappointed.
Helen:   .hhh huhhhh yeah w' ll- uh- w' ll I don'  know
         i's goin'  to be hard tuh ged away  with
         everything that' s happenin'  here,
Dora:    Mhm.
Helen:   An'  Will really wants to be at that game yih
         know
Dora:    Mm.
Helen:   and tha'  makes things a bit hard
Dora:    Mm.
Helen:   and u::hm::,
         (0.2)
Dora:    Well i's a pity.
Helen:   °Yeah°
Dora:    °°yyhhh .h°°
         (0.3)
Helen:   .hhh °°b' d i' s hard°°
         (0.3)
Dora:    So w- so whad' re you doin' .
```

What is clear in the continuation of this sequence is that neither participant is treating this sequence as closed and Helen is orienting very strongly to the missing acceptance of her change of plans and continues to talk about her reasons for not being able to 'come up on the weekend'. Dora eventually provides an assessment – *Well i's a pity* – and the sequence finally moves to closing. This assessment responds to the extended reworking of the SPP being done by Helen and provides an additional element which was missing in Dora's earlier *oh* SCT. She has now taken a stance towards the telling, rather than treating it as just information.

Non-minimal post-expansion

Non-minimal post-expansions are designed to project further talk beyond their turn and are made up of sequences with FPPs and SPPs of their own. A non-minimal post-expansion or post-sequence, therefore, is designed to project at least one further turn beyond itself. These non-minimal expansions take a number of different forms, each of which undertakes a different interactional project following the SPP.

Post-second repair

Problems of hearing or understanding can occur as easily in SPPs as in FPPs and so there is a need for a location for repair of these problems immediately after completion of the turn in which the trouble occurs. For troubles occurring in an FPP, such repair occurs in post-first insert expansions. For troubles occurring in an SPP, the repair occurs as a post-second post-expansion. Apart from differences in their sequential placement, these two phenomena are essentially the same: they are both other-initiated repair sequences (Schegloff, 1992b; Schegloff *et al.*, 1977).

```
(46) [Car conversation]
     Nick:    on- [ which] day' s your anniversary?
     Sasha:   sixth. June.
     Nick:    the sixth,
     Elvis:   yeah,
```

Here, where Sasha answers Nick's question, the answer provides a trouble, which is resolved by Nick launching a repair sequence (a repetition) after the SPP, providing a candidate answer for the repair. Sasha confirms the candidate hearing, completing the repair sequence. As was the case with post-first insert expansion, post-second repairs can also be implicated in disagreements. In this case, the repair does not break contiguity in the way insert repairs do, because there is no projected next activity which they serve to delay. However, these repairs still have features which make them appropriate as pre-disagreements.

(47) [KM:1:20–28]
```
      Kay:      .. n so I w' z wondering if you c' d fill in for
                her for a while in the morning
      Marion:   .hh Well, y- (0.3) well y' know things are a
                bit busy Sad' day >morning n so I don' know if
                I c' d do it,< We have to take the kids to
                soccer at eleven, [ n then
   →  Kay:                        [ At eleven?
      Marion:   (.) Yeah, b' t p-perhaps I could do it for a
                while before that
```

In extract (47), Kay's *At eleven?* is performed as a repair following talk which rejects a request. The repair here may deal with a problem of hearing, but it also withholds talk which would complete the sequence, such as an *okay* or assessment. The result of the talk is however a redoing of the SPP in a more preferred way. Repair initiations indicate a trouble, but they do not always indicate what the trouble is: the trouble could be a problem related to agreement as much as to any other possible trouble source. Post-second repairs, therefore, allow a position for prior speakers to redo the problematic utterance to make it more acceptable (Schegloff, 1992b) or for delaying the production of some challenge to the SPP itself by its recipient.

Rejecting SPPs
Post-expansion provides a location for challenging an SPP, for disagreeing with it or for rejecting it, without initiating a repair sequence. Disagreement in this case is done immediately, without allowing a possible location for a prior speaker to redo a contested turn, and involves overt rather than projected disagreement. This occurs in extract (48).

(48) [Lunch]
```
      Joy:      So yuh had any ideas abou' where we' ll go,
      Harry:    W' ll there' s: always la Piazza tha' s close.
   →  Joy:      B' d i' s expensive.
      Harry:    U-w' ll no' reall-<they have lo' s- lots of
                things thad' re not too expensive,
                (.)
```

```
Joy:      Bu::p' haps we should thing abou' something
          tha' s a bi' cheaper (.) [ c' z (there' s)
Harry:                            [ w' ll w- w- whad
          about that Chine:se place.
Joy:      Yeah thadded be a lo::t bedder.
Harry:    Okay: we' ll do that'
Joy:      tha' s good
Harry:    °yeah°
Joy:      °° (mm) °°
```

Here, Joy challenges Harry's choice of a restaurant and Harry follows this with a disagreement with Joy's challenge about how expensive the restaurant is. The post-expansion then continues with further disagreement from Joy. In the final turn of the extract, Harry moves from the series of disagreements to providing an alternative possibility: an apparent acceptance of Joy's rejection of the restaurant. Joy now agrees with Harry's choice and the sequence moves towards closing. Here the sequence proceeds in an orderly way in which the SPP speaker provides a defence of his original SPP and rejecting the grounds on which it was rejected. This provides one possible trajectory on which rejections after an SPP can be dealt with. Alternatively, the SPP speaker can accept the rejection of the original SPP and provide an alternative SPP for the initiating FPP. This is, in fact, what Harry eventually does in the face of Joy's continued rejection of this original SPP. A similar acceptance occurs in (49), but in this case immediately after the rejection.

(49) [STIII:2:1]
```
    Kate:     Whad is there tuh drink¿
    Fiona:    W' ll there' s:some lemona:de in the fridge.
    Kate:     Nah I meant a dri::nk.
    Fiona:    Awrigh' then whad aboud a glass uh wi:ne.
    Kate:     Yeah tha' s more like it.
```

Here Fiona accepts Kate's rejection of her initial SPP (*awrigh' then*) and produces the alternative SPP taking into account the basis for the original rejection. In the above examples, there are then two possible trajectories for such a sequence – acceptance or rejection of the disagreement – each of which is implemented in the SPP speaker's next turn after a disagreement or rejection. What the SPP speaker does in this turn leads to a different overall shape for the post-sequence. In particular, if the SPP speaker rejects the prior rejection the post-sequence is typically expanded beyond the initial rejection turn as in (48), while the post-expansion is briefer if the rejection is accepted.

FPP reworkings

The cases of expansion discussed so far have been examples where the talk expands in some way on the basis of the SPP; however, sequences can also be expanded by reworking the FPP as a consequence of a dispreferred SPP (Davidson, 1984).

```
(50) [(Davidson, 1984) NB:52]
     P:        Wul lissid- (.) uh:: d' you wah me uh come
               down' n getche t' [morrow er anythi] ng¿
     A:                          [ N o: d e a: r.   ]
               (.)
     A:        No:, [ I' m fine.    ]
→    P:             [ To the store] er any[thing,
     A:                                   [.hh   I' ve    got
               evrything bought dear,
```

In extract (50), A rejects P's offer to come down and get her, and after this rejection P, at the arrowed line, reworks the offer in a different way. Davidson (1984) argues that in such reworkings of FPPs, the speaker does work to attempt to deal with the shortcomings of the original FPP – that is, they constitute a form of repair after the SPP (Jackson and Jacobs, 1980). These FPP reworkings are, of course, also FPPs and they make an SPP a relevant next: that is, the rejector is provided with a place in which s/he can either reject again or 'repair' the rejection. In (50), this is done by making the purpose of the offer more explicit; however, the reworking also receives a dispreferred second, although this time with a warrant for the rejection which orients to the reformulated version of the FPP *.hhI've got evrything bought dear,*.

In extract (51), the rejection is replaced in the subsequent version of the SPP with an acceptance.

```
(51) [Davidson (1984) Computer]
     A:        Oh I was gonna sa:y if you a:y if you wannid
               to:,=.hh you could meet me at U.C.Be: an' I
               could show yih some a' the other things on
               the compu:ter, (.) maybe even teach yuh how
               tuh program Ba:sic er something.
               .Hhh
               (0.6)
     B:        Wul I don' know if I' d wanna get all that
               invo:lved, hh .Hhh! [ (.Hh)
→    A:                            [ It' srillyinteresti:ng:.
               (0.2)
```

```
A:         I showed Tom how tuh pro- (.) how doo uh
           program a:. hhh the computer doo: make a
           ra:ndom number cha:rt, eh heh! .Hh An' that
           rilly turned 'im o:n,
           (.)
B:         Hih! heh! huh! huh! huh! (.) .hhh ((sniff))
           We:ll,=how 'bout if I do meet you in the
           computer centre tomorrow then.
```

Here, A offers to show B some things on the computer and teach him about programming; however, B rejects the offer with *Wul I don' know if I'd wanna get all that invo:lved.* A then reworks the FPP by doing an additional inducement after the original FPP has been rejected. This inducement at the same time reinstitutes the offer FPP as still relevant: that is, by providing an inducement for B to accept the invitation, A is not orienting to the rejection SPP as ending a sequence. A's talk is therefore a subsequent version of the invitation, which requires a subsequent version of the response. B's second response accepts the offer. As in extract (50), the FPP reworking in extract (51) does work to overcome the shortcomings in the original FPP and provides a place for the SPP to be redone in the light of this additional work. In both these examples, the talk produced is a single sequence: a single project is being pursued through the stretch of talk under consideration, rather than the talk consisting of two independent sequences with the same adjacency pair type, and, therefore, the reworking of the FPP is a post-expansion of the base sequence, not a new sequence.

Post-completion musings

Post-completion musings are a class of utterances which have the status of being demonstrably related in some way to the preceding talk, but which at the same time do not appear to be treated as an expansion of the sequence. The utterances have an ambiguous status therefore in terms of being of the sequence. They achieve this status, according to Schegloff (1988a), because they are designed to be 'out aloud' mutterings which have an ambiguous status between being publicly available talk and private thinking out loud.

(52) [JSK:11:8ii]
```
           (0.2)
Dora:      We'll i's a pity.
Helen:     °Yeah°
Dora:      °°yyhhh .h°°
           (0.3)
```

```
→ Helen:    .hhh °°b' d i' s hhard°° hhh
            (0.3)
   Dora:    So w- so whad' re you doin' .
```

Helen's very quiet °°*b'd i's hard*°°, which repeats some of the prior talk (see extract (45) for the previous talk), offers a diagnosis or evaluation of the larger stretch of talk it follows and is designed as a comment on the sequence which has just played out. Moreover, it is not designed to receive a response and does not in fact get a response. It has a semi-private character. It is at the same time designed to come after the sequence, not to be a part of the sequence it follows. The sequence has been closed down prior to this talk, and the ensuing silence does not challenge this as an ending. In addition, while the talk is appended to the sequence it does not relaunch the sequence, nor does it progress the sequence. It follows silence and audible breathing and is inserted into the breathing as a very low-volume, breathy element. Helen's contribution, therefore, is done as an element of talk after a sequence is completed, but which still orients to the action which was under way in that sequence, expanding the talk still further. It is possible for the post-completion musing to engender further talk; for example, it may be rejected or contested as a comment on the prior talk, but it does not appear to be designed to generate such talk, rather it is an opportunity to 'have the last word'.

Post-expansion and preference

Most of the types of non-minimal post-expansion we have discussed above have occurred in the context of dispreferred SPPs or are themselves dispreferreds, such as disagreements. It appears that preferred SPPs are sequence-closure relevant and typically no further talk needs to be done in the sequence. Alternatively, post-expansion after preferred SPPs is likely to be minimal and therefore not designed to extend the sequence. However, dispreferred SPPs frequently occasion further talk in the sequence in which the implications of the dispreferred are played out and problems of misalignment are dealt with. Dispreferred SPPs are therefore expansion-relevant turns. This expansion relevance in turn creates an interactional problem for speakers. While preferred responses provide a readily available way to close their sequence, dispreferreds do not. This means that participants must solve the problem of closing long sequences which have extended well beyond a dispreferred SPP.

Topicalization

While the expansions discussed so far have dealt with issues arising from SPPs in which there has been some problem which needs to be resolved, not all post-expansions do this. Speakers may also prolong a sequence of talk after a base SPP by marking the SPP itself as something of interest about which they would be prepared to continue to talk. These forms of talk, often called *newsmarks* (Heritage, 1984a; Jefferson, 1981), include devices such as repeats (full repeats, partial repeats or pro-form repeats) of the previous talk and tokens such as *really*, or questions such as *Did you?*, etc., often preceded by *oh*. In producing one of these devices, a speaker registers the talk not just as information, but also as news, and projects the possibility of further talk about this news.

```
(53) [Lunch]
     Harry:   S-whadded yih end up doin' on Friday night,
     Joy:     Y-.hh huh we decided tuh go tuh a rest' rant
              in th' end.
     Harry:   Did yuh?
     Joy:     Yeah,
```

There appear to be some differences in the way *oh*-prefaced topicalizations and unprefaced topicalizations run off and the form of the topicalization also has an effect on the way a sequence unfolds (Heritage, 1984a; Jefferson, 1981). *Oh really?* topicalizations typically have a structure in which a telling (such as the answer to a question) is followed by the topicalization. The topicalization typically leads to a reconfirmation of the telling by the original speaker and an assessment by the recipient which may end the sequence, as in extract (54).

```
(54) [Jefferson (1981) NB:IV:7:5–6]
       M:     How many cigarettes yih had.
              (0.8)
       E:     NO:NE.
  →    M:     Oh really?
  →    E:     No:.
       M:     Very good.
```

In this extract, the telling is done as the answer to a question and the topicalization is an expansion after this SPP. E's *no:.* reconfirms the prior *NO:NE.* and this in turn receives the assessment *very good*. *Oh really* topicalizations, therefore, may not typically engender a large amount of talk following the news. While expansions after *oh really?* are often limited, Schegloff (1995b) has indicated that quite lengthy expansions may occur in post-expansions launched by *oh really?*.

Where the topicalization is an *oh*-prefaced partial repeat, the outcome is typically different: in this case, further talk about the news normally follows after the topicalization. This talk may be volunteered by the teller of the original news either immediately after the topicalization or it may be solicited by the recipient of the announcement in the place of a sequence-terminal assessment (Jefferson, 1981).

(55) [ST:S:21A]
```
      Sarah:   So:: what d'yih have planned for the
               weekend.
               (.)
      Sally:   Well not much c'z John's mum's prob'ly com-
               ing over
  →   Sarah:   Oh is she?
  →   Sally:   Yeh she's goin' up north soon 'n she wanded
               tuh see: the kids before she went n: that,
```

In (55), Sally volunteers further talk on the news immediately following the topicalization. This talk follows immediately on from the reconfirmation (*yeh*) and as such, Sally's turn expands the talk beyond the pattern described for *oh really?*-type topicalizations. In (56), however, the news teller does not volunteer further talk beyond the reconfirmation of the telling in the turn following the topicalization, and further talk is instead solicited by the news-recipient.

(56) [ALX:45]
```
      Annie:   Yih ever been tuh Queenscliff,
      Sue:     Yeah we hadda coupla days there las' summer
      Annie:   O:h did you?
      Sue:     Yea:h.
      Annie:   An' didjuh li:ke it?
```

Jefferson (1981) also notes that topicalizations which do not have *oh* prefaces typically lead to still different sequences, as in extract (57).

(57) [Lunch]
```
      Harry:   S-whadded yih end up doin' on Friday night,
      Joy:     Y-.hh huh we decided tuh go tuh a rest' rant
               in th' end.
  →   Harry:   Did yuh?
  →   Joy:     Yeah,
  →   Harry:   Uh huh.
```

```
→ Joy:       Yeah we thoughd id would be best yih know
             with everyon[e n]' how they all have tuh eat=
  Harry:               [mm.]
  Joy:       = diff'ren things:: a ni:ghmare tryin' to
             have dinner ad'ome.
```

Here Harry's topicalization takes the form of a partial repeat using pro-forms: the pronoun *you* and the pro-verb *did*, without an *oh* preface. Joy provides a confirmation of her prior telling (*yeah,*) after which Harry, the news recipient, produces an acknowledgement token rather than an assessment as was the case in (54) or a solicitation of further talk as in (56). His contribution to furthering the talk is therefore minimal. In this case, Joy follows the acknowledgement token by volunteering further talk on the subject. Based on cases such as those above, Heritage (1984a) argues that *oh*-prefaced partial repeats show a greater commitment of the recipient of the news to do more talk about the news than do other forms of topicalization. In cases where talk is not *oh* prefaced, further talk about the news is usually either curtailed or volunteered by the original teller.

Sequence-closing sequences

In sequences which have a lot of post-expansion, the organization of the sequence becomes less clear or less orderly as the post-expansion proceeds. This poses a problem in post-expansion of how a sequence is to be closed. While pre-expansion and insert-expansion orient to an upcoming SPP as a potential closing of a sequence, post-expansions do not have a projected completion point which can serve to constrain the trajectory of the sequence. This means that participants in talk need to achieve closure for these sequences in the absence of a projectable future point which provides for closure of the sequence. Such a problem occurs in the sequence below, which has already been discussed in another context.

```
(58) [JSK:11:8ii]
     Dora:    An' d' yuh think you'll still be able tuh come
              up on the weekend¿
     Helen:   Uh .hh well no I don' think we'll be able tuh
              do it this weeken'.
     Dora:    O↓uh.
              (0.6)
```

```
Helen:    It's uh:m [s-
Dora:            [Y're  dad  will  be  so::
          disappointed.
Helen:    .Hhh huhhhh yeah w'll- uh- w'll I don' know
          i's goin' to be hard tuh ged away with
          everything that's happenin' here,
Dora:     Mhm.
Helen:    An' Will really wants to be at that game yih
          know
Dora:     Mm.
Helen:     and tha' makes things a bit hard
Dora:     Mm.
Helen:    and u::hm::,
          (0.2)
→ Dora:   We:ll i's a pity.
→ Helen:  °Yeah°
→ Dora:   °°yyhhh .h°°
          (0.3)
Helen:    .hhh °°b'd i's hard°°
          (0.3)
Dora:     So w- so whad're you doin' .
```

In this sequence, Helen's cancelling of a prior arrangement to which it appears she was earlier committed, is expanded at length after the SPP. The sequence is closed by the deployment of a sequence specifically designed to close such long sequences. Schegloff (1995b) identifies this sequence as having three basic elements. (1) An initial turn, typically an assessment, summary or an aphoristic formulation of the upshot or outcome of the sequence (see also Button, 1991b), which proposes closing for the sequence. Such proposals for closing typically take up a cognitive, evaluative or affective stance on the sequence which has been unfolding. In extract (58) this is done by Dora's assessment *we:ll i's a pity*. (2) In the second turn, the recipient of the proposed closing may either collaborate to close down the sequence or alternatively withhold compliance or even resist closing. A speaker who is collaborating with closing produces a response which aligns with or agrees with the prior turn. Agreement or alignment provides a go-ahead response for closing. This means that a preferred response is closing relevant in such sequences. This is what Helen does in extract (58) with her *°yeah°*. A speaker who resists the proposed closing continues to speak in the sequence for which closure has been proposed. Withholding collaboration is done by silence. Any non-collaborative response at this point will terminate the sequence-closing sequence. (3) If the speaker in the second position produces a 'go-ahead' response, the speaker who proposed closing may produce a third turn in which s/he produces some closing token or assessment and thereby ratifies the prior speaker's alignment with the proposed closing: Dora's °°*yyhhh .h*°°. The usual form of this sequence is then a minimally expanded adjacency pair. In this same turn s/he may also produce the initiation of a new sequence. This does not happen in extract (58), and Dora launches the new sequence some time after her ratifying the closing of the previous sequence. It is usual for the volume of each successive turn in this sequence to decrease, with a return to louder talk at the launching of the new sequence, as it does in extract (58).

In extract (59), we can see the trajectory of talk which resists the proposed closing.

```
(59) [Schegloff (1995a) TG 10:19–11:02]
        Ava:         [ I play-] I ] go down the gym en fool
                     arou:n, yihknow.
        Bee:         [ Mmm
        Ava:         [ .hhh
                     (0.2)
        Ava:         Bud uh.
                     (0.7)
a→ Ava:              Y' know it jus' doesn' seem wo(h)rth i(h)t
                     hh!
b→ Bee:              ((sniff))
c→ Bee:              .hh Whad about (0.5) uh:: (0.8) Oh yih go
                     f::- you- How many days? You go five days a
                     week. Ri[ ght?]
        Ava:                 [Y e ]ah.
        Bee:         .hh Oh gray- .hhh
        Ava:         .hh
```

In this extract, Ava moves to close down the talk at arrow a with an assessment, Bee however resists, firstly by withholding alignment with the proposal for closing (arrow b) and then by taking up further talk on the topic (arrow c).

Conclusion

This chapter has dealt with ways in which sequences composed of an adjacency pair can be expanded to create larger stretches of coherent talk in which a single project is being undertaken and its possible trajectories and consequences are being worked through (Schegloff, 1990). The coherence of such sequences is established on a base adjacency pair which constitutes the core action with reference to which other talk is understood as being related. Much of the talk involved in expansion deals with questions of preference and functions as a way of avoiding or dealing with dispreferred second pair parts. This is the case with type-specific pre-expansions, pre-second insert-expansions and several types of post-expansion. Expansion also provides places in which the interactional work of repair can be done. The three positions for expansion – pre, insert and post – effectively allow for the possibility of a single-base SPP being expanded into quite lengthy sequences of talk. Moreover, as each expansion type typically involves a sequence of its own, expansion can be prolonged and each expansion sequence may itself be expanded in some way.

7 Repair

Repair in conversation

Repair refers to the processes available to speakers through which they can deal with the problems which arise in talk. The idea of repair has already been raised several times in the preceding discussion, as repair is relevant to all levels of talk from the turn-taking system to sequence organization and preference. All levels of conversation are potentially subject to difficulties and conversation as a self-regulating system needs to have available practices for dealing these. Repair is itself a mechanism of conversation: a set of practices designed for dealing with the sorts of difficulties which emerge in talk. Like other aspects of the conversational system, the practices of repair are independent of the nature of the thing which needs to be repaired.

Repair is a broader concept than simply the correction of errors in talk by replacing an incorrect form with a correct one, although such corrections are a part of repair (Jefferson, 1987; Schegloff *et al.*, 1977). In order to emphasize the broad nature of repair as a conversational phenomenon, conversation analysis uses the term *repair* rather than *correction* to indicate the overall phenomenon of dealing with problems in talk and the terms *repairable* or *trouble source* to indicate the thing in talk which needs to be repaired (Schegloff *et al.*, 1977: 363). In fact many cases of repair seem to involve situations in which there is no error made by the speaker at all. This is the case for example when a speaker begins a word search because the appropriate lexical item is not available at the time when it is needed, as in extract (1).

```
(1) [May and Jo]
  → May:            [ she's gone to::. ho:h. wait and till
                 I show you on the map where she's going.=
     Jo:         =right.
```

In this extract there is clearly a conversational problem. The current speaker should be producing talk, but needs more time to do so. This problem is repaired by deploying talk indicating that the speaker is searching for the relevant word: a lengthening of the vowel of *to::* and audible breathing. This talk allows the speaker to continue as the current speaker and for her speech to be heard as relevant to the turn under way. It also allows her the time to retrieve the missing word and so to continue her turn to completion, although this is not what happens in this example; rather May adopts another strategy for communicating the information for which she is searching, using a map.

Conversational repair aims at success and in the vast majority of cases, successful repair is achieved very quickly (Schegloff, 1979b). It is also important to bear in mind that repair may fail. That is, not every repair initiation inevitably leads to a repair.

```
(2) [Autodiscussion 26 (Schegloff et al., 1977)]
a→ K:      didju know that guy up there et- oh What the
           hell is' z name usetuh work up' t (Steeldin-
           ner) garage did their body work.for' em.
           (1.5)
b→ K:      Uh:::ah, (0.5) Oh:: he meh- uh, His wife ran
           off with Jim McCa:nn.
           (3.2)
c→ K:      Y' know ' oo I' m talking about,
c→ M:      No:,
           (0.5)
   K:      °Oh:: shit.
           (0.5)
   K:      He had. This guy had, a beautiful thirty-two
           O:lds.
```

In this extract, K initiates a repair sequence (*self-initiated repair*) around the name of a participant in his telling *that guy up there* (arrow a). This initiation is not repaired by either participant and is followed by a silence of one and a half seconds. After the gap, K provides additional information for identifying the 'guy' (arrow b) and this is followed by an even longer silence. K then explicitly makes a try for M to identify the 'guy' but this fails (arrow c) and after a further pause, M abandons the repair with °*Oh:: shit.*

Types and positions of repair

Schegloff *et al.* (1977) have proposed a model of the mechanism for repair in conversation which makes a central distinction between who initiates repair and who makes the repair. Repair can be initiated by the speaker of the repairable (*self-initiated repair*) or it may be initiated by its recipient (*other-initiated repair*). In addition, a repair can be made by the speaker of the repairable item (*self-repair*) or it may be made by the recipient of the item (*other-repair*). In combination, these possibilities allow for four types of repair:

1. *Self-initiated self-repair*: in which the speaker of the repairable item both indicates a problem in the talk and resolves the problem.
2. *Self-initiated other-repair*: in which the speaker of the repairable item indicates a problem in the talk, but the recipient resolves the problem.
3. *Other-initiated self-repair*: in which the recipient of the repairable item indicates a problem in the talk and the speaker resolves the problem.
4. *Other-initiated other-repair*: in which the recipient of the repairable item both indicates a problem in the talk and resolves the problem.

The distinction between self- and other-initiation is important interactionally. Obviously, it is important that either party to talk be able to initiate repair, as certain problems in talk are problems for the speaker, while others are problems for the recipient. However, they do not seem to be two independent repair initiation processes, but rather they are related to each other in an organized way (Schegloff, *et al.*, 1977). The two types of repair initiation deal with the same sorts of trouble sources in talk and this remains true even though some types of repairable items are usually associated with self-initiation (for example, grammatical errors) while others are typically associated with other-initiated repair (for example, problems of hearing). These associations are a result of the distribution of the types of repairs, not of a rule in the conversational system. It is possible for repairs of grammatical errors to be initiated by the recipient and problems of hearing to be initiated by the speaker. An example of self-initiation and other-initiation working on the same trouble source can be seen in the following extracts.

(3) [SBL:3:1:2 (Schegloff *et al.*, 1977)]
    B: -then <u>more</u> people will show up. Cuz they
    →   won't feel obligated to sell. tuh buy.

(4) [GTS:3:42 (Schegloff *et al.*, 1977)]
    → A: Hey the first time they stopped me from
                selling cigarettes was this morning.
                (1.0)
    → B: From <u>sell</u>ing cigarettes?
      A: From buying cigarettes. They [said uh

In extracts (3) and (4), the trouble source is a problem of word selection; in both cases the use of *sell* instead of *buy*. In extract (3), the repair is initiated by self and in extract (4) it is initiated by the other. Self-initiation and other-initiation are specialized for which participant in the conversation identifies a trouble in prior talk. They are not specialized for the type of trouble to be repaired.

These types of repair interact with sequential locations for repair, so that some types of repair are typically found in the same position or the same sequence type in conversation. Locations for repair are locations relative to the trouble source and repair is designed to resolve the trouble as quickly as possible. It is possible to identify the following positions for repair:

1.   within the same turn as the trouble source (*same turn repair*);
2.   in the transition space following the turn containing the trouble source (*transition space repair*);
3.   in the turn immediately following the trouble source (*second position repair*);
4.   in a third positioned turn (*third position repair*);
5.   in a fourth positioned turn (*fourth position repair*).

These positions for repair interact with repair initiation in such a way that each position is specialized to provide for a particular participant to initiate the repair. This means that self-initiation and other-initiation are also organized in terms of their sequential position. The two types of initiation are ordered so that possibilities for self-initiation precede possibilities for other initiation (Schegloff *et al.*, 1977), as in

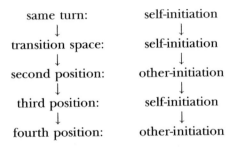

same turn: self-initiation
    ↓   ↓
transition space: self-initiation
    ↓   ↓
second position: other-initiation
    ↓   ↓
third position: self-initiation
    ↓   ↓
fourth position: other-initiation

What this ordering provides is a set of alternating possibilities. As each of these possible positions is available for repairing the same types of trouble source, they can be seen as a set of ordered possibilities for initiating repair with the speaker producing the trouble having the first opportunity to initiate a repair, either within the current turn, as in extract (5), or just after the current turn in the transition space, as in extract (6).

(5) [AN:04:03]
→ Anna: oh so then he is coming back on Thur- on
           Tuesday

(6) [SBL:3:1:2 (Schegloff *et al.*, 1977)]
   B: -then <u>more</u> people will show up. Cuz they
→   won' t feel obligated to sell. tuh buy.

In these extracts, the trouble source is identified by and repaired by the current speaker and no further repair work would seem to be necessary on this repairable. Where repairables are not dealt with in the speaker's turn, however, the recipient may initiate a repair in the second position, as in extract (7).

(7) [GTS:3:42 (Schegloff *et al.*, 1977)]
   A: Hey the first time they stopped me from
           selling cigarettes was this morning.
           (1.0)
→ B: From <u>selling</u> cigarettes?
   A: From buying cigarettes. They[said uh

Talk in the second position may indicate that there was a problem with the original turn. Responses to turns at talk are opportunities to display understanding or misunderstandings of prior talk (Schegloff, 1992b). This means that talk in a turn in the second position may indicate a trouble source in the earlier turn. Where this is the case, the speaker of the original trouble source may initiate repair in the next turn, in third position in relation to the original turn, as in extract (8).

(8) [SBL:1:1:12:11 (Schegloff *et al.* 1977)]
```
      Hannah:  and he' s going to make his own paintings.
      Bea:     Mm hm,
  →   Hannah:  and- or I mean his own frames.
      Bea:     yeah,
```

In this extract, Hannah's repairable *paintings* is not taken up by Bea and in so doing she shows that she has understood paintings as unproblematic for her. Hannah now repairs the trouble source from her own turn in third position. While talk in the second position may indicate a misunderstanding, it is also possible that such a mis-understanding may not become apparent until the third position. In this case, the recipient of the original turn may initiate repair in the next turn, or in fourth position relative to the original trouble.

(9) [EAS:FN (Schegloff, 1992b)]
```
      M:       Loes, do you have a calendar
      L:       Yeah
      M:       Do you have one that hangs on the wall?
  →   L:       Oh you want one.
      M:       Yeah
```

In extract (9), L's turn is in fourth position relative to the original repairable and indicates a trouble source in the original turn: L has not understood this as a pre-request, but rather as a question. Her answer *yeah* does not reveal that her understanding has been problematic and M produces another turn relevant to his project of requesting. From M's turn in third position, L identifies a problem in her version of the action under way and repairs this, showing she now has a new under-standing of M's original turn.

Schegloff *et al.* (1977) point out that the fact that other-initiation typically occurs in the next turn after the trouble source is not an accidental artefact of turn-taking. It is possible for repair to occur *during* the turn in which the trouble source occurs: that is, it is possible for a recipient to interrupt the current speaker during the current turn; however, other-initiated repair does not typically occur during the turn in which the repairable item occurs. Where a current turn is interrupted to deal with a trouble source, this is overwhelmingly done through self-repair. What this means is that the normal first possible position for other-initiation is not simply the next turn, but it is also *no sooner* than the next.

(10) [GJ:FN (Jefferson, 1972))
     Steven: One, two, three, ((pause)) four five six,
              (pause) eleven eight nine ten.
 →   Susan: Eleven? eight, nine, ten?
     Steven: Eleven, eight, nine, ten?
     Susan: Eleven?
     Steven: Seven, eight, nine, ten?
     Susan: That's better.

In this extract, Susan's other initiated repair would clearly be possible before Steven reaches the number ten, but does not initiate the
repair until the prior turn has occurred. Furthermore, Schegloff *et al.*
(1977) also argue that other-initiation may often be delayed in its own
turn allowing an expanded transition space in which self-initiation
could potentially occur. This means that it is not simply true that other-
initiation is found after self-initiation, rather the repair system is
organized to achieve such an ordering.

Same-turn repair

Repair initiated by the current speaker in the same turn as the trouble
source initiation is accomplished by non-lexical perturbations in
speech (Schegloff, 1979b; Schegloff *et al.*, 1977). These perturbations
are sensitive to the environment in which they are deployed and consist
of cut-offs sound stretches, items such as *uh* and *uhm* and pauses.

Cut-offs are interruptions of the word (or sound) under way and
typically take the form of a glottal or some other stop. The cut-off
therefore works to stop the next sound due from being articulated.
Usually a cut-off is used to initiate repair on some trouble source which
has already been produced in the turn so far. That is, it is placed after
the repairable item or post-positioned (Schegloff, 1979b).

(11) [AN:04:03]
     Anna: oh so then he is coming back on Thur- on
              Tuesday

In this extract, Anna interrupts her production of the word *Thursday*
and substitutes the word *Tuesday*. The cut-off serves to suspend the
ongoing production of the trouble source itself and Anna backs up her
turn to recommence the problematic element. Cut-offs often interrupt
the projected syntax of the turn, as in extract (12).

(12) [Car conversation]
```
Sasha:    poor Ron,=he' s always like- even (.) when he
          was married and happy he still (.) was always
          h[avin problems or something
```

In this extract, Sasha's turn so far projects one particular trajectory for her talk *he's always like-*. This trajectory is cut off and a new trajectory begins *even (.) when he was married and happy* projecting a different turn shape and a different possible completion. As such, talk after a cut-off may be consistent with the turn so far or it may produce a complete syntactic disjunction with the earlier components of the turn (Schegloff, 1979b).

Uh, uhm and pauses are repair initiations which occur outside word boundaries and stop the articulation of the next word due in the turn. They are typically used to repair a next element in the talk. These repair initiations are syntactically congruent with the projected TCU (Schegloff, 1979b).

(13) [Moon 6:132]
```
→ Tommy:    . . . You haven' t u:h added up any of these
            answers, (0.3) or anything like that yet.
  Pete:     A::h (.) no (.) not ye:t,
```

In this extract, Tommy projects a structure *haven't* plus participle, but delays his talk with *uh* after *haven't*. Tommy's trouble seems to be that the next element in his projects sentence is not readily available to him and he needs a bit more time to search for it. He then produces the next item *added*, continuing the projected format of the turn.

Sound stretches have as one of their functions initiating repair, especially a search for some unavailable item. A sound stretch is therefore employed within a word, but serves to initiate repair of some next element (Schegloff, 1979b).

(14) [AB:01:17]
```
Ben:      an so we wen' to: the::: La Paella restaurant
```

In this extract, Ben produces a sound stretch on *to:* and a much longer one on *the:::*. The object of the search here is the name of a restaurant, which is the relevant next item to be produced in the turn. Again this repair is syntactically congruent with the projected turn and like *uh*, etc., it serves to delay the production of a problematic item and gain time for a search.

The association of cut-offs with repair of a previous trouble source and other repair initiators with an upcoming trouble source is not always true. Speakers are able to convert their repair from one type to another (Schegloff, 1979b). For example, a repair may be initiated to repair a particular trouble, such as a missing word, but may end by recasting an earlier part of the talk in order to avoid a missing element, as in (15).

```
(15) [PB 3–4:6 (Schegloff, 1979b)]
    Merle:    So how's Michelle.
              (1.0)
    Robin:    They brought her ho:me.
              (0.7)
    Robin:    She hadda wait up the:re fo:r- u-she:'s been
              there since eight uh' clock this morning and
              at six thirty she called me ... (0.5) Said
              'Please com'n get me ...
```

In this extract, the sound stretches on *the:re and fo:r* indicate that a search is a likely next activity. The object for the search is for a duration of time, signalled by the *fo:r*. However, this search for a duration is not carried through and the projected format of the turn is aborted. Instead the turn is recast, moving to an earlier point and now projects the starting and finishing times for Michelle's wait. The repair initiation starts by projecting repair to a next element, but ends by repairing a previous element and in so doing avoids the need to produce the missing element.

The various types of repair initiations are often found in combination as a *repair segment* (Schegloff, 1979b). There are several examples of such segments in extract (16).

```
(16) [Car conversation]
a→ Sasha:    o:h. we saw some briyant ones recently, like
             uhm (1.0) oh what was that one about- (0.4)
b→           like Double In- (.) Indemnity= n like lots of
             movies from the thirties that ha- had amaz-
             ing plot lines?
             (0.9)
             some of them were really full on: like um:
             (0.3) A Place in the Sun?
```

At arrow a, Sasha initiates a search for a missing name of a film with *uhm* and combines this with a lengthy pause. At arrow b, she begins the name of the film *Double Indemnity*, but cuts off her talk and follows this with a brief pause before backing up and producing *Indemnity*. Here then she is using a collection of repair strategies to deal with the production of a problematic item.

Self-initiated repair in the same turn as the trouble source is usually resolved by the same speaker in the turn. In fact all of the extracts discussed so far are cases of *self-initiated self-repair*. However, a repair initiated by the current speaker in the same turn as the trouble source may be repaired by the recipient in a next turn (*self-initiated other-repair*). This repair may be solicited, as in (17); or not, as in (18).

(17) [Car conversation]
```
Sasha:   like this man: (0.8) was um (0.6) out in a
         boat and his wife drowned or something, and
         (0.6) he did d-=was it he didn't do it (.)
         Elly¿
Elvis:   yeah.
```

In this extract, Sasha is recalling the plot of a film she has seen with her boyfriend Elvis. She cuts off her talk at *he did d-* and immediately asks for verification of her recall of the plot, which is given by Elvis. Sasha's talk here seems designed to included Elvis as someone who knows about the event because he has shared the experience. Goodwin (1987) has shown that such displays of uncertainty and requests to a knowing recipient to provide assistance in dealing with uncertainty are useful devices for dealing with instances of shared experiences in interaction. Repairs, then, like that in extract (17), can be used in interaction to deal with more than just problems of recall. They can also be deployed to resolve other interactional needs which emerge in talk.

(18) [BC:Green: 88 (Schegloff *et al.*, 1977)]
```
B:       He had dis uh Mistuh W- whatever k- I can't
         think of his name, Watts on, the one thet
         wrote[ that piece,
A:            [ Dan Watts
```

Here, B is having difficulty finding a name. He cuts off production of the talk at *W-* and at *k-* and indicates his difficulty *I can't think of his name,* and makes another try at the name, *Watts on,* following this by a clue to the person's identity. At this point, A provides the repair.

There are cases of same-turn repair in talk where an initial attempt at repair does not lead to a successful repair and the speaker initiates a further repair on the same trouble source. Most of the instances in which more than one repair is initiated for the same trouble source are

cases of two repair initiations and cases of more than two repair
initiations are increasingly rare as the number of initiations increases
(Schegloff, 1979b). It appears that the organization of repair in conversation does not allow speakers unlimited time in which to affect a
repair. These instances of multiple repairs of the same trouble source
are orderly in their production and each successive repair appears to
be ordered in relation the previous attempts at repair. Schegloff
(1979b) has identified a number of features of this orderliness, all of
which orient to progressing the turn under way and to displaying that
each repair attempt has made progress towards solving the trouble.
This orderliness reveals that the organization of repair is not done with
relation to what precedes the attempt at repair, but is also sensitive to
the whole series of repairs on a single trouble source.

One way in which a speaker may organize a series of repairs on the
same trouble source is for each next attempt to repair the trouble to
add something to a prior attempt.

(19) [TG:492–493 (Schegloff, 1979b)]
```
     Bee:      That' s why they have us in this building-we
               finally got a' .hhh a roo:m tihday
  →            in-in the leh- a lectchuh hall,
```

In this extract, Bee's first try cuts off after *in-*, her second try adds
further elements, *the leh-*, and her third try adds *ctchuh hall,* to her
second. At each try her turn continues to progress slightly towards its
projected completion.

(20) [NYI:228–229 (Schegloff, 1979b)]
```
     Bonnie:   why? because they hg- because they have-
               because they asked you first.
```

In extract (20), Bonnie progresses her turn by replacing an element
in one try with a new element in the next, *have* becoming *asked.* As
such, her turn continues to progress although she is continuing to
initiate repair on the same item. In so doing, while she doesn't add
anything further to what the turn is projecting, she does show that her
talk is moving towards a resolution of the trouble. In extracts (19) and
(20), there is actually a combination of both adding further material
and changing elements. In (19), Bee not only continues to add talk,
but changes *the* into *a.* In (20), Bonnie starts with a cut off *hg-*, which
appears to be the beginning of *have* followed by a stop and first adds
the rest of *have* and replaces it with *asked.* Schegloff (1979b) argues that

this progression from a try which operates on the previous try by adding material or by changing an element is an orderly progression which is readily found in conversation.

Many of the examples discussed so far show that when a speaker repairs talk in the same turn, s/he may repeat a bit of the talk preceding the repairable item. Schegloff (1979b) argues that in successive tries to repair the same trouble source, each try commonly backs up less far than previous tries.

(21) [TG:492–493 (Schegloff, 1979b)]
```
      Bee:      That's why they have us in this building-we
                finally got a' . hhh a roo:m tihday
→               in-in the leh- a lectchuh hall,
```

In this extract, for example, Bee's first repair attempt backs up to *in* while her second repair attempt backs up only to the article *a.* In so doing, it shows progression at both ends of the try.

If the repair does not progress after subsequent tries, the speaker is in a sense 'marking time' in the production of the talk under way. Marking time refers to a repair in which each attempt at the trouble is the same as previous attempts: the first repair is like the original, and the second like the first. While this happens in conversation, the second try usually adds a more explicit marker of a search, such as *uh* and in so doing converts the repair into forward repair of some missing element rather than a redoing of an earlier trouble.

(22) [TH:20–21 (Schegloff, 1979b)]
```
      W:        An:'e took the inside out'n found it uz full
                of- full of- uh:- calcium: deposits . . .
```

Here W's two tries *full of- full of-* show no progress in moving towards a resolution of the trouble with nothing changed and nothing added to the prior tries. After *uh:* he no longer backs up, but rather searches for a new element *calcium: deposits* and moves forward in this projected turn.

A try which is not identical with the immediately prior try but with an earlier try still is a regressive trajectory in talk rather than a progression in the talk under way. Where this occurs it regularly turns out that this regressive try is the last try produced by the speaker, as in (23).

(23) [Upholstery shop]
```
      Vic:      En I grab a pail, en I put-. hh I see- ah- put
                all the glass in the pail,
```

In this extract, Vic abandons the projected turn with *I see* in his first repair and returns to the earlier *put* format. Something similar happens in extract (24).

(24) [Car conversation]
```
→ Sasha:   o:h. we saw some briyant ones recently, like
           uhm (1.0) oh what was that one about- (0.4)
→          like Double In- (.) Indemnity=n like lots of
           movies from the thirties that ha- had amaz-
           ing plot lines?
           (0.9)
           some of them were really full on: like um:
           (0.3) A Place in the Sun?
```

Here, at arrow a, Sasha initiates a search for a missing name of a film following *like*. She then begins to solicit help in the search, but cuts off this, pauses and provides an answer, backing up to her original turn shape again with *like*, abandoning the immediately prior projection.

Repair initiated within the same turn can also be used to deal with interactional problems other than those related to the talk of the speaker him/herself. This is the case for some recycled turn beginnings. Goodwin (1981: 57) has identified a rule in conversation according to which a 'speaker should obtain the gaze of his recipient during a turn at talk'. Where a speaker obtains a recipient's gaze early in the turn this is unproblematic; however, where this does not occur, the lack of a gazing recipient needs to be repaired. Recycled turn beginnings are closely linked to repairing such problems, as in extract (25).

(25) [(C. Goodwin, 1981)]
```
   Barb:   Brian you' re gonna ha[v- You kids' ll have to go
→ Brian:
                               [ X_____
```

In this extract, Barbara begins her turn without having a gazing recipient, but Brian later moves his gaze to Barbara (at the X). Barbara does not complete her original talk, but begins a new sentence at the point where she receives her recipient's gaze. Goodwin (1981) argues that in talk it is preferred to have a gazing recipient because a gazing recipient is displaying to the speaker that s/he is acting as a hearer. This means that a speaker with a gazing recipient is not only speaking, but is also being attended to. In this extract, therefore, by restarting a turn, Barbara is able to produce an entire turn at talk which is attended to. Such restarts are therefore repairing an interactional problem rather than a language problem. Goodwin also demonstrates that the fit between gaze and recycled turns is not always as neat as in extract (25). In some cases, the gaze of a recipient is not obtained until after a restart, as in extract (26).

```
(26) [(C. Goodwin, 1981)]
    Lee:     Can you bring- (0.2) Can you
    Ray:
    Lee:     bring me here that nylo[n?
    Ray:                             [X_
```

In this extract, Lee does not get his recipient's gaze until almost the end of the turn. However, while Lee does not secure Ray's gaze until late in the turn, his restart still seems to be associated with securing a gazing recipient. This can be seen more clearly in extract (26') which shows when Ray begins to move his gaze to the speaker.

```
(26')   [(C. Goodwin, 1981)]
    Lee:     Can you bring- (0.2) Can you
    Ray:                      .........
    Lee:     bring me here that nylo[n?
    Ray:     ....................[X_
```

Here, the recipient's gaze begins to move just after Lee's restart and gaze direction and restarting talk continue to be closely related. Goodwin argues that turn restarts and gaze are related in two alternative ways. A restart may allow a speaker to produce new talk with a gazing recipient where such gaze has not been available earlier in the turn. A restart may also be used to request the gaze of a recipient. Goodwin argues that these restarts function as a special type of *summons–answer* sequence in these contexts. Goodwin also provides further support for such an analysis through cases in which the restart does not secure a recipient's gaze, as in extract (27).

```
(27) [(C. Goodwin, 1981)]
                             Restart (1)
                                 ↓
    Eileen:  I ask him, (0.1) I ask him if he- (0.4)
                    Restart (2)
                        ↓
    Debbie:
    Eileen:  could-If you c[ould call ' im when you got in
    Debbie:  ............[X
```

In this case, the first restart does not secure the recipient's gaze and Eileen continues her turn for a little way before restarting again. At the second restart, Debbie begins to move her gaze to Eileen and the turn moves to completion with no further restarts. When Debbie's gaze has been secured, Eileen stops producing restarts and produces a coherent TCU.

Goodwin argues that restarts are not the only devices which can be deployed in this way. He also provides examples in which pauses seem to function in the same way.

```
(28) [(C. Goodwin 1981)]
     Michael: Who kno:ws, .hh (-[- - -) nu:mbers and letters
     Don:         . . . . . . . . . . . . . . .  [X_____
```

In this extract, rather than a restart, Michael pauses in the middle of his ongoing turn. This pause is shown by a series of dashes in Goodwin's transcription, where each dash represents 0.1 second. Michael secures Don's gaze during the pause and resumes speaking when he has secured Don's gaze, waiting during the pause for a recipient who is moving his gaze towards him to complete this. The structure here is a [Beginning] + [Pause] + [Continuation] rather than a new start. Such pauses can also be found in conjunction with other self-initiated repair devices such as *uh/uhm* or lengthened sounds, as in extracts (29) and (30).

```
(29) [(C. Goodwin 1981)]
     Anne:    When you had that big
     Jere:
     Anne:    uhm:, ( -------- + -[ -) tropical fish tank.
     Jere:    . . . . . . . . . . . . . . . . .  [ X_____
```

```
(30) [(C. Goodwin 1981)]
     Ethyl:   I had a who::le:: (- - - -[ - - - -+- -) pail full of
     Jim:                         . . . . . .  [ X_____
```

In these two extracts, the devices which precede the pause, *uhm:,* in extract (29) and the sound stretch on *who::le::* in extract (30), function to request the gaze of a recipient in a similar way to the ways in which restarts can work. After each of these devices and during the pause, recipients begin orienting their gaze to the speaker and after the recipients' gaze has been secured the talk continues. The pause therefore provides a space in which the recipient's gaze can be obtained before the talk continues.

Goodwin (1981) points out that the central difference between restarts and pauses is the way they run off: that is, they both interrupt a turn in progress and differ only according to whether the turn is restarted or not after the interruption. The restarting or continuing after the interruption is again relevant to gaze, but in this case the speaker's gaze. There appears to be an interactional order for organizing gaze between a speaker and a recipient which places the interaction importance of a recipient gazing at a speaker higher than a speaker gazing at a recipient. Where a recipient is gazing at a nongazing speaker there appears to be no interactional problem and repair is not needed. However, where a speaker is gazing at a nongazing recipient, repair is required. Goodwin has demonstrated that this feature of gaze organization is implicated in the ways in which restarting and continuing are deployed after an interrupted turn. This can be seen in extracts (31) and (32).

```
(31) [(C. Goodwin, 1981)]
     Lee:      . . . . . . . . . . . [ X_____
               Can you brin[g- (0.2) Can you
     Ray:                              . . . . . . . . .
     Lee:                 _____
               bring me here that nylo[n?
     Ray:      . . . . . . . . . . . . . . . . . . . . . [X_
```

```
(32) [(C. Goodwin, 1981)]
     Barbara:
               Uh, my kids (- - -[- - - -) had all these
     Ethyl:                  . . . . [X_____
     Barbara:                  . . . . . . . . . . . . [X_____
               blankets, and quilts and slee[ping bags.
     Ethyl:    _____
```

In extract (31), Lee is gazing at a non-gazing recipient. He interrupts his talk and, after the interruption and a brief pause, his recipient begins to move his gaze towards the speaker. At this point, Lee restarts his turn and continues it through to the end. In extract (32), Barbara is talking to a non-gazing recipient, but has not yet begun to gaze at her recipient. She interrupts her talk and secures her recipient's gaze before continuing, her gaze reaching her recipient much later in the turn. Instances of the coordination of talk and eye gaze such as these provide evidence that restarting is specialized for speakers who are gazing at non-gazing recipients and that continuing is specialized for non-gazing speakers with non-gazing recipients. Goodwin (1981) further shows that no perturbation in talk is found where a speaker's gaze reaches a gazing recipient; that is, where there is no trouble to repair.

Transition space repair

The next structurally provided place at which self-repair can be done is within the transition space after a TCU containing the trouble source (Schegloff *et al.*, 1977). In other words it is possible for a speaker to begin a repair after the first possible completion of the TCU and effectively extend their turn as a multi-unit turn in order to carry out repair. While the end result is for the current speaker to initiate the repair within the turn in which the trouble occurs, transition space repair works differently from repair initiated before the first possible completion of a TCU. Transition space repair can be done with no explicit repair initiation marker, other than further talk in the transition space, as in extracts (33) and (34).

> (33) [SBL:3:1:2 (Schegloff *et al.*, 1977)]
>   B: -then <u>more</u> people will show up. Cuz they
>   →   won't feel obligated to sell. tuh buy.

> (34) [GTS 4:1 (Schegloff *et al.*, 1977)]
>   → Ken: Hey why didn't you show up last week. Either
>   of you two.

In neither of these extracts is there any evidence of the speech perturbations or of repair marker such as *uh* or sound stretches which accompany within turn repair. The repair is both initiated and completed by the addition of talk in the transition space. Sometimes transition space repair is accompanied by a very reduced transition space (for example latching, as in (35)). This reduced transition space shows an orientation to the need to get an additional TCU to provide for repair before speaker change can be effected.

> (35) [Lunch]
>   Joy: Well yuh see I w' z talking with Carol and she
>   said she wannid to come along=wu-<u>Em</u>ma did.

Here Joy initiates a repair on a problem of person reference: *she* is interpretable here as *Carol* and she latches the repair immediately after possible completion of her TCU.

In other cases, speakers may deploy devices such as *uh* and *uhm* indicating that a repair is being initiated in the transition space. These devices serve to gain speakership in the transition space and provide for time to carry out the repair by indicating a repair on some next item. This can be seen in extract (36).

```
(36) [KC–4:14 (Schegloff et al., 1977)]
      A:          ...well I was the only one other than the
  →               uhm tch Snows [ uh Mrs. Randolph Snow?
      B:                         [ ( )
      A:          (uh huh)
```

In this extract, the *uh* is placed in the transition space and leads to two next speakers self-selecting. The *uh* also serves to initiate a word search which is produced in the new TCU.

Transition space repair may also be initiated by a device such as *I mean*, as in extract (37).

```
(37) [NJ:4 (Schegloff et al., 1977)]
      N:          She was givin me a:ll the people that were
  →               go:ne this yea:r I mean this quarter y' [ know
```

Speakers may also use a *not X, Y* format for initiating transition space repair, as in extract (38).

```
(38) [GTS 1:28 (Schegloff et al., 1977)]
      Louise:  Isn' t it next week we' re outta school?
      Roger:   Yeah next week.
  →            No [ not next week, [ the week after
```

Both the *I mean* and the *not X, Y* formats locate the repairable in the prior talk, with the *not X, Y* format doing so more explicitly than the *I mean* format.

Transition space repair may be a delayed repair of the trouble in the immediately prior TCU. Repair is usually initiated as soon as possible after the repairable has been produced, and for repairables within a turn, this position is most likely to be inside the TCU itself (Schegloff, 1997). In extract (34) above, therefore, the repair of the problem in reference of *you* is delayed until after the full TCU has been completed. However, many cases of transition space repairs are repairs of the terminal element of the prior TCU (extracts (33) and (36)–(38)), and such repair has to be initiated in the transition space. Most transition space repairs seem not to be delayed repairs, but rather repairs on terminal elements of the turn (Schegloff, 1997).

Second position repair

Repair in second position, that is, in the turn following the trouble source, is initiated by the recipient of the trouble source. Second position is the first structurally specified place for other-initiated repair (Schegloff, 2000b). Many of these other-initiated repairs are spread over two turns, being initiated in second position and completed in third position relative to the trouble source: they form sequences of an FPP initiation and an SPP repair. Such second position repairs, therefore, equate with the post-first insert sequences and post-second repair post-sequences discussed in Chapter 6.

Speakers use a range of turn-constructional devices to initiate repair in second position and these devices are fundamentally different from those employed in self-initiated repair (Schegloff *et al.*, 1977).

One common way for next speakers to initiate repair in second position is to use *huh?* or *what?* as in extracts (39) and (40).

```
(39) [CD:SP (Schegloff et al., 1977)]
      D:          Wul did' e ever get married ' r anything?
   →  C:          Huh?
      D:          Did jee ever get married?
      C:          I have // no idea


(40) [Lunch]
      Harry:      Aren' t you suppose to go up there with John
                  though?
   →  Joy:        Wha' ¿
      Harry:      Aren' t you goin' up there with John.
      Joy:        Na:h that fell through weeks ago.
```

These forms indicate that there is a problem in the prior talk, but give no indication of the nature of the trouble source itself. This means that they are a very generic way of initiating repair in second position. A more specific type of repair initiation consists of question words such as *who, where* and *when*.

```
(41) [BM:FN (Schegloff et al., 1977)]
      B:          By the way, I haveta go ta Lila' s.
   →  A:          Where?
      B:          Lila' s ta get ( )
```

(42) [Lunch]
```
        Harry:   So I guess I'll see yuh this afternoon.
    →   Joy:     When?
        Harry:   Oh I'm comin' tuh the planning meeting.
                 =Roger can't make it.
```

These forms are more specific than the earlier one's because they not only indicate that the preceding talk contained something problematic, but give some indication of what the trouble source was. Partial repeats serve a similar function in locating the trouble source in the prior talk.

(43) [TG 1:7–14]
```
        Ava:     [ <I wan] 'dih know if yih got
                 a-uh:m wutchamacawllit. a:: pah(hh)khing
                 place °th's morning' . .hh
    →   Bee:     a pa:king place,
        Ava:     mm hm,
```

Partial repeats may also be done with a question word (Schegloff *et al.*, 1977), as in extract (44).

(44) [Election]
```
        Gary:    so what' d' ya think of the news.
    →   John:    what news?
        Gary:    yihknow about the election;
        John:    o-*uh* 's te::rrible isn' it,
```

These partial repeats, by including an element of the prior turn, indicate even more strongly the nature of the trouble source.

Another frequent type of repair initiation found in second position consists of *you mean* with a possible understanding of the trouble in the prior turn.

(45) [Lunch]
```
        Joy:     Kerry's no good. She's haven a fight with
                 Sally.
    →   Harry:   Yih mean Sarah dontchuh. Those two are
                 always fightin'
        Joy:     Yeh.'s a bitch isn' it,
```

Here Harry not only initiates the repair but also provides a try-marked (*dontchuh*) candidate correction for the repairable, together with a warrant for his repair item. This correction is accepted by Joy in the next turn. The try-marking serves to mitigate the force of the correction but the corrective value of this repair initiation still exists. The *you mean* format for second positioned repair, therefore, represents a strong form of repair initiation. The types of other-initiation discussed here are ordered in terms of their relative strength in terms of their ability to locate the repairable in the prior talk. *What?* and *huh?* are quite weak, indicating only that there was some trouble while *you mean* plus a possible understanding is a very strong locator of the trouble source. Schegloff *et al.* (1977) have identified a preference for stronger over weaker forms of repair initiation. One piece of evidence for this is that weaker repair initiations may be interrupted and replaced with stronger ones, as in extract (46).

(46) [DA:2 (Schegloff *et al.*, 1977)]
    B: How long y' gonna be here?
    A: Uh- not too long. Uh just till Monday.
→ B: Til- oh yih mean like a week f' m <u>tomor</u>row.
    A: Yah.

In this extract, B begins what appears to be a partial repeat of *till Monday*, but interrupts this turn and repairs it to a stronger *you mean* plus possible understanding format. Such moves from weaker to stronger repair initiators are also found where multiple other-initiations are performed on the same repairable, as in (47).

(47) [HS:FN (Schegloff *et al.*, 1977)]
      A: I have a: – cousin teaches there.
      D: Where.
      A: Uh:, Columbia.
a→ D: Columbia?
      A: Uh huh.
b→ D: You mean Manhattan?
      A: No. Uh big university. Isn't that in Columbia?
      D: Oh in Columbia.
      A: Yeah.

In this extract, D initiates a repair on *Columbia* with a repeat (arrow a) indicating this as a trouble source in the prior turn. When A continues with an unrepaired version of this, D upgrades the repair initiation to a *you mean* plus possible understanding format. In this case, the possible understanding is rejected by A, who backs up the original *Columbia* and this is now accepted by D.

The extracts examined so far are all cases of other-initiated self-repair, in which the speaker who produced the original trouble provides the repair of the trouble. In some cases, the repair work done by this speaker is quite minimal, as in extracts (45) and (46), where the speakers simply assent to the possible understanding provided by the recipient of the trouble. While the substance of the repair is provided by the recipient, the actual repair is not achieved until the speaker who produced the trouble has accepted the proposed repair. Such possible understandings are not themselves repairs: they are only candidate repairs which do not have the force of repair until they are accepted by the speaker of the trouble. The fact that repair in such sequences is achieved by the speaker of the trouble is seen clearly in extract (47) where the possible understanding produced by D is rejected.

Not all second position repair involves other-initiated self-repair as in the cases discussed so far. Other-initiation may also be resolved by other repair produced in the same second position turn. Jefferson (1987) calls these sorts of repairs *corrections*. Corrections have their own sequential properties, which vary according to whether the correction is *exposed* or *embedded*. In *exposed correction*, the other-initiated other-repair is produced in second position by the recipient of a trouble, as in extract (48).

```
(48) [SF:II:7 (Jefferson, 1987)]
     Larry:    They' re gonna drive ba:ck Wednesday.
  →  Norm:     Tomorrow.
     Larry:    Tomorrow. Righ[t.
     Norm:                   [M-hm,
     Larry:    They are working half day.
```

In this extract, the activity under way in the prior turn, in this case a telling, is discontinued and the correction itself becomes the activity which is being pursued by the following talk. The talk devoted to the activity of correction may be quite short as in extract (48), in which the correction is provided by Norm with no other talk, other than Larry's acceptance. However, the correction talk may be lengthier as in extracts (49) and (50).

```
(49) [GTS:II:2:ST (Jefferson, 1987)]
     Ken:      and they told me how I could stick th-uh:
               Thunderbird motor? (0.5) in my Jeep? and I
               bought a fifty five
               [ Thunderbird motor.
  a→ Roger:    [ Not motor, engine.
```

```
        Roger:      You speak of [ electric motor and gasoline engine.
  b→    Ken:                     [ Okay
  b→    Ken:        Engine. [ Okay-
        Al:                 [ Internal combus:tion.
        Ken:        Alright, So [ lookit,
        () :                    [ mhhh
        Ken:        I moved this thing in the Jeep, yesterday . . .
```

In this extract, Ken's telling is disrupted by a correction sequence in which the correction itself *Not motor, engine.* is followed by an explanation of the difference between the two terms. Jefferson (1987) calls such talk *accountings*, which take the trouble and treat it in some way. According to Jefferson (1987), accountings typically include activities such as complaining, instructing, admitting, apologizing, accusing and ridiculing, all of which are activities related to the activity of correcting itself. The correction talk here also includes the intervention of an additional speaker, Al, who also engages in the activity of correction. These actions occur even though Ken accepts the correction twice (arrows b). To close the correction and re-establish the telling, Ken produces talk which explicitly marks a shift in focus in the talk through *Alright* and *so*. *Alright* here is a change-of-activity token, which Gardner (2005) argues indicates a marked shift of activity and *so* marks a shift in topic (Rendle-Short, 2003; Schiffrin, 1987), away from the correction talk to the prior telling.

(50) [DP:32–33:ST (Jefferson, 1987)]

```
        Jan:        I guess they paid two-twenty for the house
                    and two thousand for the ki:l.
        Beth:       Mm::,
        Jan:        Technically,
  →     Ron:        (It' s a) kil:n.
        Jan:        Kil:n, I don' t know how to say it,
        Ron:        You always say kil.
        Jan:        I don' t know I thought that' s righ[t.
        Beth:                                          [Ye[ah.
        Ron:                                             [It' s
                    like-
        Ron:        Is that right? You say kil?
        Beth:       Kil:n. I don' t know I' ve heard both . . .
```

In extract (50), the talk is expanded by an accounting (Jefferson, 1987) involving complaining about the speaker's competence, *You always say kil.* In all cases of exposed correction, regardless of what other talk may be done, Jefferson (1987) argues that there is a basic sequential structure. This structure consists of:

a.   A speaker produces some object (X)
b.   A subsequent speaker produces an alternative (Y)
c.   The prior speaker produces the alternative (Y) (accepts correction)

In the extracts above, the acceptance is usually done by a repetition of the corrected item, in some cases with some other talk showing acceptance of the corrected version. It is also possible, however, for the correction to be rejected, as in extract (51).

(51) [Office II:4]
         Anna: An' we have a meeting this afternoon
    → Barry: It' s tomorrow afternoon
         Anna: No it' s <u>this</u> afternoon. They had to bring it
                         forward.

In this extract, Anna rejects Barry's correction, restating her original version and providing an account for the rejection. To account for this, the sequential structure above requires an additional component:

c'   The prior speaker produces the original (X) (rejects correction)

Exposed correction, therefore, has two possible trajectories X-Y-Y and X-Y-X, to account for the possibilities that in the third turn, the speaker of the original trouble source can either accept the correction and produce the alternative (Y-Y) or s/he can reject the correction and restate the original item (Y-X).

In *embedded correction*, there is a similar sequential structure, but the talk runs differently, as in extracts (52) and (53).

(52) [GTS:II:60 ST (Jefferson, 1987)]
         Ken: Well-if you' re gonna race, the police have
                         said this to us.
         Roger: <u>That</u> makes it even <u>bet</u>ter. The <u>chall</u>enge of
    →   running from the <u>cops</u>!
         Ken: The cops <u>say</u> if you wanna race, uh go out at
                         four or five in the morning on the freeway . . .

In extract (52), Ken says something that Roger treats as a trouble: *police.* Roger provides an alternative form, *cops,* and Ken in his next turn adopts Roger's alternative. In terms of the discussion in extract (52), in which teenagers are talking about their pastime of hot-rodding in city streets, the problem with the form *police* seems to be the fact that it is a standard language term rather than the less standard and less respectful *cops*. In cases such as this, the alternative forms provided by a next speaker function as a type of correction, although the correction is more 'off the record' than in exposed correction. These types of correction can also be resisted or rejected by the recipient of the correction, as in extract (53).

```
(53) [SBL:3:6:4 (Jefferson, 1987)]
       Adele:   Do you think they might go tomorrow,
       Milly:   Oh I don' t think so,
       Adele:   Oh dear. They' re [ (          )
       Milly:                     [ No I don' t think until
                after uh after new years now cause uh, New y-
                - New Years is tomorrow eve [ isn' t it.
  →    Adele:                               [ it' s  tomorrow
                night uh huh
       Milly:   Yeah tomorrow eve,
```

Here the trouble source is *eve*, in *tomorrow eve*, for which Milly provides the alternative *night*, with contrastive stress. However, in her further talk Milly continues to use the form *eve*. The corrections in these two extracts are like exposed corrections in that they have very similar sequential arrangement:

a. A speaker produces some object (X)
b. A subsequent speaker produces an alternative (Y)
c. The prior speaker produces the alternative (Y) (accepts correction) (extract (52))
c' The prior speaker produces the original (X) (rejects correction) (extract (53))

These extracts both have the same sorts of structure based on repeating sequences which demonstrate either the acceptance of an alternative form (*police-cops-cops*) or the rejection of an alternative form, by repeating the original form (*eve-night-eve*). However, embedded correction differs from exposed correction in that it does not disrupt the action under way, but rather is incorporated (embedded) into it. The talk is not about the correction and the ongoing action is not changed while correction happens. Embedded correction does not

allow for accountings as these are really only possible if the talk is
directed to the action of correction.

In the examples so far, the format of the correction is initiated by the
recipient of the trouble and when the prior speaker accepts or rejects
the correction, s/he does so following the same format as the one
initiated by the speaker. This outcome is not inevitable. Embedded and
exposed correction is actually achieved collaboratively by the
participants. There are also instances in the talk in which a speaker
initiates correction in one format, but the correction gets done using
the other, as in extract (54).

(54) [Office II:5]
```
       Barry:   the girls in our office are really busy now so
                I don' t like to give them too much more to do
  →    Anna:    you mean the women
       Barry:   well they' re all doin' so much now an' I need
                to get someone else to take on some of the
                admin load. The women just have too much to do.
```

Here, the trouble source is Barry's use of the word *girls* to describe
the female employees in his office. Anna produces a correction in an
exposed correction format, *you mean the women*. At this point Anna's
talk is dealing with the work of correction. Barry, however, does not
enter into the correction talk, but goes on with his telling, shifting to
an embedded format, but accepting the correction to *women*. Jefferson
(1987) argues that, by converting the format to an embedded one,
speakers are precluding the possibilities for accountings for the
repairable in their earlier talk.

Third position repair

Third position, after an interlocutor's response to a previous turn,
allows for the possibility of repairing a trouble in understanding of a
prior turn demonstrated by the recipient's response to it. This type of
repair can be seen in extract (55).

(55) [CDHQ, I, 52
(Schegloff, 1992b)]
```
       Annie:   Which one::s are closed, an' which ones are
                open.
```

```
     Zebrach: Most of' em. This, this,
              [ this, this ((pointing))
  →  Annie:   [ I ' on' t mean on the shelters, I mean on the
              roads.
     Zebrach: Oh! (8.0)
     Zebrach: Closed, those' re the one' s you wanna know
              about,
     Annie:   Mm[hm
     Zebrach:   [Broadway
```

In this extract, Annie asks a question in her first turn, which receives an answer in the next turn. Zebrach's answer in turn reveals something about how he has interpreted the question, and in particular the referent of Annie's *ones*. Zebrach's turn is sequentially appropriate for his understanding of Annie's question turn and is built to be responsive to this turn. He does not display a problem of understanding. In her next turn, the third turn, Annie treats Zebrach's understanding of her first turn as problematic and acts to repair the understanding.

Schegloff (1992b) has proposed a four-component format for third position repair, consisting of:

1.   a repair-initiating component
2.   an agreement/acceptance component
3.   a rejection component
4.   the repair proper

These components have a canonical ordering, 1–4, and as Schegloff (1992b) shows, this ordering is the result of speaker's practices in constructing repair turns in third position.

The *repair-initiating component* commonly has the form *no* (extract (56)), possibly repeated as *no no* or *no no no*. *No* may also be found in combination with *oh* as *oh no* (extract (57)) and occasionally *oh* alone may be used to initiate the repair (extract (59) below).

(56) [NYI, 6–7
(Schegloff, 1992)]

```
     Bonnie:  Because I' m not even sure if we' re goin' to
              have it yet because a buncha people say
              [ maybe, maybe,
     Jim:     [ Yeah
     Bonnie:  ' t' s buggin me. (1.5)
     Jim:     Oh uhh hh I' m sorry, Ihh
```

```
  → Bonnie:   No, that's okay, I mean y' know I can under-
             stand because- this was just a late idea that
             Barb had.
```

(57) [Office 4:1]
```
      Joe:    Have the papers arrived yet,
      Mary:   uh-Nuh nothin's come down from admi[n so far.
  → Joe:                                          [Oh no I-
             uh not- Have the papers arrived yet.
      Mary:   Oh you mean the newspapers,
      Joe:    Yeah.
      Mary:   No they don' usually get here until ten.
```

These turn-initial *no*s have a superficial appearance of being disagreements with the prior turn. However, they do not seem to be
constructed as disagreements. Firstly, after issuing a *no* the speaker
deals with a trouble source in their own prior talk, not with features of
the second positioned talk itself. Secondly, disagreement is not
ordinarily done with a direct *no*, especially at the start of the disagreeing turn. As has been seen in chapter 5, disagreements tend to be
done in a mitigated form and are usually pushed late in their turn
(Pomerantz, 1984; Sacks, 1987). This means that Bonnie's arrowed
turn in extract (56) cannot be seen as a disagreement with Jim's prior
apology, but rather as the initiation of a repair on a misunderstanding
of her own prior turn. The same is true with Joe's response in extract
(57). *Well* is also possible as a repair initiator in third position repairs,
but Schegloff (1992b) indicates that where *well* is found the repair
moves directly to the repair proper, without the other sequential features found with other initiators.

(58) [GHY:II:09–10]
```
      Gary:   Yuh got anymore screws.
      Harry:  Yeah I got lo:ts.
  → Gary:    Well, I wanted one
      Harry:  O:h okay.
```

There, Gary's third positioned turn begins with a *well* and moves
immediately to a recharacterization of his prior turn as a request, not
an enquiry.

The *agreement/acceptance component* is usually found where the
original turn has been treated as a complaint and the next speaker has
responded with a response such as an apology or an excuse: a response
which is sequentially relevant for a complaint (Schegloff, 2005). In this

case, the speaker accepts the complaint and then proceeds to deny that
the turn was intended as a complaint, as in extract (59).

```
(59) [NB (Schegloff, 1992b)]
      Agnes:    I love it.
                (0.2)
  a→ Portia:    Well, honey? I'll pob'ly see yuh one a' these
                day:s.
      Agnes:    Oh:: God yeah,
      Portia:   [Uhh huh!
      Agnes:    [We-
      Agnes:    B't I c- I jis [couldn' git down[ there.
  b→ Portia:                   [Oh-            [Oh I know
                I'm not askin [yuh tuh [come dow-
      Agnes:                   [Jesus. [I mean I jis- I didn'
                have five minutes yesterday.
```

In this extract, two sisters have been having problems getting together and the telephone call from which the extract is taken involves a
comment from Portia (at arrow a) about another failure to do so.
Agnes treats this turn as a complaint and responds by providing an
excuse for her not coming down. At arrow b, Portia's turn is constructed first to accept Agnes' excuse for not getting together (*I know*)
and then moves to rejecting the interpretation of her first turn as a
complaint. Bonnie does the same in extract (56), in which her repair
turn, *no, that's okay*, accepts Jim's earlier apology, before dealing with
the problem in understanding this apology demonstrates.

In the *rejection component*, the speaker overtly rejects the understanding of the first turn revealed by the recipient's response to it.
There are a small number of possible formats that speakers usually use
to do this rejection. One common format is *I don't mean X*, where X
identifies the problematic item in the trouble source. This format is
used to repair problems with reference (Schegloff, 1987b). This use
can be seen in extract (60).

```
(60) [CDHQ, I, 52 (Schegloff, 1992b)]
      Annie:    Which one::s are closed, an' which ones are
                open.
      Zebrach: Most of 'em. This, this,
                [this, this ((pointing))
    → Annie:    [I 'on't mean on the shelters, I mean on the
                roads.
      Zebrach: Oh!
```

Here, Annie is dealing with a problem in understanding the reference of *ones*. Her turn, which does not begin with a repair initiation, rejects Zebrach's interpretation of the reference as *on the shelters*, before repairing the reference in her turn. Another common format for rejecting a prior speaker's understanding of a turn is the *I'm not X-ing* format, where X names an action which the prior speaker has understood the talk to be doing. This format deals with problems in which the talk in second position shows a problem of sequential implicativeness; that is, where the next speaker's talk is not sequentially appropriate to the prior speaker's expressed understanding of the trouble source (Schegloff, 1987b). This can be seen in extract (61) from a group therapy session.

(61) [GTS
(Schegloff, 1992)]
```
        Dan:       . . . See Al tends, it seems, to pull in one or
                   two individuals on his side (there). this is
                   part of his power drive, see. He's gotta pull
                   in, he can't quite do it on his own. Yet.
        Al:        W' l-
        Roger:     Well so do I.
  →     Dan:       Yeah. [ I'm not criticizing, I mean we'll
        Roger:          [ Oh you wanna talk about him.
        Dan:       just= = uh look, let's talk.
        Roger:     Alright.
```

In this extract, Dan's arrowed turn accepts Roger's response to a perceived criticism and then rejects this interpretation with *I'm not criticizing*, where *criticizing* is a formulation of Roger's understanding of the trouble source. This same format is also found in extract (59) above, where Portia formulates Agnes' understanding of her talk as *not askin [yuh tuh [come dow-* and rejects this interpretation using the *I'm not X-ing* format.

The third common format is less specific in its design than the previous two. In the two preceding formats the speaker indicates an explicit understanding of the nature of the misunderstanding which has occurred. That is, Annie shows an explicit understanding of the referential problem in extract (60), while Portia and Dan show explicit understandings of their interlocutors' perception of their trouble source turns in extracts (59) and (61). In the third format for rejection, however, the misunderstanding is not named, but is referred to using a pro-form such as *that: that's not what I mean, I don't mean that,* etc., as in extract (62).

(62) [Lunch]
```
    Joy:     I have so much to do at the moment i' s gonna be
             tight fitting something else in, yih know.
             (0.2)
    Harry:   Well I don' mean that yih have to [ do-
→   Joy:                                        [ No uh-' as
             no' what I meant=I jis- (.) I jis' think I' ll
             have to do something tuh make room for i' .
             Yih know reprioritize.
```

In this extract, Joy's turn indicates that there has been a problem in misunderstanding her first turn, but gives no explicit formulation of what the problem is. She overtly rejects Harry's understanding of her talk without naming it. Schegloff (1992b) argues that this format does not show a problem in understanding the nature of misunderstanding which has occurred, but rather some potential problem in expressing the understanding.

The *repair proper* is the component which is most likely to be found in any third position repair, although it too may be absent (Schegloff, 1992b). In the repair proper, the speaker takes up the problem that the recipient's response has revealed and modifies the prior turn in some way to deal with the problem. Schegloff identifies a number of ways in which this repair is commonly done. The speaker may repeat the prior turn with some modifications, such as prosodic marking, to display that the prior turn is being made clearer.

(63) [Office 4:1]
```
    Joe:     Have the papers arrived yet,
    Mary:    uh-Nuh nothin' s come down from admi[n so far.
    Joe:                                         [oh no I' m
→            uh not- Have the papers arrived yet.
    Mary:    Oh you mean the newspapers,
    Joe:     Yeah.
    Mary:    No they don' usually get here until ten.
```

Joe initiates repair with *oh no* and repeats his prior turn with stress on *papers* and falling intonation. Joe's contrastive stress on the word *papers* here is the only additional information he gives about what the word means. The stress indicates only that a different sort of papers is meant. Mary then reformulates this as *newspaper* and responds to this new understanding of the trouble source. Another possible format for the repair is a contrast with the recipient's understanding of the trouble source, usually introduced by *I mean,* as in extract (64).

(64) [CDHQ, I, 52 (Schegloff, 1992b)]
```
     Annie:    Which one::s are closed, an' which ones are
               open.
     Zebrach: Most of 'em. This, this,
               [this, this ((pointing))
 →   Annie:    [I 'on't mean on the shelters, I mean on the
               roads.
     Zebrach: Oh!
```

Speakers may also repair a trouble source in this position with a more specific formulation of the trouble source, as in (65).

(65) [CDHQ, I, 46–47
(Schegloff, 1992b)]
```
     Lehroff:   What is the weathuh. Out in the area now.
     Zebrach:   No winds, er its squalling, rain, the
                winds are probably out of north,-west, at
                uh estimated gusts of uh sixty to sixty five
                miles an hours.
     ():        (Whew!)
     Zebrach:   Sustained winds of thirty five to forty five
                miles per hour. and uh anticipated
                duration,
 →   Lehroff:   How is the wah- weather period outside. Is
 →              it- rain(ing)? uh windy? or what?
     Zebrach:   ('s what I said). 's windy?
     ():        (  )
     Zebrach:   An' it's raining.
     Lehroff:   S' an' it's raining,
     Zebrach:   An' it's raining.
```

Here, Lehroff repeats his trouble source turn with modified prosody and follows this with a list of specific features of his general question about the weather in a non-technical way. Repairs may also be done by redoing the trouble source as an explanation of the prior turn, as in extract (66).

(66) [BC (Schegloff, 1992b)]
```
     Host:     and now, dear hearts, let's go to the next
               call. Shall we?
     Host:     Good evening, WNBC,
     Caller:   Good evening, this is uh, oh boy.
     Host      ehh heh heh hyah [hyah!
 →   Caller:                    [No I was listening to the
               commercial, and I'm just kinda- confused
               fer a min[ute.
     Host:              [Sorry about that, it's a little
               rattling.
```

In the repair turn, the Caller provides an explanation of his earlier talk and addresses the Host's understanding of it as something which was designed to be laughed at.

A final type of repair identified by Schegloff (1992b) is a characterization of the trouble source as serious or non-serious. This repair is designed to address this one particular problem of understanding and is associated also with withdrawing from the sequence in which the trouble occurred. Schegloff (1992b) notes that such repairs do not occur with *I mean*.

```
(67) [TG 1:7–14 (Schegloff, 1992b)]
      Ava:          [<I wan]' dih know if yih got a-uh:m
                    wutchimicawllit. A:: pah(hh)hking place
                    °th' s mornin' . .hh
      Bee:    A pa:rking place,
      Ava:    Mm hm,
              (0.4)
      Bee:    Whe:re.
  →   Ava:    t! Oh: just anypla(h)ce? I wz jus' kidding
              yuh.
      Bee:    Nno?=
```

In extract (67), Bee's response shows that she is treating Ava's first turn as a serious question, but is having difficulty in understanding the question as one to which she can give an appropriate answer. She deals with the problem through a series of insert repairs, which do not succeed in resolving the problem. Ava repairs the problematic understanding by characterizing her question as *kidding*, as non-serious.

The components Schegloff (1992b) has identified for third position repair are not obligatory in constructing any repair turn, and any element may be omitted from a particular repair turn. While no component is necessary for a repair, the components themselves are ordered as initiation, acceptance/agreement, rejection and repair and this ordering can be seen as achieved by participants through their orientation to this ordering.

The cases discussed so far are all instances in which a repair is initiated by a speaker in the turn after a prior speaker has demonstrated some problem in the understanding of a trouble source. Schegloff (1997) describes another trajectory for self-initiated repair after a next speaker's turn, as in extract (68).

```
(68) [TG 286–289 (Schegloff, 1997)]
      Bee:    Y' have any cla- y' have a class with Billy
              this term?
```

```
      Ava:        yeah, he's in my Abnormal class.
      Bee:        Oh yeah, [ how
  →   Ava:                 [ Abnormal Psych.
```

In this extract, Ava's repair follows Bee's turn, but it does not respond to problems of hearing and understanding emerging from this turn. Rather, Ava is performing an operation on her first turn without reference to Bee's talk. Ava's repair, therefore, is not really in third position as it is not designed sequentially to follow Bee's second positioned turn. Schegloff (1997) terms this *third turn repair* to distinguish it structurally and sequentially from *third position repair*. These third turn repairs, in fact, seem to have more in common with transition space repair than with third position repair as they are often repairs on terminal components of the trouble source turn. The difference between the two is that some talk by a next speaker intervenes between the trouble source and the repair. The principal difference between the two repair formats is, therefore, the presence or absence of talk by a next speaker after the trouble source turn. The phenomenon here is a little like Jefferson's analysis of overlapping talk where the overlap occurs just after the beginning of a new TCU (see chapter 4, extracts (18) and (19)). In these cases, she argued that the onset of the talk just after the commencement of another TCU could be attributed to a pause in talk occurring just prior to the beginning of the overlapping turn. It appears that something similar is happening in the case of third turn repair.

(68')   [TG 286–289 (Schegloff, 1997)]
```
      Ava:        yeah, he's in my Abnormal class.
      Bee:        Oh yeah, [ how
  →   Ava:        (_____) [ Abnormal Psych.
```

In (68') Ava's talk appears to be constructed to have an intra-turn pause *yeah, he's in my Abnormal class. ((pause)) Abnormal Psych*. However, at the end of Ava's turn she has reached a TRP and Bee legitimately becomes the next speaker. Ava, however, identifies a trouble with the reference of her *abnormal* and works to correct it after Bee has started. The repair needs to be as close to the trouble source as possible; however, for Ava this can only come in a third turn, because Bee has already begun to talk. Third turn repair, therefore, demonstrates the vulnerability of the transition space for doing repair and the need to get the repair done quickly for this format to come off in the transition space itself.

There is an additional interactional issue involved with third turn repair, which distinguishes this repair format from transition space repair. In these repairs, the next speaker has produced a second positioned turn which demonstrates understanding of the prior talk. The subsequent repair in third position can imply that this claiming of understanding of the turn was not right at the point where the turn was produced. This can be seen in extract (69).

```
(69) [BC:Gray, 42–43
(Schegloff, 1997)]
      Call:    I never saw a single piece of action while I
               was there.
      Brad:    Mhhm,
      Call:    I was (manning the) civil affairs, and I had
               a very good time.
      Brad:    Mm hm,
  →   Call:    Nothing uh lewd in any- by way of a good time,
               I mean
      Brad:    Yes, [ I know what you mean
      Call:         [ (Perfectly) honest good time.
```

In this extract, Brad's second positioned talk is the *mm hm*. While this may not be a full turn, but rather a quasi turn which passes up an opportunity to take a turn at this point, it does nonetheless show that the prior talk has been received as unproblematic and as such has been 'understood' (Schegloff, 1982). Call's third turn repair changes the possible interpretation of *a good time* and Brad's response *Yes, I know what you mean* seems to be designed to address any implications that his prior understanding may no longer be appropriate. Transition space repair, however, does not need to deal with such interactional difficulties as the repair is effected before any display of understanding by the recipient has occurred.

Third turn repair and third position repair are structurally different repair positions. Third turn repair refers to a phenomenon in conversation in which repair is done in the third turn from the trouble source, but it is not designed to be second to a recipient's response to the trouble. Third position repair is designed in relation to a recipient's response to a trouble source. While this is commonly found in the third turn after the trouble, this is not the only place in which third position repair can occur. That is, third position repair is commonly done in the third turn, but is not *necessarily* done in the third turn (Schegloff, 1992b). Extract (70) is an example of a repair which is found after a second positioned response, but is not in the third turn after the trouble source.

```
(70) [FD,IV,66
(Schegloff, 1992)]
    Dispatch:  Now what was that house number you said=
               =[you were-
    Caller:    =[No phone. No.
    Dispatch:  Sir?
    Caller:    No phone at all.
→   Dispatch:  No I mean the uh house number, [ Y-
    Caller:                                    [ Thirdy
               eight oh one?
    Dispatch:  Thirdy eight oh one.
```

In this extract, Dispatch's repair is positioned after the caller's SPP response to an FPP question *Now what was that house number you said.* The caller's SPP is, however, not in the turn immediately following its relevant FPP as it is delayed by an insert repair sequence. Nonetheless, the caller's turn *No phone at all* is designed as second to the FPP and the arrowed repair is both a repair of the FPP and designed as a sequentially next turn after the SPP.

Fourth position repair

Fourth position repair is very infrequent as most problems are dealt with before this point; however, some problems may persist. Fourth position repair allows an opportunity for a recipient of original trouble source to repair a problem of understanding which has become evident as a result of talk produced in the third position (Schegloff, 1992b). As third position repair allows a speaker of some trouble source to deal with talk which displays a problem of understanding, fourth position repair allows the recipient of the trouble to do the same, as in extract (71).

```
(71) [EAS:FN (Schegloff, 1992b)]
    Marty:  Loes, do you have a calendar
    Loes:   Yeah ((reaches for desk calendar))
    Marty:  Do you have one that hangs on the wall?
→   Loes:   Oh you want one.
    Marty:  Yeah
```

Here, Marty's original turn can be understood either as a pre-request to borrow a calendar or as a pre-request for a calendar.

Loes' action following Marty's turn indicates that she is acting on the turn as requesting her calendar, reaching for her own desk calendar as an appropriate next action for such a request. Marty then produces another form of the request designed to follow up his original turn. This new version of the talk leads Loes to re-analyse the original turn and she produces a repair turn stating this new understanding.

As with third position repair, fourth position repair deals with the sequential placement of talk relative to the actions performed by other speakers rather than simply a question of repair in a fourth turn. This can be seen in extract (72).

(72) [CDHQ:15; openings, 299 (Schegloff 1992b)]

```
       Phil:      Hello?
       Lehroff:   Phil!
       Phil:      yeh.
       Lehroff:   Josh Lehroff
       Phil:      yeh.
       Lehroff:   Ah:: what've you gotten so far. Any
                  requests to dispatch any trucks in any
                  areas,
  →    Phil:      Oh you want my daddy
       Lehroff:   Yeah, Phi[l
       Phil:               [Well he's outta town at a
                  convention.
```

In this extract, Phil understands Lehroff's identification as having been correct. Lehroff's *Phil!* is constructed as an identification and demonstrates a degree of certainty in the identification. It is not designed to elicit in any way the identity of the interlocutor, but rather to confirm recognition and therefore provides for the possibility that the identification is correct (Schegloff, 1979a). In Phil's following turn, in which he accepts the identification, he displays his understanding that Lehroff's identification has worked. This talk is then followed by an identification sequence which runs off without a problem and in which the caller identifies himself and has this identity registered by the answerer (Schegloff, 1979a). The talk then moves to the first topic. Lehroff's move to first topic at this point is based on his understanding of the earlier identification sequence having identified his intended interlocutor and the turn is constructed for this interlocutor. The turn is, therefore, in third position in relation to the identification of Phil, although not the third turn in the talk (72').

(72') [CDHQ:15; openings, 299
(Schegloff, 1992b)]

Lehroff:	Phil!	first position
Phil:	yeh.	second position
Lehroff:	Josh Lehroff	third position

.

.

.

| Phil: | Oh you want my <u>daddy</u>. | fourth position |
| Lehroff: | Yeah, Phi[l | |

Lehroff's turn, however, indicates that there has been a problem in the identification sequence and this is repaired by Phil in the next turn, or in fourth position in regard to the trouble source *Phil!*

Fourth position repair consists of two components. The first component is a change of state token *oh* reflecting a new understanding of the talk under way (Heritage, 1984a). The second is a recharacterization of the trouble source addressing the problem of understanding, *you want one* in extract (71) and *you want my daddy* in extract (72). Reanalyses of the trouble source such as these are usually confirmed by the speaker of the original trouble source and this reconfirmation leads to a new response to the matter of the trouble source (Schegloff, 1992b). The recharacterization may, however, be omitted and the repair turn constructed with the change of state token and the revised response.

Fourth position repair is sometimes found in conjunction with third position repair, as in extract (73).

(73) [Office 4:1]

	Joe:	Have the papers arrived yet,
	Mary:	uh–Nuh <u>no</u>thin' s come down from admi[n so far.
	Joe:	[oh no I' m
→		uh not- Have the <u>pa</u>pers arrived yet.
→	Mary:	Oh you mean the <u>news</u>papers,
	Joe:	Yeah.
	Mary:	No they don' usually get here until ten.

Here, Joe produces a third position repair dealing with Mary's misunderstanding of his original turn and Mary follows this with a fourth position repair in which she also addresses the problem of understanding and confirms her new understanding. These two repair positions are used to perform the same operation on the prior talk.

The multiple repair space

The above discussion shows that any utterance can be repaired at a number of points in the following talk and the form the repair takes determines which position the repair will occupy. Schegloff (1992b) describes this series of possible positions for repair as a *repair initiation opportunity space* consisting of four positions which normally occupy the four turns following the repairable item. The repair space, however, can be longer if some intervening talk expands the sequence involved. As all talk is subject to repair, each turn can be seen as being followed with a repair space of its own and, in an ongoing conversation, each turn becomes a site for many possible repairs of preceding turns. This set of multiple possibilities for next turn repair can be schematized as (Schegloff, 1992b: 1327):

Turn 1	A:	Q1			
Turn 2	B:	A1	2nd position repair on T1		
Turn 3	A:	Q2	2nd position repair on T2	3rd position repair on T1	
Turn 4	B:	A2	2nd position repair on T3	3rd position repair on T2	4th position repair on T1
Turn 5	A:	Q3	2nd position repair on T4	3rd position repair on T3	4th position repair on T2
Turn 6	B:	A3	2nd position repair on T5	3rd position repair on T4	4th position repair on T3

In this schematization, A initiates talk at turn 1 with a question FPP. At turn 2, B may either provide an answer SPP or initiate repair on the turn. In turn 3, the alternatives available to A are to produce further sequentially relevant talk after B's answer (e.g. another question) or A may initiate second position repair of B's answer turn, or third position repair of A's turn 1 in response to B's answer turn. In turn 4, B may also be able to continue to produce sequentially relevant talk or may use the turn to repair earlier talk in turns 1–3. The possibility that repair will be initiated on turn 1 is still available at turn 4, as is the possibility for repair on either of turns 2 or 3. Each next turn has the same set of possibilities trailing after earlier turns. This means that, at any next turn, a speaker has a space in which to begin repair on a number of prior turns. The multiple repair space is further expanded by the possibility of initiating repair within the same turn as a trouble source. Any turn, therefore, may provide space for repairing both itself and a number of preceding positions within the talk so far.

The preference for self-repair

Schegloff *et al.* (1977) have identified a preference for self-repair in conversation. They argue that this preference is not simply a matter of an overwhelming number of instances of self-repair, but also that the system is designed to achieve self-repair. One feature of the system that favours self-repair is that the positions in which self-repair can happen precede the positions in which other repair can happen, providing a structurally first opportunity for speakers to repair their own trouble sources. The first two possible repair positions (within the turn and within the transition space) are allocated to the speaker. In conjunction with third position repair, this means that three of the five possible locations for repair are provided for the speaker who produced the trouble source and that these three positions represent three of the four possible spaces. The preponderance of locations for possible self-repair is further supported by the overwhelming success of repairs themselves. This means that many repairs are resolved before the possibility of other repair even arises.

Furthermore, the division of repair work into initiation and repair also allows for further possibilities for self-repair. Other-initiated repair does not automatically lead to other-repair; rather other-initiated repair most commonly leads to self-repair. In particular, second position other-initiated repair is usually designed to provide for self-repair. In the discussion above, most other-initiated repair techniques are techniques for indicating that there was a trouble in the prior talk, but do not perform any operations on that talk. In some cases, such as *huh?* or *what?* other-initiated repair does no more than indicate that there has been a trouble while in other cases (e.g. question words and partial repeats), the repair initiator more explicitly identifies the trouble source. These second position turns are typically occupied only with initiating repair and pass the work of the repair itself to the next positioned turn, that is, they pass the repair back to the first speaker who produced the trouble source. This means that other-initiated repair is usually designed to achieve repair in two turns: an FPP which initiates a repair sequence and requires talk from its recipient and constrains this talk to the work of repair. Other-initiations, therefore, are designed primarily to achieve self-repair.

This means that the four repair types discussed above – *self-initiated self-repair, self-initiated other-repair, other-initiated self-repair* and *other-initiated other-repair* – are not interactionally equal options. There is a strong preference for some of these types over the others. The preference does not affect who initiates repair. The need to deal with trouble in talk applies equally to all participants if conversation is to work as a self-regulating system. This means that self-initiation and other-initiation are alternatives responding to different interactional needs. Self-repair and other-repair, however, are not alternatives in the same way, and the preference organization involved in repair is such that self-repair is favoured over other-repair. Other-repair is, therefore, a dispreferred. As with other dispreferreds, other-repair usually shows interactional modifications which affect the turn shape in which other-repair is found. Other-repairs are often done in a mitigated way. They may contain makers of uncertainty, as in extract (74), or they may be produced in question form, as in extract (75).

```
(74) [JS:II:219–20 (Schegloff et al. 1977)]
     Ben:      Lissena pigeons
               (0.7)
     Ellen:    [ Coo-coo::: coo:::
 →   Bill:     [ Quail, I think.
     Ben:      Oh yeh?
               (1.5)
     Ben:      No that's not quail, that's a pigeon.
```

```
(75) [JS:II:97 (Schegloff et al. 1977)]
     Lori:     but y' know single beds' r awfully thin tuh
               sleep on.
     Sam:      What?
     Lori:     Single beds. [ They're
 →   Ellen:                 [ Y' mean narrow?
     Lori:     They' re awfully narrow [ yeah.
```

In these extracts, the modification of the talk leads to other correction having a form in which the correction is not asserted, but rather put forward either to be accepted or rejected by the prior speaker. They have a *correction invitation format* (Sacks and Schegloff, 1979) in that they allow for the possibility of the prior speaker to disagree with the version being proposed, as in fact happens in extract (74).

Conclusion

Repair is a fundamental part of conversation and reveals clearly the nature of conversation as a self-organizing and self-righting system based on rules which operate and are managed locally by participants. The repair mechanism discussed here is a relatively simple device which can be employed by participants to deal with troubles as they emerge in talk. It is simple in that a single mechanism can be used to deal with a very broad range of troubles and the mechanism itself is independent of the nature of the problem as a speaker perceives it. While repair is simple, the mechanism is also highly organized, providing multiple possibilities for repair to be carried out on prior talk as interaction reveals a trouble at some earlier point. Thus, while repair is designed to deal with troubles as quickly as possible, it is also sensitive to the possibility that a trouble may not be realized to be problematic until talk has progressed. Repair is also an interactionally sensitive mechanism which, while designed to deal with multiple types of trouble and allowing any participant to initiate repair once s/he has identified a trouble, is constrained by social as well as linguistic considerations.

8 Opening Conversation

Introduction

The discussion so far has focused on the practices through which conversation is managed and maintained by speakers. However, in order to use these practices, speakers must have begun a conversation. The beginning of a conversation does not just happen. Like other things in conversation, the opening of a conversation between two or more participants must be interactionally achieved. This chapter will investigate how the opening of a conversation is achieved. Most work to date on conversational openings have focused on the opening of telephone conversations and this makes a useful starting point for a more general discussion of conversational openings because the interactional issues involved are made more obvious by the limitations involved in telephone talk. In particular, the opening of a telephone conversation is done by participants who do not have access to non-verbal cues which rely on visual aspects of communication (eye gaze, expressions, etc.) and everything has to be done through sound.

Openings in telephone conversations

In examining the first few moments of a telephone opening, a regular pattern of talk emerges similar to that found in extract (1):

```
(1) [Tel11:1–3]
                ((ring))
    Anna:       Hello?
    Cal:        Oh hi:.
```

On the basis of this extract we can make the following observations: the telephone rings, the recipient of the call (the answerer) speaks and after this the caller speaks. It is this quite simple structure which has to be accounted for first of all in understanding a telephone opening. Schegloff (1968) has observed that this pattern can potentially be accounted for by a distributional rule which says that the answerer speaks first. A further refinement of this rule would include a restriction of the sorts of talk which happen at this point. Typically in everyday calls in English the answerer's talk takes the form *hello*, although other sorts of talk, such as a self-identification by name or telephone number are also possible. This demonstrates that the sorts of talk which are usually performed as the first turn at talk in a telephone conversation are restricted to a small set of possible utterances.

Schegloff (1968) challenges the validity of the distributional rule as the organizing basis of telephone openings by considering what can potentially happen if the distributional rule is violated; that is, if the answerer picks up the phone, but does not speak. Where this happens, the caller may speak after a pause, as in extract (2):

```
(2) [Gran:3:1–3]
                ((ring))
                (0.8)
       Call:    Hello?
```

In this extract, the caller's first turn *hello?* is the same as the sort of talk routinely produced by answerers as their first turn. Schegloff argues that the caller is now acting like an answerer by speaking first and using part of the limited subset of options available to answerers, while the answerer is acting as a caller by not speaking in first position. While both the caller and the answerer use *hello* is this position, the function of the two *hellos* is different. A caller's *hello* in this context must be viewed as an attempt to check whether or not the channel of communication has been established. This *hello* is, therefore, an attempt to repair the problem of a missing answerer's turn (Hopper, 1992). The argument at this point is that the repair can be affected by supplying the missing talk as it is understood in terms of the distributional rule. If the role reversal begun by the caller is to continue, the answerer should now offer talk typical of a caller's turn. Such talk, Schegloff argues, typically takes one of a limited number of possibilities.

One possibility is the form of a *hello* token, along with some expansions as in *hello, this is Harry*. Such talk, however, produces an interactional problem for the answerer-as-caller. Real callers have access to different information from that available to real answerers: callers know the likely identity of their answerer, but answerers do not know the likely identity of callers. (Technological changes from the time at which Schegloff was writing now allow answerers to know the likely identity of a caller from electronic displays of telephone numbers for incoming calls.) While the caller's *hello* turn has provided a voice sample on which to base a possible identity of the caller, this can only be done if the caller is known to the answerer. As such, a true caller can construct a self-identifying turn in a way which is suitable for their recipient depending on factors such as the relationship between the caller and the answerer, the degree of intimacy, etc. (Schegloff, 1979a). The answerer-as-caller, however, cannot construct such a self-identification as s/he does not have the necessary information to know how to formulate it. Another possibility is to produce a simple unexpanded *hello*. This is done in situations where the callers have a relationship which is close enough to allow for the expectation that the caller will be able to identify the recipient from a voice sample (Schegloff, 1986). Again, the answerer does not have the necessary information to know if this is a viable option in constructing the next talk. A further possibility is that a caller may produce a *hello* token, along with an identification of the recipient, and again the answerer cannot do this as s/he does not yet know the identity of the caller and has little information with which to make the identification. A final possibility is that the caller may produce a 'reason for call' (Sacks, 1992: 773–9) and again answerers-as-callers face an interactional problem as they as yet do not know the reason for the call.

Such violations of the distributional rule cannot be resolved by a role reversal and a redistribution of speakers' roles according to the distributional rule. The distributional rule may, therefore, be an adequate description of what happens in most telephone openings, but it is not an adequate account of the ways in which participants organize their talk to achieve a telephone opening. Deviant cases, in which the distributional rule is not adhered to, provide evidence for a different explanation of the structure of telephone openings. In returning to the deviant case given above (given here as extract (3)), it is possible to see how these structures are achieved by participants.

(3) [Gran:3:1–7]
```
                 ((ring))
                 (0.8)
       Call:     Hello?
                 (0.2)
→ Answ:          °Loh?°
       Call:     Is that Sally?
       Answ:     Yes
```

In this extract, the answerer's arrowed response, a *hello* token, is a typical answerer's response, even though it is delayed in its turn. To understand what is happening in this extract, it is necessary to look beyond the distributional rules formulation of who speaks first. In fact, the first spoken turn is not the first action in a telephone opening. Telephone openings begin with the ringing of the telephone, and while this ringing is not speech as it is usually considered, it is a communicative action performed by one of the parties to the conversation: the caller.

The caller is faced with an interactional task in attempting to begin a telephone conversation: s/he must secure a non-present co-participant for the conversation. The ringing of the telephone is the caller's attempt to secure an interlocutor. This indicates that the telephone's ringing is a technologically enacted case of a summons turn: like other summons, it is an attempt to get the attention of another participant in order to undertake further talk (Nofsinger, 1975; Schegloff, 1968, 1986). As was seen in Chapter 6, summons turns are first pair parts which require a second pair part to complete their sequence. The second pair part in telephone openings is the answerer's *hello.* This *hello* is not a first turn, but rather it is produced as a second to a prior action. The answerer's *hello* is, therefore, to be understood not by a telephone conversation-specific distributional rule, but rather as an instance of the broader phenomenon of sequence organization adapted to the technological reality of telephone mediated talk.

In extract (3), the caller's *Hello?* can be understood not as a doing of a missing turn, but rather as a redoing of the summons in the absence of an answer turn. The *hello,* therefore, is a repair which is achieved by redoing the first pair part, and as such it is an unexceptional form of repair within the context of sequence organization: FPPs are routinely redone in the absence of an SPP, or of some sequentially related talk (Schegloff, 1968). The answerer's turn, then, is the supplying of the missing SPP and the completion of the sequence begun with the ringing of the telephone.

The ringing of the phone and the picking up of the handset may appear to be automatic actions; however, this does not deny that the answering of the phone is socially constructed. For example, the picking up of the phone may be enough to open the channel for communication in the sense of establishing the electronic connection, but it is not, as has been seen, sufficient to establish interaction between the caller and the answerer. For this to happen, some talk is required. The talk signals not simply that the channel for communication has been established in the sense that communication at a distance can now take place, but also that there is an available recipient for that talk. It is the mechanical and the spoken elements together which construct the beginning of a telephone conversation. This socially constructed nature is also true of the way in which the ringing occurs: Schegloff (1986) observes even the ringing of the telephone itself is socially as well as mechanically shaped. He cites three basic ways in which the ringing of the telephone is socially constructed. Firstly, answerers typically allow the telephone to ring several times before they answer it, even when they could answer it immediately. Answering the telephone very quickly is, therefore, unusual and may become the subject of talk as in extract (4).

```
(4) [208 (Schegloff, 1986)]
                ((ri-))
        Joan:    Hello?
        Cheryl:  Hello:.
        Joan:    Hi:.
  →     Cheryl:  .hh Y' were you s(h)itting be the phone?
        Joan:    No, I'm (0.3) I'm in the kitchen, but I wz
                 talking to a friend of mine earlier. I was
                 just putting (0.2) my fried rice on my plate
                 to go eat lunch.
```

Here, Joan's very quick response becomes topicalized as *Y'were you s(h)itting be the phone?* and engenders further talk in which there is some account of the sooner-than-normal answer to the call.

In addition, the ringing of the telephone is not usually too delayed. Schegloff (1986) notes that people who are distant from the phone usually hurry to answer it. A lengthy ringing of the telephone may lead to an interpretation that 'no one is at home' (Schegloff, 1968, 1986) and as a result the caller may hang up. Each ringing of the telephone can be viewed as one iteration of the summons and Schegloff (1968) has proposed a terminating rule for redoing summons turns: that is, summons turns are not redone until they succeed, but rather are terminated in the face of repeated failure. While there is no rule as to what constitutes too many rings, it is clear that the greater the number of rings, the greater the possibility that there is no one to answer the phone and the greater the likelihood that the caller will hang up. Therefore there is a pressure to answer the telephone relatively quickly, although not too quickly. If the telephone rings too many times, this too may become the topic of talk in the call, as in extract (5).

(5) [Tel5:1-]
```
            ((ring))
Aaron:      Hello?
Sue:        Oh you are the:re.
Aaron:      Yeah.h
Sue         'S jus' that I wz about to hang up I thought
            y' were out or something.
Aaron:      No, I wz just doin' stuff upstairs and I had
            tuh come down tuh get the phone.
```

In this extract, Aaron's delay in answering the telephone becomes the first topic in the call, and the unusualness of the prolonged ringing becomes an issue in the caller's first turn *Oh you are the:re*. This is framed with a change of state token *oh* (Heritage, 1984a) indicating that Aaron's answering is being treated as something new or unexpected in the context and is contrasted, therefore with a 'not at home' interpretation. The accountableness of the delayed ringing becomes the topic of subsequent talk with both Sue and Aaron providing possible candidate reasons for not answering sooner: Sue's interpretation being 'no one at home' and Aaron's warrant being that he was far away from the phone when it rang. In both cases, they are orienting to a delayed answering as being something that is interpretable and which needs explanation.

Schegloff (1986) also observes that answerers typically orient their picking up of the phone to either the completion of a ring or to a midpoint in the ring. Some people wait until a ring is completed, while others usually answer just after a ring has begun. This behaviour has no significant interactional consequences; however, it demonstrates that participants have an orientation to rings as distinct features rather than responding to ringing as a continuing mechanical process.

The ringing of the telephone is a special form of summons specific to telephone conversations and the same is also true of the answer response *hello*. In other summons–answer sequences there are a wider range of answer responses including *what, yeah* and non-verbal responses. However, *hello* is not normally replaceable by other answer forms in telephone openings. The absence of non-verbal responses is obviously a result of the non-visual nature of the medium; however, the absence of the other possible responses is not explainable by any constraint imposed by the technology, but rather it is a socially imposed constraint in telephone interactions. *Hello* has emerged as the default way to answer a telephone, at least in domestic contexts (Hopper, 1992).

Other answer types are found in telephone conversations, but these are usually limited to specific contexts and contrast with *hello* as the most usual answer form. One possible answer turn is *yes* or *yeah.* Schegloff (1986) argues that *yeah* is used when the answerer is 'superconfident' about the caller's identity. It is most common in contexts where a telephone call has been ended so that some task may be done, with an undertaking to call the other back immediately the task has been completed, as in extract (6).

(6) [Tel19:178-]

Brian:	Okay, (.) look I' ll jus get the file and I' ll call you right back,
Tom:	<u>O</u>kay.
Brian:	it' ll only take a minute.
Tom:	' kay.
	((ring))
Tom:	Yeah,
Brian:	Yeah I' ve got it n you' re right . . .

A further possibility in this context is *hi*, as in extract (7).

(7) [Friedman 1979: 56 (Schegloff, 1986)]

Mom:	terrific, listen, I' ll call you back.
Ed:	Okay
Mom:	All right, in about one minute.
	((ring))
Ed:	Hi.
Mom:	Hello there. I just got some more coffee. We um went to see the Rhineholts last night.

Again in this extract, the answerer's response shows a high degree of certainty about the identity of the caller. This association is interesting because semantically *hi* is normally considered to be an informal version of the greeting *hello* and has no semantic link with *yes* (Schegloff, 1986). In the cases of *yes/yeah* and *hi*, the answerer is orienting to the current conversation as a resumed or at least foreshadowed conversation and the selection of these answer tokens displays this orientation (Schegloff, 1986). This is clearly seen as a mutual orientation in extract (6), in which the caller immediately continues with talk relevant to the prior conversation, omitting any further interactional work such as establishing identity, greeting or other actions which we shall see are relevant parts of a telephone opening.

One further possible answer type in telephone conversation is self-identification as in extract (8).

(8) [Ling3:1–2]
```
                ((ring))
     Answ:      Linguistics department
```

Self-identifications are usually, but not exclusively, associated with institutional contexts. These answers to summons will be considered more fully later in the context of issues of identification.

The summons–answer sequence addresses the interactional problem of availability for talk (Schegloff, 1968). However, telephone openings involve more than just a summons–answer sequence. As noted above, the summons–answer sequence is a pre-sequence which is designed to secure further talk and, as such, the *hello* response makes some further talk by the caller a relevant next action. It is now necessary to characterize the nature of the talk which follows the summons–answer sequence.

Identification

Securing an interlocutor is only one of the interactional problems that participants face at the beginning of a telephone call. As mentioned in the discussion above, telephone calls begin with differential access to information. The caller knows both his/her own identity and the likely identity of the answerer, although where there are several possible answerers for any given number, the exact identity of the answerer is still an unknown. The answerer, however, knows only his/her identity and the identity of the caller is at best speculative and more typically unknown. Having secured an interlocutor, it becomes important to confirm the identities of the parties in the conversation before the conversation can proceed. This means that identification work is a relevant next action once the channel for communication has been opened and each party to the conversation must identify the other before the interaction can proceed. The first possible place that identification work can be done, therefore, is in the caller's first turn (Schegloff, 1979a).

Identification is achieved when one party recognizes the other. This recognition is based on the information available to the participants. In a telephone conversation, this information may be quite limited: the caller knows the possible set of answerers at a given telephone number, however; at the beginning of the caller's first turn, the answerer has no information as yet on which to base an identification. Having received the answerer's *hello* turn, the caller also has a voice sample on which to base further recognition. On the basis of this information, it is quite

possible for a caller to recognize an answerer, as can be seen in
extract (9).

(9) [Tel5:1–3]
```
                ((ring))
    Kate:       He:llo::,
    Jill:       KATie::[:!
```

Schegloff (1986) argues that answerers orient to their response
token as being available for recognition through the use of *signature
hellos*: a particular delivery of the *hello* token which is relatively standard
across occasions and therefore allows for recognizability in opening
contexts. A trouble in the signature hello may become a problem for
recognizability, as in (10), or it may occasion accounts for why the hello
sounds different, as in (11) and (12).

(10) [Tel24:1–9]
```
                ((ring))
    Sue:        *H' llo::,*
                (0.2)
    Joe:        Sue?
    Sue:        Yeah.
    Joe:        's Joe
    Sue:        Hi:.
→   Joe:        I didn' recognize your voice.
    Sue:        O:uhgh I go' such a co:l'.
```

(11) [Tel4:1–3]
```
                ((ring))
    Faye:       hhhH' llo::?. ghh
→   Gale:       Hel-yih sound outta breath.
```

(12) [Wong:NNS,3 (Schegloff, 1986)]
```
    Answ:       Hello,
    Call:       Tch Hi Mei Fang?
    Answ:       (Hmm?)
    Call:       This iz Joan Wright.
    Answ;       Hi [ How are you.
→   Call:          [ Did I wake you up?
                (0.4)
    Answ:       No.
                (0.2)
→   Call:       Oh: you soun:ded as if [ you might have=
    Answ:                              [ (no really)
→   Call:       =been (0.2) resting.
```

```
                 (0.2)
Answ:            I have a cold.
Call:            Oh:::
                 (0.4)
```

In both extracts (11) and (12), recognition is successfully achieved by the caller on the basis of the voice sample given by the answerer, in combination with knowledge the caller has about the possible identity of the answerer for that given number. Schegloff (1979a) argues that identifications are achieved through a 'recognitional source' and a 'recognitional solution'. In these extracts, the recognitional source is the voice sample provided by the answerer in the answerer's first turn, the recognitional solution is the naming of the answerer by the caller. This naming displays recognition and does this strongly and overtly (Sacks and Schegloff, 1979). These successful recognitions involve more than a cognitive act of recognition, they have a social dimension as well. The rapid recognition of the answerer by the caller invokes a relationship between the caller and the answerer which is close enough for the two participants to be able to recognize each other easily, quickly and with a minimum of information (Schegloff, 1979a, 1986). Rapid recognition invokes 'we know each other well' and this in itself has interactional consequences, if the caller can recognize the answerer, the answerer should be equally able to recognize the caller.

Here there is an issue of preference in identification. Schegloff (1986) argues that there is a strong preference for recognition by the other over self-identification in English-language telephone openings. Requests for a self-identification, such as *Who is this?*, are not frequent in telephone openings and can be highly vulnerable to topicalization and may be accountable, as in extract (13).

(13) [Tel7:1–17]
```
                 ((ring))
Cindy:           Hello:,
Dale:            hHi.
                 (0.6)
Cindy:           uh- hu-Who is this?
Dale:            H've you forgotten me already?
                 (0.2)
Cindy:           uh hh Uh-yNo: [ I- uh
Dale:                          [ huh  huh  Now  I'm  rea(h)lly
                 offe(h)nded [ hh
Cindy:                       [ Bu-
                 (0.3)
```

```
Dale:      I' ll let yuh off the hook. I' s me Da:[le.
Cindy:                                          [ DA:LE
           OH MY ↑GO::D=I didn' expect- I didn know you
           were back[ in the country]
Dale:                [ huh huh hhh] Long time no [ see huh?
```

Here Cindy is unable to identify Dale from his voice sample in his
first turn. She pauses, as much a sign of a dispreferred as of a problem
of recognition, and then produces a request for self-identification. This
does not produce the requested recognition, but rather leads to teasing about the accountability of not having recognized the caller.
Eventually, Dale self-identifies in a turn which encodes the interactional dilemma with which Cindy is faced: *I'll let yuh off the hook. I's me
Da:[le.* Cindy's response involves ratifying her recognition by repeating
Dale with marked prosody, and includes a warrant for her inability to
recognize him earlier and unassisted: he is an unexpected caller and as
such not one of the recognizable set of potential callers (Schegloff,
1986). Cindy's talk also encodes surprise through the loudness and
heightened pitch of her response and through the construction *OH
MY↑GO::D=*. Cindy's request for self-identification *Who is this?* cuts to
the heart of the interactional problem for the answerer. The answerer
has few clues to the identification of the caller, as callers may be either
known or unknown to the caller. Dale's *hHi* implies that the caller is a
known caller and gives a small voice sample to provide for recognition.
When Cindy fails to recognize her caller from among the set of
potential known callers, she is placed in an interactionally difficult
position; one which a request for self-identification does not resolve.

The discussion so far, demonstrates that recognition is far more than
a cognitive activity; it is also a socially constructed activity and the ways
in which recognition is achieved has social consequences. It is now
necessary to consider the possible forms of talk found in caller's first
turns which have a bearing on questions of identification and recognition. Schegloff (1979a) notes that in his corpus of approximately 450
telephone calls, there are only nine component types of caller first
turns, which may occur either alone or in combination with another
component. Greeting tokens are a very common turn type in the
caller's first turn.

```
(14) [Tel7:1-3]
                ((ring))
      Cindy:    Hello:,
  →   Dale:     hHi.
```

```
(15) [Tel11:1–3]
                ((ring))
    Anna:       Hello?
→  Cal:         Oh hi:.
```

Callers may also produce the name of the recipient and this may be done in a number of ways. Names may be try-marked: callers may answer with the answerer's name, or the name of the presumed answerer or with a relevant address term, such as *Mum* in example (16) with a rising question intonation or with a quasi-intonation contour which has a terminal rise, but to a lesser pitch peak.

```
(16) [Tel19:1–3]
                ((ring))
    Carla:      hello.
→  David:       Carla?
```

```
(17) [Tel12:1–3]
                ((ring))
    Betty:      hello.
→  James:       hh mum?
```

Name components may occur with other intonations which do not have an interrogative force, such as with an assertive, exclamatory or terminal intonation contour.

```
(18) [Tel5:1–3]
                ((ring))
    Kate:       He:llo::,
→  Jill:        KATie::[ :!
```

```
(19) [Tel2:1–3]
                ((ring))
    Andy:       H' llo?
→  Gary:        hHi Andy.
```

Callers may also orient to the circumstances of the call itself through a question or a noticing concerning the answerer's state.

```
(20) [NB#105 (Schegloff, 1979a)]
    P:          Hell::o,
→  A:           Are you awa:ke?
```

(21) [Tel4:1–3]

```
              ((ring))
   Faye:      hhhH' llo::? .ghh
→  Gale:      Hel-yih sound outta breath.
```

Immediately following the answerer's turn the caller may introduce the first topic or the reason for the call.

(22) [T&T3:1–3]

```
              ((ring))
   Tom:       Hallo:[:
→  Terry:          [You'll   never   guess   wha'   just
              happen:d.
```

Callers may request to speak to another person other than the answerer.

(23) [Gran:2:1–3]

```
              ((ring))
   Kim:       Hu:llo::
→  Gran:      Hello:. Is your mother there?
```

(24) [ID#289 (Schegloff, 1979a)]

```
   M:         Hello:,
→  C:         May I speak to Bonnie,
```

Callers may also self-identify. Self-identifications are usually found in combination with some other components.

(25) [Tel:11:1–3]

```
              ((ring))
   Anne:      hello:,
→  Sue:       hi mum, it's me
```

(26) [Tel:10:1–3]

```
              ((ring))
   Frank:     h'llo:,
→  Jay:       hi, it's Jay
```

They may ask questions regarding the identity of the answerer.

(27) [LL#27 (Schegloff 1979a)]

```
   L:         Hello:,
→  M:         H'llo, is this Kitty?
```

(28) [Tel5:1–3]
```
    Kim:      Hu:llo::,
  → Lee:      Oh hallo, is that Kim is it?
```

Finally callers may produce jokes or joke versions of the other component types, including mimicking features of the prior turn, giving intentionally inaccurate identifications or by producing their turn in a deliberately humorous way.

(29) [RJ1:1]
```
    Tom:      Hello:?
  → Roberta:  I'm a f:airy princess.
    Tom:      hHuh you? a fairy princess?
    Roberta:  Well my daughter says so.
```

(30) [ID#287a (Schegloff, 1979a)]
```
    Ba:      Hello¿
    B:       Hello¿
    Ba:      Hello?
    B:       Hello?
    Ba:      Hi Bonnie.
    B:       Hi he [ hheheheh ' hh
    Ba:            [ heheh
```

Schegloff (1979a) notes that the overwhelming majority of caller's first turns are made up of greetings, others' names with interrogative intonation and others' names with declarative intonation or combinations of greetings and one of these two naming components. While only some of the possible turns overtly address questions of identification, Schegloff argues that all nine types of caller first turns are oriented to the issue of identification. This can be seen in the case of greetings, in which no overt identifying talk is produced, but where the recognition of participants in the talk is fundamentally at issue. Schegloff (1979a) argues that, in face-to-face interaction, greetings are not simply the beginning of an interaction, but rather they are the conclusion of other interactional work associated with identification: that is, greeting is a relevant action only after identificational work has been done. In face-to-face interactions, a difference in recipient design can be seen between forms such as *excuse me*, which are designed to begin interactions with people who are identified as strangers, and forms such as *hello*, which are not so designed. As greetings are adjacency pairs, a greeting FPP invites a greeting SPP and makes such an SPP the relevant next action in the talk. Therefore, a greeting can display recognition of a recipient by its speaker and invite reciprocal recognition of the speaker by the recipient as the relevant next action and the sequence organization involved here is fundamentally linked to the achievement of the social outcome of recognition.

In telephone calls, the production of a greeting in the caller's first turn can be seen in this context. At this point in the talk, the answerer has provided a voice sample on the basis of which s/he may be identified by a familiar caller. The caller's greeting displays recognition of the answerer on the basis of the voice sample and invites reciprocal recognition of the caller by the answerer. In producing the greeting, the caller also provides a brief voice sample, providing the answerer with information on which to base the recognition. The answerer does the work of recognition by providing a greeting SPP, as in extract (31).

```
(31) [Tel4:1–3]
                ((ring))
      Tina:     H' llo:,
  → Sue:        hHi.
  → Tina:       Oh hi:.
```

Here, Sue's *hHi.* displays recognition of Tina, while Tina's return greeting displays reciprocal recognition. The *oh* which prefaces the greeting is a further indication that more than just greeting is occurring at this point. The *oh*, as a change-of-state marker (Heritage, 1984a), registers that Tina now knows something that she did not know earlier and this new state of knowledge is that she now knows the identity of her interlocutor. In this extract, recognition is achieved through very minimal resources. The terminal intonation on the two greeting turns indicates further certainty of the identification. The talk here, therefore, makes very strong claims about recognizability because it has been accomplished with very limited amounts of information (Schegloff, 1986). Strong displays of recognition can also be achieved by following the greeting with a name with falling intonation, giving evidence of the recognition which has been made, as in extract (32).

```
(32) [Tel2:1–3]
                ((ring))
      Andy:     H' llo?
  → Gary:       hHi Andy.
```

Alternatively, the greeting can be omitted and the recognition can be done by the naming, with a falling intonation, as in extract (33).

```
(33) [Tel5:1-3]
                    ((ring))
        Kate:       He:llo::,
    → Jill:         KATie::[:!
```

Having been the recipient of one of these displays of recognition, the answerer has two possible actions: s/he can either produce a display of recognition, following the trajectory established by the FPP or s/he can produce a request for identification. Here then, there are issues of preference organization with a display of recognition following the preference for agreement by following the trajectory established by the prior recognition (Sacks, 1987) and the request for identification being dispreferred. Recognitions are typically done immediately as in extract (34).

```
(34) [Tel5:1-4]
                    ((ring))
        Kate:       He:llo::,
        Jill:       KATie::[:!
    → Kate:                  [ JI:::LL::.
```

Where recognition is not done, it is usually prefaced by a pause, and perhaps other devices delaying the question in its turn, as in extract (35).

```
(35) [Tel7:1-5]
                    ((ring))
        Cindy:      Hello:,
        Dale:       hHi.
    →               (0.6)
    → Cindy:        uh- hu-Who is this?
```

Here, Cindy's pause withholds a recognition that hasn't been achieved and here the question is prefaced by disfluencies which further delay the production of her *Who is this?* The pause thus indicates a problem which is both cognitive and social. It displays both that recognition has not been achieved and that a preferred SPP cannot be produced. The caller at this point may speak to resolve the problem, as in the extract below.

```
(36) [Tel8:1-3]
                    ((ring))
        Rob:        Hello?
        Sam:        Hi: Ron.
```

```
→                    (0.3)
→ Sam:        I' s Sam
   Ron:        Oh Hi Sam. Yih sound diff' rent.
```

Here, Sam backs down from the trajectory his first turn established: that recognition can be achieved on the basis of the minimum information of a short voice token. In so doing he adds more information on which to base recognition, in this case his name, and reduces his claim to being recognized on the basis of voice alone. Ron provides the recognition in his next turn and also provides a warrant for having failed to achieve recognition earlier on the basis of the voice sample Sam had provided: the voice sample was in some way defective as a basis for recognition.

In cases where the talk proceeds to a *who is this?* question, the question functions as the FPP of an insert sequence to initiate a repair on the sequence in progress. The question indicates a trouble in the prior turn, in this case the claim that recognition can be achieved on the basis of a voice sample alone, and provides the prior speaker with an opportunity to repair the trouble (Schegloff, 1979a). The SPP can then be produced once the trouble has been repaired, as in extract (37), where Annie proceeds directly to the hitherto missing SPP immediately after the repair of the problem of identification.

```
(37) [Tel12:1–3]
                    ((ring))
      Annie:        H' llo::,
      Bill:         Hi Annie.
                    (1.0)
      Annie:        u:h=Who is this?
      Bill:         I' s Bill[y
      Annie:                 [Oh Billy hi::.
```

The strong preference for recognition in sequences such as the ones examined above gives rise to the possibility of claiming recognition by returning the greeting even where it hasn't been achieved (Schegloff, 1979a). This can be seen as paralleling the cases of token agreement in other types of dispreferreds discussed in Chapter 5: that is, the preferred action is done as a precursor to the dispreferred. The false claim of recognition may gain extra time and/or extra talk so that recognition may be achieved by the answerer at a later point and a false recognition may avoid the problem becoming known to the other participant. However, there are some cases in which a false recognition may be seen clearly in the talk:

```
(38) [EN#183 (Schegloff, 1979)]
                 ((ring))
        A:       Hello
        B:       Hi:
   →    A:       Hi: (0.3) Oh Hi Robin
```

Here, A's second turn contains a greeting term *hi:* which claims recognition. A brief pause and then an *oh*-prefaced greeting and the caller's name follow it. The *oh* here marks success and success just now in recognizing the caller (Heritage, 1984a; Schegloff, 1979a) and demonstrates that the prior claim of recognition was false.

In the discussion above, it has been argued that a greeting or a name with falling intonation or a combination of these is a strong claim for recognition and that it makes an equally strong reciprocal claim of recognition a relevant next action. However, names can also be delivered with a rising intonation, in which case the issues for recognition appear to be less stringent (Schegloff, 1979a). These identifications are designed to encode an element of doubt about the accuracy of the recognition and are try-marked (Sacks and Schegloff, 1979) by the intonation as a best attempt at recognition on the basis of the voice sample given.

```
(39) [Tel12:1–3]
                 ((ring))
        Betty:   hello.
   →    James:   hh mum?
        Betty:   Hi James.
```

However, it is equally the case that the answerer's turn will not be addressed to the recognition of the caller, but rather to confirming the tentative identification made in the caller's prior turn, as in extract (40). In these cases, it is usual to find a self-identification by the caller in the immediately following turn.

```
(40) [Tel19:1–5]
                 ((ring))
        Carla:   hello.
   →    David:   Carla?
        Carla:   Yeah,
        David:   It's David.
```

In cases such as (39) and (40), the caller's identification is marked as tentative even when the identification has proved to be correct. In other cases, however, there is real evidence of uncertainty in these identifications with rising intonation, as in (41).

(41) [MDE Supp (Schegloff, 1979a)]
```
M:        Hello?
E:        Tina?
M:        This is Martha.
```

Here the recognition is in fact false and the caller has failed to identify the recipient. Examples such as these indicate that a short voice sample may not be adequate for identification, even when the participants know each other well (Rose and Duncan, 1995).

The form with rising intonation, regardless of its correct or incorrect identification of the answerer, has sequential consequences which are quite different from names produced with falling intonation. In the latter case, recognition of the caller becomes the required next activity, while in the former case, only confirmation or disconfirmation of the answerer's identity is required as a next action. This means that names with rising intonation allow the possibility that the recognition of the caller will be delayed beyond the immediate next turn. Schegloff (1979a) argues that naming with rising intonation functions as a pre-sequence, with a self-identification as the projected base sequence. Pre-sequences work to avoid dispreferred actions and so naming with rising intonation works as a pre-sequence by projecting self-identification, but by allowing the possibility of doing a more preferred recognition before this self-identification takes place, as occurs in extract (39) above. Schegloff (1979a: 51) argues that try-marked address terms function as pre-sequences by:

1. providing a voice sample;
2. displaying doubt about the recipient's ability to recognize the speaker on the basis of the voice sample alone;
3. providing a position in the next turn for the recipient to display recognition if recognition is achieved on the basis of the voice sample;
4. providing an option in the next turn for talk which does not explicitly show a failure to achieve recognition;
5. projecting a place in the next turn but one for the caller to self-identify if recognition is not achieved on the basis of the voice sample and displayed in the answerer's turn.

The pre-sequence therefore allows for the possibility of a preferred recognition turn, but retains the possibility of a less preferred self-identification if the preferred outcome is not achieved.

Sacks and Schegloff (1979) argue that in cases of recognition there is a preference to 'oversuppose and undertell'. That is, in referring to people, speakers design their talk so as not to tell the recipient what s/he ought to suppose the recipient already knows. This means that it is possible for speakers to be in a position where they assume that the recipient knows a person and can identify that person by name, but may have doubts about whether this is truly the case. Where such a doubt is held, speakers try-mark their reference. In the case of these try-marked identifications in telephone openings, however, it is not really a case of problems about whether or not the answerer will be able to make the identification of the try-marked address term as the recipient him/herself is the supposed referent of the address term. In this case, the problem of identity lies in the possibility for recognizing the caller on the basis of a voice sample. Therefore, the try-marking here is not addressed to problems for the recipient knowing who the recipient is, nor to problems in the speaker knowing who the recipient is, at least in many cases, but rather to problems in the recipient knowing who the speaker is (Schegloff, 1979a).

Try-marked address terms lead to a number of possible outcomes. One possibility is 'evidenced recognition' (Schegloff, 1979a) in the next turn, as in (42).

```
(42) [Tel12:1–3]
                ((ring))
      Betty:    hello.
  →   James:    hh Mum?
      Betty:    Hi James.
```

In this case, the answerer has achieved recognition on the basis of the voice sample, and with other information, such as the recipient-designed address term *Mum* which invokes a small set of possible callers, and exhibits the recognition unambiguously through the address term. By providing recognition of the caller here, Betty displays that the try-marked *Mum?* is not problematic and in so doing accepts the recognition. Where this happens the recognition in the answerer's turn blocks the sequence from proceeding to a self-identification by the caller and no further identification work is relevant in the talk. A second possibility is for 'unevidenced recognition' in the next turn through a greeting, as in extract (43), or an *oh*-prefaced greeting, as in extract (44) (Schegloff, 1979a).

(43) [Tel14:1–4]
```
              ((ring))
    Helen:    Hello:,
    Gay:      Helen?
 →  Helen:    Hi.
```

(44) [Tel19:1–4]
```
              ((ring))
    Will:     H' llo.
    Val:      Will?
 →  Will:     Oh hi.
```

In this case, both answerers claim recognition without explicitly displaying it. The addition of *oh* upgrades the claim to recognition by marking a change of state. The greeting terms may be upgraded by the addition of other components, such as *how are you* FPPs, which advance the opening past identification work by requiring the relevant SPP, or they may be upgraded by prosodic features such as amplitude, pitch or duration (Schegloff, 1979a). In cases of unevidenced recognition, especially where it is not upgraded, the caller may proceed to self-identification in the immediately next turn, as in (45).

(45) [Tel14:1–5]
```
              ((ring))
    Helen:    Hello:,
    Gay:      Helen?
    Helen:    Hi.
 →  Gay:      It' s Gay.
```

The most common group of responses to try-marked address terms is a *yes* response. These responses are very weak as recognitions and are usually treated as failures of the pre-sequence to achieve recognition and typically proceed to a self-identification by the caller, as in (46).

(46) [Tel19:1–5]
```
              ((ring))
    Carla:    hello.
    David:    Carla?
    Carla:    Yeah,
 →  David:    It' s David.
    Carla:    Hi.
```

In some cases, however, callers may withhold self-identification after a *yes* response, as in (47).

(47) [CF#171 (Schegloff 1979a)]
```
        C:        Hello.
        J:        Hello, Charlie?
        C:        Yeah?
  → J:        Did I wake you up?
        C:        No. It's alright.
```

Schegloff (1979a) argues that the withholding of self-identification in this position is further evidence of the strength of the preference for recognition. When the response to a try-marked address term is weak, talk other than self-identification may be produced in response and may get recognition in their following turn, as in (48).

(48) [Gran:11:1–3]
```
                  ((ring))
        Cal:      H:ello,
        Gran:     Calvin?
        Cal:      Yeah.
        Gran:     You're home already?
        Cal:      Yeah Gran.
```

In other instances callers may mark time in the conversation until an identification comes, as in (49), while in others no overt identification using address terms ever occurs.

(49) [JG#66 (Schegloff, 1979a)]
```
        J:        Research Design
        P:        Jim?
        J:        Yeah.
        P:        Wha' d' ya say.
        J:        Oh:: not much.
        P:        What's doin.
        J:        Not a damn thing Jeff.
```

It is important to remember that the act of self-identification is not the same as a recognition. While self-identification provides a more informative recognition source, it may not lead to recognition being achieved. In some cases, self-identifications may be followed by a pause, which reflects a problem in achieving recognition and responding with a display of recognition, as in (50).

(50) [LL#31 (Schegloff 1979a)]
```
        L:        H' llo:,
        B:        H' llo Lana?
```

```
     L:        Yeah?
→  B:        This' Brigette.
→             (0.3)
     L:        Hi.
```

In this case, recognition comes only after a gap. In other cases, callers may further upgrade their self-identification by providing more information as a source for recognition such as last name (51) or some other identificatory information (52).

(51) [LL#25 (Schegloff, 1979a)]
```
     L:        H' llo:,
     M:        Laura,
     L:        Ye:s,
→  M:        It's Peter. (0.7) Williams.
     L:        HI: just a minute, let me close the uh thing
```

(52) [Tel8:1–6]
```
                 ((ring))
     Jeff:      Hello,
     Hana:     Jeff?
     Jeff:      Yeah,
     Hana:     It's Hana. (0.3) u-Kay's friend,
     Jeff:      Oh hi,
```

In both these examples, the pause after the identification is treated as a trouble which is repaired with further information. The further information comes as an increment to the prior talk, converting the pause following the identification into an intra-turn pause and in both cases recognition is achieved following the expanded recognition source. Where recognition is still not achieved, answerers may produce a *who is this?* question, as in (53).

(53) [Tel13:1–12]
```
                 ((ring))
     Ilene:    Hello:,
     Kay:      Ilene?
     Ilene:    Yes,
     Kay:      This's Kay. (0.5) Fisher.
                 (0.3)
→  Ilene:    uh-Who?
     Kay:      Kay Fisher (.) from the school.
     Ilene:    uh Hello.
     Kay:      I'm k-calling to see (.) if you can come to
                 the meeting Monday ni:ght.
     Ilene:    Oh Ka:y, oh yes I'm coming.
```

In this extract, the expanded self-identification does not lead to a recognition and Ilene requests the identity of the caller after another pause. This leads to a restatement of the expanded identification with the further information that she is *from the school*. This in turn receives a *hello* response claiming recognition. The response here, however, appears to be a deception and recognition is only achieved during the speaker's next turn, leading to the expressed recognition *oh Ka:y*, which is marked as a change of state; that is as recognition just now.

The discussion of try-marked address terms gives a framework in which we can understand questions about the identity of the answerer found in a caller's first turns. These questions seem to function as elaborated versions of try-marked address terms, as in (54).

```
(54) [Tel5:1–3]
                    ((ring))
        Kim:        Hu:llo::,
  →     Mona:       Oh hallo, is that Kim is it?
        Kim:        Yeah.
        Mona:       It's Mona.
        Kim:        Oh hello.
        Mona:       Hello, is you mother there.
```

In this case, Kim is no longer a resident at the number being called and as such is not an expected answerer. Mona's first turn, with its *oh-*preface and tag question does not seem to be designed as uncertainty about the identity of the answerer, but rather as a form of pre-sequence for a later self-identification. The elaborated form of the pre-sequence may be related to the unexpectedness of the answerer, in this case. The existence of a pre-sequence designed to project self-identification indicates that self-identification earlier in the opening can be delayed until at least the fourth turn at talk (that is the caller's second turn). Given this possibility, it is not unsurprising that Schegloff (1979a) argues that the caller's first turn is not the main place in which self-identification occurs. Nonetheless, self-identification can be found in the caller's first turns. In some cases, these self-identifications are self-identifications in form only as they do not really identify the caller, as in (55).

```
(55) [Tel:11:1–3]
                    ((ring))
        Anne:       hello:,
  →     Sue:        hi Mum, it's me
```

In examples such as this, recognition is still done primarily on the basis of a voice sample as the form *it's me* does not provide explicit self-identification in the same way a name does. Sue's turn here does provide some extra resources for recognition: it is a longer voice sample than a simple *hello*. It also potentially constrains the possible range of people from whom the voice sample could come, as self-identifications of the type *it's me* are used in contexts of very high degrees of familiarity, especially among nuclear family members (Schegloff, 1979a).

In other cases overt self-identification is found in a caller's first turn. In this case the identification is usually followed in the same turn by some other turn component. The additional turn component is typically an FPP and so it is this component, not the identification, that determines the sequence which follows from the turn. Such identifications appear to be designed for instances where recognition is problematic and is known to be problematic. This may be the case, for example, in switchboard situations in which the answerer is not the intended recipient and where the caller and answerer may not have any prior relationship. Switchboard situations will be discussed further below, but the context can be seen in (56) in which the answerer is not the person who is the descried interlocutor (Hopper, 1991).

(56) [Gran4:1–3]
```
            ((ring))
   Gran:    Hello?
   Beth:    Hello this is Beth. Is Tim there?
```

Here, Beth's *hello* shows that she has identified the answerer, at least as not being her intended recipient. She immediately produces a self-identification, which may be warranted by an expectation that this particular answerer may not be able to identify her, and perhaps could not be expected to be able to do so. Beth's turn not only provides identification, but by requesting some other interlocutor, she provides a potential account of why she may be unknown to the answerer.

Self-identification by the caller may be used to pre-empt opening work and to do some relevant identification work prior to beginning some other matter, as in (57).

(57) [Tel:10:1–3]
```
                ((ring))
     Frank:    h'llo:,
   → Jay:      hi, it's Jay. Look I've got a problem
               here . . .
```

In this extract, the motivation for dealing with all identification work and the reason for the call in the caller's first turn seems to be to underline the urgency of the problem. The doing of as much relevant interactional work as possible at the first available slot in the talk allows for the trajectory of the opening to be curtailed in order to do other things. In this case there is a pre-emption of the sequence, which is done for an action motivation. (This will be discussed further when in the context of pre-emption below.)

The discussion above has considered the matter of identification as it occurs in everyday telephone calls. It is now time to consider the case of telephone calls in institutional contexts where issues regarding identity are different. It has already been observed that in institutional contexts, the summons–answer sequence may have as its SPP an identification, as in (58).

```
(58) [Ling3:1–2]
                ((ring))
      Answ:     Linguistics department
```

In these contexts, the initial answerer's turn does not simply provide a voice sample as a resource for recognition, but also provides explicit self-identification. Schegloff (1986) argues that this convention is so strong that failure to provide an identification can lead to an assumption that the call has reached a wrong number, as in (59).

```
(59) [FN (Schegloff, 1986)]
      Answ:     Hello?
      Call:     'HeLLO' !?
      Answ:     Yeah. 'Hello' .
      Call:     Wuh- Is this 657-6850?
      Answ:     No, this is 657-6855.
      Call:     Oh. Well, you have a very lovely voice.
      Answ:     Why thank you. Am I supposed to be a business
                firm?
      Call:     Yes that's right, that's exactly right. I'm
                calling my office. They never answer with
                'hello' .
```

The use of self-identification in openings in institutional contexts is, however, more than a simple matter of convention. It is motivated by the interactional context in which it is found. In institutional contexts, the answerer is not answering as the owner of the phone, but rather on behalf of the business or office which does own the phone. In this context, a caller cannot expect to identify an answerer on the basis of a voice sample alone and this means that a caller cannot know on the basis of an answer such as *hello* whether or not s/he has reached the correct number (Schegloff, 1986). In a context in which it is not interactionally possible to do recognition on the basis of a voice sample, recognition has to be achieved in some other way: an appropriate resource for identification has to be provided and this appropriate resource is the formulation of the identity of the business or office to which the telephone number is assigned.

Greetings

In the above discussion, it was seen that greetings are fundamentally linked to recognition work in telephone openings and that much of the work of recognition is done through the exchange of greetings. However, not all recognition work is done as an exchange of greetings and greetings are not solely means for achieving recognition, as is the case in extract (60).

```
(60) [247a (Schegloff, 1986)]
                  ((ring))
        R:        Hallo,
        C:        Hello Jim?
        R:        Yeah,
        C:        's Bonnie
  →  R:           Hi,
  →  C:           Hi, how are yuh
```

In this interaction, there are four *hello*-like words distributed over four turns. However, it would be inappropriate to call each of these a greeting as they have quite different functions: the answer to the summons, the *hello* in the try-marked identification and the paired *hi*s at the end. While the first of these paired *hi*s is related to recognition, the second is not. R's *hi* is in fact doing two things: it is both claiming recognition and it is greeting. The greeting is then accomplished as an adjacency pair. Sacks (1975) has noted that greetings are not properly repeated and so wherever multiple examples of *hello*-like tokens occur, they typically have very different functions in the interaction. However, Schegloff (1979a) has noted that, in some cases, greetings may be repeated, but where this is the case, they are usually humorous or teasing.

Greetings are adjacency pairs (Sacks, 1975) and the initial *hi* turn requires an SPP for completion. As such, while much recognition work is done through the exchange of greetings, it is also possible that greetings may be done once recognition has been achieved. When greetings are being used as greetings they serve to put the participants in the conversation into a state of ratified mutual participation (Goffman, 1963). Sacks (1975: 64) has argued that greetings are 'ahistorically relevant'; that is, they are deployed by people regardless of what previous interactions or relationship may exist between them. This means that greetings themselves are designed primarily for beginning conversation, not for other social or interactional goals, even though, as has been seen, other things, such as identification, may also be done with greetings.

In some cases, greetings may be substituted with other turn-shapes, which still have a greeting function, most commonly *how are you?*-type turns, as in (61).

(61) [Op3:1–2]
```
    Joan:      How' re yuh goi[ng,
    Brian:                    [Hi:.
    Joan:      I haven' t seen you for a:ges.
```

Where this happens, the *how are you?* is used where a greeting would normally occur, but at the same time, the greeting is not seen as absent: rather the contribution is treated as a greeting and is responded to as a greeting. Moreover, Brian's response *Hi:* is not treated by Joan as a problematic answer to her *How're yuh goi[ng,* and she does not try to repair it.

'How are you?' sequences

Not all *how are you?* tokens are greetings, as in extract (61), and in many cases the *how are you?* is found after a greeting sequence and/or it is treated as a question rather than a greeting. The question *how are you?* and its variants in telephone openings function as enquiries about the current state of the participant and are designed to get an answer. Schegloff (1986) notes that this is slightly different from other contexts in which 'how are you?' can function as a greeting substitute (cf. Sacks 1975). *How are you?* sequences are typically *exchange sequences*; that is, once the first question is launched and answered, it is usual for the recipient of the first question to launch a reciprocal sequence, as in (62).

```
(62) [Tel19:1–4]
                 ((ring))
      Will:      H' llo.
      Val:       Will?
  →   Will:      Oh hi. How' re things,
  →   Val:       Okay n how' re you.
  →   Will:      Okay=
      Val:       =That' s good.
```

How are you? questions may receive a response which is either positive (e.g. *terrific*), negative (e.g. *awful*) or neutral (e.g. *okay*) and these possible answers have different sequential outcomes. Neutral responses are closure-relevant and are typically followed by talk on a next subject, or if relevant by a reciprocal *how are you?* (Schegloff, 1986). At most, neutral responses engender assessments as sequence closing thirds, as in the second sequence in (62). These neutral responses effectively pass up opportunities to talk on this topic and allow the conversation to move on to other matters. Highly positive and negative answers to the question routinely lead to sequence expansion and further talk on the topic (Sacks, 1975).

```
(63) [Tel8A:1–7]
                 ((ring))
      Kim:       Hullo.
      Sam:       Hi!
  →   Kim:       Hi. How' re you:.
  →   Sam:       Re:ally grea:t.
  →   Kim:       Why?
      Sam:       Well I just had some really good news . . .
```

In extract (63), Sam's *re:ally grea:t.* is a highly positive response to the question and rather than passing up an opportunity to talk, indicates that there is something tellable about how she is. Kim's response positions her as a recipient for this tellable and this then becomes the first topic of the call. Similarly, where a response to the question is negative, a similar trajectory is found, as in (64).

```
(64) [Tel11:1–8]
                 ((ring))
      Kay:       ' Llo?
      Sue:       Hi Kay
  →   Kay:       Oh hi=How' re you,
  →   Sue:       ' Kay, n you,
```

```
→ Kay:      Sstre:ssed.
→ Sue:      Stressed,=wha' s a matter.
```

Here Kay answers with a negative formulation of her state as stressed and this becomes the topic of the following talk, as Sue provides an opportunity for a further telling with her question. Kay as the answerer in this call is therefore allocated the first topic in the talk, although it is Sue who initiated the call and presumably has a reason for making the call, which would typically become the first topic (Sacks, 1992: I: 773–9). By producing a negative response here, Kay has introduced her own tellable as the first mentioned matter in the conversation.

The prosody with which a response is delivered may affect the way in which it is treated sequentially. Prosodic features which mark the response as very upbeat or as depressed commonly engender sequence expansion in the same way as positive or negative responses. Where there is a mismatch between the lexicon and the prosody, e.g. where the lexicon is neutral but the prosody is negative, the prosody is usually taken as the 'true' response (Schegloff, 1986).

(65) [Tel*B:1–8]
```
                ((ring))
       Kim:     Hullo.
       Tom:     Hi
→ Kim:          Hi. How' re you:.
→ Tom:          Fi:ne,how' re you,
→ Kim:          .hhh hhh. ↓o:ka:y:hh.,
→ Tom:          W-what' s up with you.
```

Here Kim gives a neutral response *okay* but it is realized in a highly marked way. The *okay* is preceded by a sigh and is produced slowly, at a lower pitch and with an exhalation at the end. These features of the talk mark the *okay* as other than neutral although the form does not: it is like an 'off the record' negative response. This response is pursued by Tom as a negative response and he positions himself as a recipient for a trouble telling.

Telephone opening sequences

The discussion above has outlined a series of four sequences which form a core for opening telephone conversations (Schegloff, 1986):

1. a summons–answer sequence: addressing the interactional task of establishing the channel and the availability of the participants for the interaction;
2. an identification/recognition sequence: establishing the identity of the participants in the conversation;
3. a greeting sequence: ratifying participation;
4. *how are you?* sequences: provide opportunities to make some state of being a matter for talk in the conversation or to pass this up as a relevant action at this point in the talk.

Each of these sequences is usually achieved in either a two-turn adjacency pair or in three turns as an adjacency pair with a sequence-closing third. These sequences form a sequence of sequences which are organized relative to each other. They can be organized serially so that each turn at talk deals with one part of the sequence and the sequence progresses turn by turn, as in (66).

(66) [Tel14:1–5]
```
             ((ring))
Helen:   Hello:,
Gay:     Helen?
Helen:   Hi.
Gay:     It's Gay.
Helen:   Oh Gay.
Gay:     Hi.
Helen:   Hi:
Gay:     How are you?
Helen:   Fine.
Gay:     Good.
Helen:   How're you?
Gay:     Okay
```

Alternatively, they may be organized in an interlocking way so that a single turn may contain parts of two or more sequences, as in the arrowed turns in (67).

(67) [Tel17:1–5]
```
               ((ring))
    Chris:   Hello:?
    Dan:     Hi Chris?
→   Chris:   Hi Dan, how're you
→   Dan:     Okay. How're you doin.
    Chris:   Can't complain.
```

In some cases, interlocking can also take the form of a single TCU which functions as both the completion of the prior sequence and the start of the next sequence as in (68)

(68) [Tel16:1–5]
```
                ((ring))
       Dan:     H' llo:¿
       Tom:     Dan?
  →    Dan:     Hi.
       Tom:     Hi. How' re you.
       Dan:     Okay. N you?
       Tom:     Not bad.
```

In this extract Dan's _hi._ is both the SPP to Tom's try-marked address term and also the FPP of a greeting exchange. Interlocking sequences produce openings in fewer turns, but also reassign roles of the answer and caller in relation to the various sequences. In extract (66) above, all sequences except the reciprocal _how are you_ are initiated by Gay, the caller, who as a result of this reciprocation ends as the final speaker of the opening. In extract (67), Chris, the answerer, is the initiator of the first _how are you?_ sequence and the final speaker in the opening. In (68) Dan, the answerer, launches the greeting sequence and Tom launches the first _how are you?_ sequence in the same turn as his return greeting and is the final speaker in the opening.

This core can be seen as the normal way in which a telephone opening runs off. However, telephone openings do not always have all of the components discussed above and some openings are shortened by one or other speaker initiating a first topic before the opening has worked its way to conclusion. Schegloff (1986) argues that there is a structural motivation for answerers to pre-empt opening sequences because it is normally the caller who initiates the first topic after an opening sequence. Answerers who have something to tell or something to do in the call may therefore want to initiate this before the completion of the opening sequence assigns the role of first speaker after the opening sequence to the caller. At the same time, callers may orient to the possibility that an answerer may pre-empt the first topic and attempt to initiate their own tellable or doable before this gets pre-empted by the answerer. It is possible therefore for pre-emption to occur at various points in the opening.

Pre-emption by answerers

Answerers may pre-empt the first topic in their answer to the second *how are you?* sequence. Schegloff (1986) treats this as a weak form of pre-emption because the *how are you?* sequence seems to be designed to allow for this possibility. However, producing a non-neutral response in this position allocates the first topic to the answerer, not to the caller.

```
(69) [268 (Schegloff, 1986)]
        Marylin:   Hello:,
        Irene:     Hello, Marylin
        Marylin:   Yes it is.=
        Irene:     =Oh this is Irene.
   →    Marylin:   Oh HI.=How're you do:in.
   →    Irene:     Heh Okay.=How about you.
        Marylin:   Okay, pretty goo:d. I've been busy:
                   bu(h)t,. hh [ other
        Irene:                 [ Are you tea:ching¿
```

In this example, Marylin comes to be the recipient of the final *how are you?* FPP because she has produced a turn which includes both a greeting component and a latched *How're you do:in.* which also pre-empts a second greeting. As such, while the pre-emption of first topic does not come until the very end of the opening, some interactional work has also been undertaken by Marylin to be the recipient of the last *how are you?*. Recipients may also pre-empt the first topic in response to the first *how are you?*, as in (70).

```
(70) [95 (Schegloff, 1986)]
        Marcia:    Hello,
        Tony:      Hi Marcia,
        Marcia:    yeah?
        Tony:      This is Tony
        Marcia:    HI Tony.
        Tony:      How are you,
   →    Marcia:    Ohhhh hh I've got a paper b- (0.2) the yearly
                   paper due tomorrow,
        Tony:      How about that.
        Marcia:    heheheh. hh I can tell you a lot ab(h)out
                   th(h)at . . .
```

Here, Marcia recognizes Tony through a greeting FPP which does not receive an SPP, except in so far as *how are you?* questions can function as greetings (Sacks, 1975). Tony's first *how are you?* sets him up as the recipient of the second *how are you?* and Schegloff (1986) argues

that it is a response to a possible pre-emption by Tony to use the
second *how are you?* to launch his first topic that Marcia uses the first to
pre-empt first topic for herself. In both examples (69) and (70), the
pre-emption is not a unilateral activity, but rather something that is
strategically introduced into the unfolding talk.

In addition, pre-emption may also be done by producing talk which
departs from the sequence currently under way to introduce some new
action into the talk, thereby deleting the previous talk from having a
further role in the sequence.

```
(71) [Tel21:1–11]
                  ((ring))
        Ann:      He:llo:,
        Kate:     Hi Ann.
        Ann:      Hello. How' re you?
 →      Kate:     I' ve been tryin to ring you a:ll da:y.
        Ann:      Oh I w' z working today.
        Kate:     O:hh. I [ thou-
        Ann:             [ I haddan extra shift.
        Kate:     yeah, I knew that you were usually at home
                  today.
        Ann:      So whaddid you want?
```

In this example, Kate's *I've been tryin to ring you a:ll da:y.* is not
designed as a response to the *how are you?* question, but rather introduces a new sequence with a new FPP and it is this new sequence which
becomes the first topic of talk. In fact the interrupted *how are you?*
sequence does not get done at all. Here, Kate tells something about
her experience which prompts an account from Ann about where she
has been, launching this as the topic of talk (Pomerantz, 1980). The
topic is occasioned by the context of the telephone call itself and uses
the reporting of this call as the successful call after a series of failures as
a device for pre-empting other talk.

Pre-emption by the answerer can also occur earlier in the opening
prior to *how are you?*, either during the greeting sequence or immediately after identification has been done.

```
(72) [Tel27:1–5]
                  ((ring))
        Neil:     Hello:,
        Mark:     Neil?
        Neil:     Yeah?
        Mark:     I' s Mark.
        Neil:     Hi Mark.=Where' ve yuh bee::n.
```

```
Mark:    Uh when?
Neil:    All da:y. I've been tryin to get you for like
         hou::rs.
Mark:    I w- well y' know I've sorta been in an' ou:t
         all day.
```

In (72), Neil, the recipient of the call, produces a greeting and in the same turn produces immediately afterwards a question FPP. Here he pre-empts a return greeting by including in his turn a TCU which requires a different SPP and makes that SPP the relevant next action. The talk takes up this trajectory through an insert repair and eventually moves to the required SPP.

(73) [Tel25:1–5]
```
         ((ring))
Jim:     H-hello?
Craig:   Hi Jim.
Jim:     Didjuh get my message?
Craig:   u- Yeah,
```

In (73), Craig, the caller, produces a first greeting and Jim pre-empts the second greeting to do a first task, asking about a message he has left for Craig and to raise this message as the trajectory for the first topical talk of the interaction. This pre-empts at a very early point in the talk, that is, at the first point after the answerer can make an identification of the caller, in order to ensure that his doable becomes the first action undertaken in the talk.

These examples of pre-emption by the answerer – and the examples in Schegloff (1986) – all deal with issues relating to contact between the two participants engaged in the call. The issue being dealt with seems to be the distribution of the roles of answerer and caller in this particular call and that, if some previous attempt at communication had been successful, the roles existing in this particular call may have been reversed. That is, early pre-emptions which produce sequentially unrelated turns at talk seem to deal with problems relating to a failure to establish communication at a previous attempt. The pre-emption, then, involves pre-empting the role of caller, by invoking the relevance of the status of caller for the current answerer and launching issues related to the answerer's earlier attempt(s) to initiate contact.

Caller pre-emptions

Callers can also move into first topics or other actions before the opening sequence has run its course and these pre-emptions also can be either minimal, in the sense of responding to a component of the emerging opening in such a way as to launch a first action, or it may be a more drastic departure from the opening sequence in which it occurs. Extract (74) is an example of a weak pre-emption in which the caller pre-empts the first topic as the answer to the second *how are you?* sequence.

```
(74) [Tel18:1–7]
                 ((ring))
       Sally:    Hello:,
       Sam:      Hello!
       Sally:    Hi Sam,
       Sam:      How are yuh.
       Sally:    Fine, how' re you
   →   Sam:      hhhh Oh not so good. I had this real problem
                 today at work.
       Sally:    Wha' happ' n' d.
```

In (74), Sam, the caller, launches the first *how are you?* sequence and is positioned as the recipient of the second. In the second position he produces a negative answer to the question and this becomes the first topic of the conversation. In (75), the pre-emption is slightly stronger as it occurs earlier in the opening and pre-empts a return *how are you?* sequence.

```
(75) [Tel31:1–9]
                 ((ring))
       Sam:      He:llo:,
       Dan:      Sam,
       Sam:      Hi Dan.
       Dan:      Hi.
       Sam:      How' re you,
   →   Dan:      khh. I' m pissed off.
       Sam:      Pissed off?
       Dan:      Yeah.
```

Here, the conversation proceeds with one sequential component per turn, meaning that Dan becomes positioned as the recipient of the first *how are you?* sequence. His answer to this becomes the first topic of talk and pre-empts a reciprocal *how are you?* sequence. In (76), the *how are you?* sequences are pre-empted altogether as David latches his first action to his greeting SPP and so moves the following talk out of the opening sequence.

(76) [Tel19:1–5]
```
                ((ring))
    Carla:   hello.
    David:   Carla?
    Carla:   Yeah,
    David:   It's David.
    Carla:   Hi.
 →  David:   Hi=Did you get my message?
    Carla:   Uh yeah b't I only just got home.
```

Callers can equally pre-empt openings by producing turns which are not related to the unfolding opening sequence, as in (77).

(77) [MDE (Schegloff 1986)]
```
    Marcia:  Hello?
    Donny:   'lo Marcia. [ (it's) D] onny.
    Marcia:             [ Yea :h ]
    Marcia:  Hi Donny.
    Donny:   Guess what.hh
    Marcia:  What.
    Donny:   .hh My ca:r is sta:lled.
```

In this extract, the caller is the recipient of a greeting FPP, but rather than producing a greeting SPP, introduces a first topic through a pre-telling *guess what*. In this case, as Schegloff (1986) indicates, there are additional signs of urgency in this opening, most notably the compression of the identification work into the caller's first turn.

Pre-emption by callers can also be done in the very first caller turn as in (78).

(78) [T&T3:1–4]
```
                ((ring))
    Tom:     Hallo:[:
 →  Terry:        [You'll never guess wha' just
             happen:d.
             (.)
    Tom:     What?
```

In this call, Terry introduces the first topic just before the completion of Tom's answer to the summons. This means that Tom has no recognition source available to make an identification before the first topic is launched by a pre-telling which formulates a basis for the pre-emption. However, the basis of other pre-emptions may not be so overtly displayed in other openings.

```
(79) [108 (Schegloff 1986)]
      Portia:  Hello::,
a→  Agnes:   Are you awa:ke?
      Portia:  YEA:H. I [ dis got up.
      Agnes:              [ I-
      Agnes:   Oh didjeh?
      Portia:  Yeah.
      Agnes:   .hh Weh goo:d.
b→  Agnes:   I'm alo:ne.
               (0.4)
      Portia:  [ mvh-
b→  Agnes:   Guy left me las' night.
               (1.0)
```

In extract (79), the pre-emption happens at the immediately first turn (arrow a), but the action done does not immediately signal the basis for the pre-emption: in this case the telling of bad news (arrow b). Schegloff (1986) argues that Agnes' first turn is constructed not as a pre-apology, checking if there are grounds for an apology for having woken the recipient, but rather a 'pre-calling orientation' to with-holding the call because the recipient may not be awake, but deciding to risk waking her. The formulation *are you awake?* rather than *did I wake you?* displays that the caller was willing to risk waking the recipient and therefore has a tellable which is important enough to warrant waking the recipient as a 'self-conscious' action (Sacks, 1984). The importance of the news is signalled by Agnes' attempt to start the delivery of the news in her next turn at talk *I-* although the talk here is aborted in overlap with Portia's continuation.

In the examples of very early pre-emption by callers discussed here, the basis for pre-emption is some matter of urgency which needs to be told in the conversation. Reducing the opening sequence is a display of urgency and marks this opening as one which will not be done as a routine sequence of sequences. This differs from the answerer's motivations for pre-emption, which addressed matters of contact between the participants. While the motivation for pre-empting the routine flow of the opening sequence may be different for each par-ticipant, what they both point to is the idea that an opening sequence is jointly achieved by the participants. The routine opening of a conversation is achieved as only one of a set of possible ways for doing so, not as the result of a pre-scripted interaction which precedes the real business of telephone talk (Schegloff, 1986).

Openings in face-to-face interaction

In face-to-face interaction the issues involved in opening a conversation are similar to those found in telephone openings, although the resources are not so exclusively limited to voices. In both sorts of openings one needs to secure and recognize an interlocutor. The ordering of these things, however, may be different in the two contexts.

Some face-to-face interactions begin with a summons of some sort, for example, knocking on a door or ringing a doorbell.

```
(80) [Office2]
  →                ((knock, knock))
  → Steve:    c'min.
                   (0.3)
     Harry:    Hi.
```

Like the ringing of a telephone, the non-vocal sounds are designed to secure a co-participant for a conversation (Kendon and Ferber, 1973). Again, like the ringing of the telephone, they either secure a response such as *come in* or the opening of the door, or, if they go unanswered, they may be repeated until the summoner has sufficient grounds to believe that the summons will not be answered. Such summons–answer sequences are used as the first action in an interaction where there is some barrier between the potential participants, typically a door. This barrier may mean that the instigator of the summons does not know if the other potential participant in the conversation is present, but this is not necessarily the case, as a summons can be made by knocking on an open door when the other person is in full view of the knocker.

Knocking, and similar summons–answer sequences in face-to-face interaction, do not seem to be designed with consideration of whether the participants are known to each other or not. That is, such a summons can equally be issued where the interlocutors do not know each other, as in the case of a door-to-door salesperson initiating an interaction, or when they know each other well, as in the case of friends paying a visit. These summons–answer sequences, therefore, may precede identification work by the participants, as in extract (81).

(81) [Office 4:1-]
```
A:          ((knock knock knock))
B:          Come i:n,
A:          Dr Smith?
B:          Yes,
B:          I'm Sally Jones, I'm in planning to take your
            class on Fridays, . . .
```

However, this is not always the case. In cases where a knock is given on an open door, at least one of the participants may have done some recognitional work before the summons was produced. In face-to-face interaction, unlike telephone calls, participants have an additional resource available to them – sight – to help do some of the work involved in beginning a conversation. What this means is that where participants are co-present, know each other to some degree and can see each other, recognition can be done non-verbally and may, at least in part, precede other interactional work, including the summons–answer sequence. This means that recognition may be a relevant pre-beginning in face-to-face interaction and is not contingent upon establishing communication (Schegloff, 1979a).

Kendon and Ferber (1973) argue that in face-to-face interactions in which individuals are available to be seen, sighting a potential interlocutor is the first action in establishing interaction. Such sighting involves two actions. Firstly, it does the work of identifying someone as known and secondly, it identifies the other as someone whom one wishes to greet. However, interaction cannot begin until the sighting has occurred and one participant does not typically approach another until the other has indicated s/he is aware of the first participant. If the participant is not aware of the potential interlocutor, s/he typically does something to secure this awareness. That is, s/he produces a summons of some type. This summons can be verbal or non-verbal (for example, a wave of the hand or a head gesture) (Goffman, 1963; Kendon and Ferber, 1973). The response to this summons may also be verbal or non-verbal, but the important interactional outcome of the summons–answer sequence is that the participants establish mutual eye gaze. Goffman (1963: 92) argues that this mutual eye gaze establishes an 'avowed openness to verbal statements and a rightfully heightened mutual relevance of acts', which is necessary for beginning an interaction.

Eye gaze also makes moving into a different, closer spatial config-uration a potentially relevant next action: participants for a conversa-tion normally need to be close to each other in order for the conversation to proceed (Goffman, 1963; Kendon and Ferber, 1973). In some cases, this may, however, not happen. Sacks (1975) has pointed out that a *minimal proper conversation* can consist simply of an exchange of greetings, without participants coming into closer proximity, or even interrupting other activities. Whether participants move closer or not, a greeting sequence is the typical next activity once availability and identity have been established and in face-to-face interaction this may involve non-verbal actions, such as handshakes or kisses, as well as verbal greeting tokens. The greetings are also commonly followed by an exchange of *how are you?* sequences (Kendon and Ferber, 1973).

In face-to-face conversations, therefore, the opening of the conversation is quite similar to that found in telephone openings, although it does not seem to be as strictly ordered. The initial actions in the opening involve issues of recognition and securing availability. However, because the interaction is not limited to a single communicative channel, it is not necessary to secure an interlocutor before identification or recognition can be done. In fact, recognition is typically a precursor to interaction and an attempt to establish an interaction may be undertaken as a result of having recognized a potential co-conversationalist.

Conclusion

Participants beginning a conversation use a set of devices designed to deal with the interaction problems they face in beginning a conversation. These sets of devices can be considered a sequence of sequences through which conversationalists pass as they establish their interaction and enter into a conversation. While this sequence of sequences provides a format which participants can use to begin a conversation, it is important not to consider this format to be a routine or ritual through which the participants invariably pass. Rather, this format provides a resource which conversationalists can use or modify in order to achieve interactional ends (Hopper, 1989; Schegloff, 1986). This means that deviations from the format represent a form of interactional work which achieves a different action from following more closely the sequence of sequences. If participants produce a sequence of sequences in its typical format, then, this must be seen as a interactional product achieved by the participants, rather than as a ritualized entry into a conversation. Likewise, a deviant sequence cannot be seen simply in terms of its departure from an 'expected' norm, but rather as talk designed to do some other task in the conversational opening.

9 Closing Conversation

Introduction

Closing a conversation provides a particular interactional problem. Participants need to disengage from talk in a way which does not make the relationship between participants vulnerable and which ensures that all participants to the conversation have had the opportunity to talk about all of the things which need to be dealt with in the conversation. Moreover, they have to disengage from the turn-taking system itself (Schegloff and Sacks, 1973). The turn-taking system described in Chapter 3 provides for the ongoing possibility of speaker change at every possible completion. Absences of talk after a completion are heard as silences in the conversation, not as endings of the conversation. Moreover, some silences are heard as belonging to particular speakers of whom further talk is required by the talk so far. This means that reaching the end of some bit of talk does not in itself provide for closing and absence of talk does not equate with the end of a conversation. Instead, speakers need to employ practices which are designed in such a way that they will not occasion further talk and at the same time will not be heard as a particular speaker's silence (Schegloff and Sacks, 1973). This chapter will explore the practices speakers use to end conversations.

Terminal sequences

It is readily apparent to speakers of English that a conversation is usually ended by an exchange of *goodbyes* or similar tokens and that after such an exchange a conversation is considered closed and the turn-taking system is suspended, as in (1):

(1) [ES:1:3:17–22]
    Emma: So we' ll do it at 7.30

```
Sue:      It' ll be fun
Emma:     Alright,
Sue:      Okay
Emma:     Bye=
Sue:      Bye:,
```

An exchange of *goodbyes* therefore is a terminal sequence for conversation: it declares the conversation to be at an end. This indicates that in English (as in other languages) there is a particular class of speech tokens which are used to perform closing. The issue, however, is how these tokens achieve this. One of the first things to observe about this exchange of *goodbyes* is that it constitutes an adjacency pair. The production of one *goodbye* makes the production of another a relevant next action for a co-conversationalist. The effect of such paired turns in conversational closings is that the first proposes the end of the conversation and the second accepts this. Closing is achieved with the production of the second component: the completion of the adjacency pair completes the conversation and removes the relevance of the continued application of speaker change for this conversation (Schegloff and Sacks, 1973). The use of an adjacency pair to close conversation means that closing is achieved collaboratively by the parties to the conversation. Failures to collaborate in closing (for example, by saying a first *goodbye* and immediately hanging up the telephone) have a very different interactional affect from paired closings and are potentially interpretable as expressing anger or some other emotion. Terminal components may be expanded with other tokens, such as tag-positioned address terms and endearments. Where this happens, the expansion does not affect the emerging sequence and closure proceeds in the same way as when unexpanded turns are used, although such tag-positioned utterances may be vulnerable to overlap (Jefferson, 1973).

Goodbye and similar expressions are not the only components found in the closing of conversations and several other components are found. A conversational closing is in fact a series of activities which lead up to an exchange of terminal components and the closing of the conversation. While it is true that a terminal sequence ends a conversation, it is not the case that a terminal exchange can legitimately be introduced at any moment in talk. Conversational closing is an action which orients to the completion of the current conversation as an event and must be sensitive to what is happening or potentially could happen in a conversation. One feature of conversation is that participants may have a number of things they wish to talk about in the current conversation ('mentionables') but at any point in the conversation not all mentionables may have been introduced into the talk. This means that it is important when closing a conversation to determine if all potential mentionables have been mentioned. Conversation, therefore, needs a structure which will allow participants to check if there are further things to be talked about before they close the conversation. Terminal sequences do not do this.

Pre-closing sequences

Terminal sequences are regularly preceded in conversation by talk which is designed to verify if all relevant mentionables for this conversation have been mentioned. This talk usually takes the form of a short turn such as *okay*, *alright* or *right* with falling intonation, possibly with a tag-positioned address term of endearment, as in (3) and (4).

```
(2) [ES:1:3:19–22]
  → Emma:    Alright,
  → Sue:     Okay.
    Emma:    Bye=
    Sue:     Bye:,
```

```
(3) [MM:87–90]
  → Mark:    hn' kay
  → Mary:    Okay Ma[rk
    Mark:          [Bye
    Mary:    B' bye
```

```
(4) [JSK:11:8ii]
  → Helen:   Okay Mum
  → Dora:    y-Oka[y, h.
    Helen:        [G' dby[:e
    Dora:               [Bye:,
```

These short turns meet the requirements of the turn-taking system in that speaker change occurs; however, they do not advance topical talk. They pass up an opportunity to do further talk or to introduce some new matter into the talk at this particular moment. They provide for the possibility that for the current speaker all mentionables have been mentioned and that closing to conversation could now be done. A pre-closing sequence is then one in which 'each party declines at least one opportunity to continue talking' (Schegloff and Sacks, 1973: 214) before producing terminal components. These turns therefore work to provide a place to determine whether closing could be a next activity and are known for this reason as pre-closings. At their completion a pre-closing component provides for speaker change and passes the talk to an interlocutor, who may at this point introduce some new mentionable into the conversation. This means that the turn immediately after the pre-closing provides a place in which a speaker may legitimately introduce new material rather than indicating that the conversation may move to closure (Schegloff and Sacks, 1973). As pre-closings provide a space in which new mentionables may be inserted, they do not therefore always lead to closing and are never more than *possible* pre-closings.

Pre-closings are adjacency pairs: production of a first pre-closing requires some next talk. This next talk may be a new topic or it too may be a pre-closing component. Where an interlocutor has no new mentionables to introduce into the talk, s/he too can produce a turn such as *okay*, passing up an opportunity to introduce new talk and providing for closing as the next relevant activity. We therefore have two possible trajectories for the sequence:

1.	pre-closing FPP	2.	pre-closing FPP
	pre-closing SPP		topic talk SPP
	↓		↓
	terminal sequence		continued conversation

The first trajectory makes closing a relevant next action while the second cancels the relevance of closing for this point in the conversation. In both cases the FPP provides for the possibility of closing, while the SPP either advances that possibility or cancels it.

Schegloff and Sacks (1973) argue that the pre-closing sequence and the terminal sequence form a sequence of sequences or a 'closing section' and that both sets of actions are required to achieve closing. This means that conversational closing is a two-part action. First, it involves determining whether all mentionables for this conversation have been introduced. Second, it involves agreement to end the conversation and suspend the relevance of turn-taking. It is the completion of both of these activities that constitutes a typical conversational closing.

Closing implicative environments

While the closing section itself achieves closing, there are limits on where the closing section can commence. Not all instances of *okay*, *alright*, etc., are heard as pre-closings and whether such a turn will be treated by a speaker as proposing closing or not depends on its placement in the talk in progress. Specifically, pre-closings are placed at the analysable end of a topic (Schegloff and Sacks, 1973). When one participant produces talk which closes down a topic in some way, s/he provides for the possibility that there is nothing further to be said on the current topic. This allows for the possibility of a co-participant in the conversation to move to closure of the conversation. In addition, some particular conversational actions appear regularly as last topics in a conversation and lead to closing as a relevant future activity. These actions can be considered *closing implicative environments*. The term closing implicative environment refers to sets of actions after which closing may be a relevant next activity and after which closure is a common activity but it does not imply that closure will necessarily happen after such an action. Conversational closure only happens where the participants to a conversation pass up opportunities to introduce new mentionables into the conversation. A closing implicative environment provides a place where such possibilities for passing up opportunities for introducing new talk can be located but it does not cause conversational closure.

Announcing closure

One obvious way in which a conversation may move to closure is if one of the participants announces closure as a relevant next activity at some point in the conversation. Such announcements of closure usually invoke some external circumstance which warrants ending the current conversation, with a greater or lesser degree of specificity. In addition, the circumstances which warrant ending to conversation may orient to the speaker's circumstances or the recipient's circumstances. For example, an announcement of closure such as *I've gotta go* invokes an unspecified external circumstance which affects the speaker's ability to continue in the current conversation (Button, 1991b; Schegloff and Sacks, 1973). Announcements of closure of this type may however be expanded to invoke a more specific reason for closure, as in extract (5).

```
(5) [MK 2:II]
  → Mandy:    Look Karen I gotta go now Tom' s jus' got home
    Karen:    Okay [ love
    Mandy:         [ Okay
    Karen:    B-bye=
    Mandy:    =By::e
```

Here Mandy invokes Tom's getting home as an external circumstance which warrants her ending of the current conversation. The announcement of closure, however, does not immediately lead to a terminal component, but rather leads into a pre-closing sequence where further opportunities to introduce new items of talk are passed up before the conversation is finally closed. Such announcements of closure are not unilateral declarations of closure, but rather proposals for closure as a next activity. In this extract, Karen's next turn (*Okay love*) accepts the proposed closure and at the same time is treated in the talk as the first element of a pre-closing sequence. However, it is not always the case that such an announcement of closure will be followed by a paired pre-closing sequence, and cases such as (6) can be found.

(6) [BD:II:6]

```
    Bee:    W' ll honey I' ve gotta go an get to this
            meeting.
    Dee:    Oka:y
    Bee:    Bye bye
    Dee:    Bye:
```

In this case, the announcement of closure is being treated as a pre-closing component in its own right and the closure is achieved by a pre-closing SPP followed by a terminal exchange. The pre-closing nature of such utterances is derived from their passing up of opportunities for further talk: the announcement of closure proposes that for the speaker there are no further mentionables which s/he feels relevant for inclusion in the conversation at this time. The following response can then be treated as a pre-closing component through which the recipient of the announcement also passes up the opportunity to introduce further talk. That is, in the extract above, Dee's *oka:y* does more than accept the announcement, it also expresses a stance towards that announcement: she too displays she has no more talk which she feels has to be included in the current conversation and that closure could now happen. It is equally possible for the pre-closing nature of the announcement to be rejected by a recipient, as in (7).

(7) [MF:2:IV]

```
    Fay:    Okay, w' ll I' ve gotta go.
    May:    Jus' before you do, =have yuh deci:ded about
            what you' re doin' Fri:day,
```

Here, rather than preceding to closure, May resists the trajectory established and raises a further mentionable which is relevant to the current conversation.

In many cases, the announcement of closure invokes the circumstances of the recipient of the announcement, as in the case of (8).

(8) [Clay I 5]

Mary:	and he' s going to come by himself I think
Hope:	Okay well I better let y' go now
Mary:	Alright
Hope:	Okay
Mary:	By:e Hope
Hope:	Bye

Here, Hope proposes closure with an inexplicit formulation of some external need for her recipient to terminate the conversation. Her turn is designed not to express her own needs or desires, but rather as an obligation to consider her recipient's needs or desires.

Announcements of closure are often designed specifically for the conversation in which they occur and may reintroduce material which has been raised earlier in the talk as a warrant for closing the conversation. This is the case with Bee's *I've gotta go an get to this meeting* in extract (6) above, which had been mentioned earlier in the talk. In fact the formulation of the meeting as *this meeting* is an explicit invocation of the meeting as mutually known information at this point in the conversation. Speakers can also invoke recipients' issues from earlier in the talk, as in (9).

(9) [Clay II 5]

Mary:	Okay w' ll I' ll let you get back to y' r tee vee then,
Hope:	Okay
Mary:	Bye bye
Hope:	Bye .

While announcement of closure is an explicit way in which a speaker may move a conversation to closure, the majority of closures do not seem to result from such announcements, but rather are done through closing implicative environments which make closure relevant, but without talking explicitly about closure as a relevant activity.

Arrangements

Arrangements for some future interaction between participants are very commonly found as the last topic in conversation and after an arrangement a conversation may proceed very quickly to closing (Button, 1991b; Schegloff and Sacks, 1973), as in extract (10).

```
(10) [JH:5:09–22]
     Julie:    .hh Yeah hh. (.) b' d I really won' know much
               more ' n that until Kris gives me a call tuh
               say wha' she' s gonna do.
               (0.2)
     Julie:    Then I' ll know more aboud it.
               (0.2)
     Helen:    Yeah.
               (0.2)
  →  Helen:    So lemme know w' ts happenin' when yih know.
  →  Julie:    Yeah okay I' ll call yuh then.
     Helen:    Okay:
     Julie:    Okay
     Helen     Bye [ bye
     Julie:         [ bye::
```

The achievement of closing after an arrangement occurs because of properties of arrangements as conversational actions. First, arrangements provide for a linking between the current conversation and future conversations and as such they orient to the potential vulnerability of conversational closing for social relationships. Moreover, the invoking of an arrangement implies that the next encounter between the participants will be orderly rather than accidental and is designed to show that a future encounter is both expected and desired by the participants (Button, 1991a). Secondly, because arrangements provide for a future encounter, they allow for closing of this current conversation by proposing that other potential topics for talk could be held over until the next conversation (Button, 1987). These two properties allow arrangements to be oriented to a closing implicative and for speakers to initiate closing talk as a next action on the completion of an arrangement.

Formulating summaries

One possible activity that conversationalists may engage in during talk is to talk about the talk so far: that is, they may formulate a summarized version of the talk which characterizes what has been happening in the talk so far (Garfinkel and Sacks, 1970). While these formulations may have a range of conversational functions (Heritage and Watson, 1979), one outcome of formulations is to provide a possible conclusion to the topic in progress by producing a characterization of the talk as a whole. Such formulations present the talk as a thing which is potentially complete to the point where it can be now talked about as a bounded event and if the formulation is accepted as an accurate formulation by other participants, it can be treated as a proposal that the talk under way could be concluded (Button, 1991a). Where there is agreement about the formulation, conversations may move to a close, as in (11).

(11) [WPH:5 (Button, 1991a)]
```
 →  Phil:    We::ll what I've been saying to you for the
 →           last ten minutes is that I don't like him.
 →           Yeah?
 →  Jack:    Uh-huh
    Phil:    Okay Jack
    Jack:    Okay
    Phil:    By[e
    Jack        [Goodbye.
```

Here, Phil's formulation of his own talk summarizes the gist of his talk so far and is accepted by Jack's *uh-huh*, which accepts formulation and does not add further talk on the topic in progress, and after this Phil begins a pre-closing proposing no further talk in this conversation. A similar role is played by assessments, which rather than summarizing the gist of the talk so far, characterize what has been said in a particular way. Where the assessment receives a next-turn assessment which affirms this characterization, the conversation may then move to closing, as in (12).

(12) [TS3:9]
```
    Tom:     and then we have to repeat the whole thing
             over again
 →  Sally:   It's silly
 →  Tom:     Yeah really silly
    Sally:   h. Alright
    Tom:     Okay Sal
    Sally:   Bye
    Tom:     Bye
```

Appreciations

In telephone conversations, appreciations for the call are also closing implicative. Like summaries, they have a bounding function because they design a segment of talk as potentially complete.

> (13) [Phone12:9]
> ```
>       Lucia:    Okay I' ll talk to yuh later
>   →   Fatima:   Yeah thanks for calling
>       Lucia:    Okay
>       Fatima:   Okay
>       Lucia:    Bye
>       Fatima:   Bye
> ```

An appreciation for the call after a period of time talking implies that the call has in some way reached a conclusion, because the appreciation only becomes relevant once the activity has been completed. Once a call has been appreciated, such an appreciation therefore counts as a proposal that for one of the participants there is no relevant future talk for this current conversation and that the conversation may now be completed and can move to closing.

Sequence-closing sequences

As was seen in a previous chapter, sequence-closing sequences are strongly topic-bounding and as such they may serve as the final action in a conversation before the initiation of a closing. Where sequence-closing sequences occur as a preliminary to closing, they are commonly initiated by a closing implicative action such as formulating a summary, as in (14) and (15).

> (14) [Phone1:2]
> ```
>   →   Peter:    So maybe somethin' ll turn up=
>   →   Bob:      =Yeah yeh never know when somthin' ll turn up
>   →   Peter:    °Yeah°
>                 (.)
>       Bob:      hh. Okay.
>       Peter:    Okay.
>       Bob:      G' bye
>       Peter:    Bye.
> ```

> (15) [Phone2:5]
> ```
>       Mark:     so I' m not gunna do anythin' about it now
> ```

```
Rob:      yea:::[hh
Mark:          [ °y:::e[::h°
Rob:                   [°yeah.°
          (0.2)
Mark:     Alright then.
Rob:      Okay
Mark:     Bye:
Rob:      B' bye.
```

In these cases, the sequence-closing sequence works to close down a topic and prepare the way for another action. This action could be talk on a new topic or it could be the passing up of this talk. If no new topic is generated, the talk naturally moves to closure.

Back references

Back references to material that has already been talked about may be found as the last topical talk before a closing. This is especially true of arrangements which are frequently reintroduced at the end of a conversation. The inclusion of prior material in the emerging talk may indicate that the possible new mentionables in the conversation have been exhausted at this point and there is nothing new to be introduced into the conversation, as the talk is not dealing with new items but with items already discussed. This means that a back reference passes up an opportunity to introduce something new into the talk and makes closing a potentially relevant next action. Back references to arrangements are strongly closing implicative as they additionally take on the closing implicative nature of arrangements.

```
(16) [House 5:8]
    Grant:    Then I wanna be able to do somethin' 'bout
              paintin' it
    Phil:     Yeah yuh need ta paint it
              (0.3)
    Phil:     So we'll meet up on Saturday
    Grant:    Yeah Saturday night
    Phil:     At seven
    Grant:    Yeah
    Phil:     Okay
    Grant:    Okay
    Phil:     See yuh
    Grant:    Bye
```

Back references to reasons for telephone calls are also strongly closing implicative as such a reference late in the conversation presents the call as having achieved its goals and therefore being potentially concluded for the caller who initiated the conversation.

(17) [Wentworth 2:2]
```
Mary:    Anyway I just called to see you what was
         happening
Mark:    Okay
Mary:    Okay
Mark:    Bye
Mary:    Bye
```

Moving out of closing

Not all closing implicative environments move to closing and not all closings, once they are initiated, succeed in bringing a closing to completion. An important consideration for closings is that they have to be negotiated between participants in a conversation. This allows for the fact that while one participant is prepared to close a conversation, other participants may still wish to offer further talk and, rather than moving to close the conversation, they may move out of the closing sequence to continue the conversation, as in (18).

(18) [Reef 5:3:6]
```
    Betty:    Yes. So I told that tuh somebuddy yeh know
              an' 'z I said I didn' t think it' d happen no:w
              but it did.
    Lisa:     Yeah.
→   Betty:    Okay
→   Lisa:     So we' ll see you Thursday then
    Betty:    Yeah Thursday after work
    Lisa:     At the café
    Betty:    Yeah
```

   In this extract, Lisa and Betty have bounded a conversation in their first two turns after Betty formulates a summary of her talk and Lisa accepts this. Betty then produces a first pre-closing component *okay*; however, instead of this receiving a second pre-closing component, Lisa produces a back reference to an arrangement, which leads to further talk and the closing is broken off. In this extract, the conversation initiates a closing, but the participants then move out of the closing sequence and begin new talk (Button, 1987). What happens in moving out of closing, then, is that a turn is found in a slot which could normally be occupied by a closing-related component (that is, a pre-closing component or a terminal component) and the deployment of such a turn cancels the trajectory of the closing. When participants move out of a closing, they cancel the relevance of the closing which had previously been proposed and to close the conversation at some later point a new closing sequence must be initiated. The closing work done earlier in the conversation is disregarded and it is not assumed by participants that if a closing was offered earlier in the conversation that the offer still exists once there has been a move out of the closing (Button, 1987).

Moving out may lead to a brief prolongation of the conversation, where a closing is re-established very soon after the moving out, or it may lead to much longer talk. A new closing can quickly re-establish where the talk which results from the moving out is itself closing implicative and no further work needs to be done to re-establish a closing; however, where the new talk is not closing implicative more talk is required to come to the point of closing. Button (1987, 1991b) characterizes these types of moving out as either minimal (where a participant moves out to a closing implicative action) or drastic (where participants move out to talk that is not closing implicative). He further makes the point, however, that whether or not a closing is quickly re-established or a moving out is followed by a significant amount of talk before a closing is re-established is the result of the unfolding inter-action and is not determined entirely by the nature of the interactional activity that participants move out to (Button, 1991b).

Locations for moving out

It is possible to move out of closing at any point in a closing sequence. The earliest point at which a moving out can occur is after the first pre-closing component. At this point in the talk, one participant has pro-posed closing by passing up an opportunity to introduce a new men-tionable, and provides a slot for another participant to do the same; however, rather than passing up the turn, this participant produces further talk, as in the case of (19), where the *okay* is followed by an arrangement.

```
(19) [TJT: 4:5]
     John:     Yeah n tha' s wha' I called t' tell yuh.
               (0.2)
 →   John:     Jist so y' d know if y' sa:w him.
     Tina:     Okay
 →   John:     So I' ll see you Friday
     Tina:     Yeah
```

It is also possible for a moving out to occur after the second pre-closing component. This means that although both participants indicate that they have no further talk to contribute in the current conversation, rather than proceeding to closure, a belated bit of additional talk is introduced, as in (20).

```
(20) [GATT: 4:5]
        Gina:     So that's goo::d
        Anna:     Yeah
        Gina:     Okay
        Anna:     Okay
   →    Gina:     I just thought I'd call to let you know
        Anna:     Okay
```

Further talk may also be introduced after the conversation has moved to termination by the introduction of talk after the first terminal component, as in (21).

```
(21) [PP II: 4:15]
        Pam:      Okay
        Penny:    Okay
   →    Pam:      Bye
   →    Penny:    Don't forget to pick me up on Saturday
        Pam:      No I won't
        Penny:    Okay
```

Finally, participants may move out of a closing sequence even after the final terminal component has been produced. In this case the talk is really relaunching a conversation which has been terminated rather than moving out of the closing sequence. When this happens the moving out turn is usually marked as having been suddenly remembered and this shows that in some ways relaunching a conversation after its termination is potentially accountable.

```
(22) [GHFT 7:1]
        Pete:     Okay
        Marty:    Okay
        Pete:     See ya
        Marty:    By[:e
   →    Pete:         [Oh, by the way, I forgot to tell you about
                  what happen tuh Mary.
```

Here, Pete's *oh* marks a 'discovery' of a new mentionable together with an account for introducing the tellable at this point in the conversation as a misplaced item of talk. These moving out turns are most common in face-to-face interaction where closure of the conversation does not lead to a breaking of the channel of communication. However, these may be attempted in telephone calls as in (23).

```
(23)  [GOffice]
          Fay:      Okay
          Carol:    Okay
          Fay:      Bye bye
          Carol:    Bye
    →    Fay:      O:h, CAROLE DO[N' T HANG uh –
                                [((click))
```

Here's Fay's discovery *o:h* is followed by loud talk involving an attempt to re-establish attention with a summons naming, *CAROLE*, and an attempt to prevent the closure of the communication, although her the attempt is unsuccessful.

Typical sequences found in moving out

Arrangements

Arrangements are very common in moving out and they may overspill into the closing of a conversation if the arrangement occupied a turn prior to the closing. In this case, the arrangement continues as a topic after one of the participants has offered a closing (Button, 1991b).

```
(24)  [TLAS:1107]
          Angie:    Well I' ll talk to you about it tomorrow then
          Tony:     Yeah
          Angie:    Right
          Tony:     Okay
          Angie:    By[e
    →    Tony:        [I' m looking f (h)orward t (h)o it
          Angie:    Me too:.
          Tony:     Okay
          Angie:    Alright
          Tony      Bye
          Angie;    Bye
```

An arrangement which was not the topic of the turns preceding the closing may be reintroduced in the closing itself.

```
(25) [Reef 5:3:6]
     Betty:     Yes. So I told that tuh somebuddy yeh know
                an' 'z I said I didn't think it'd happen no:w
                but it did.
     Lisa:      Yeah.
  →  Betty:     Okay
  →  Lisa:      So we'll see you Thursday then
     Betty:     Yeah Thursday after work
     Lisa:      At the café
     Betty:     Yeah
     Lisa:      Okay then
     Betty:     A' right
```

After an arrangement is produced as a moving out, the participants may move to close the conversation immediately, as an arrangement is a closing implicative environment. Such a moving out can be said to be minimal – it doesn't relaunch the conversation, although it does delay the closing. In extract (25), however, the reintroduction of the arrangement leads to four turns of arrangement talk before the closing is re-established.

Back references
Material which has been a previous topic of this conversation may be reintroduced in moving out.

```
(26) [Green 9:1]
     Joan:      and then there's nothing more to do
     Brett:     Yeah
                (.)
     Brett:     hhh. Okay
     Joan:      O:kay
  →  Brett:     I hope you get everything sorted out
     Joan:      Yeah it's a mess an' I've got s:o much to do now
```

Back references may not be closing implicative, so while they are found in moving out, they do not lead directly to re-entering a closing. What happens here is that a back reference re-topicalizes material drawn from earlier in the conversation. The next turn may now continue this topic in a manner which does not provide a closing implicative environment.

```
(27) [Green 9:1]
     Joan;      O:kay
     Brett:     I hope y' get everythin' sorted out
```

```
Joan:    Yeah it's a mess an' I've got s:o much to do
         now
Brett:   Can you get any help with it
Joan:    Dunno, b' Kate said she c'd do somethin' but
         she's only around on Mondays
Brett:   Yeah
Joan:    But I mi:ght be able to get Terry in to help
         out
Brett:   Yeah he c'd do it.
Joan:    s-So there are possibilities
→ Brett: Yeah it sounds like yer not left on yer own
Joan:    Yea:h
Brett:   Oka:[::y
Joan:        ['Kay
Brett:   Bye
Joan:    Bye
```

Here the talk continues on topic until Brett's formulation allows a new closing implicative environment, which then proceeds to a closing section which is completed.

Topic initial elicitors

A topic initial elicitor is an object which is designed to generate a new topic (Button and Casey, 1984). Topic initial elicitors explicitly provide a space for launching any mentionables which have not yet been included in the conversation and at the same time signal that the speaker is available for further talk in the conversation although s/he may have no available mentionables to continue the talk.

```
(28) [Grace 9:1]
     Diane:   So you'll come on Thursday then
     Helen:   Yeah=
     Diane:   =Okay
              (0.2)
→    Helen:   Anything else happening,
```

These objects signal availability for talk, but do not present a specific item for the next speaker to talk about. These things are quite interesting because they are oriented to the fact that a closing would be relevant at this point, but they also allow scope for a drastic movement out of a closing. There are two ways in which these topic initial elicitors can be treated in the conversation. First, the next speaker can use the turn to introduce a new topic which can lead to subsequent talk about the topic.

(29) [Grace 9:1]
```
      Diane:    =Okay
                (0.2)
→  Helen:    Anything else happening,
→  Dianne:   Oh yeah=I saw Grace the other day
      Helen:    Yea:h, how is she
      Dianne:   She's f-fine she looks a bit tired still but
                she's fine
      Helen:    'S good
```

In this case the moving out is drastic and potentially leads to extended talk on the topic before a closing is re-established. Alternatively, the next speaker may use the turn to decline to initiate a new topic. This means that the next speaker has passed up an opportunity to introduce a new mentionable in the conversation and that further talk is not necessary in this conversation. Following a decline, therefore, the closing may be reinitiated and the moving out is minimal, as closing becomes a relevant next activity on completion of the topic-seeking sequence.

(30) [Home 1]
```
      Tracy:    . . . but it's okay now=
      David:    =Yeah (.) °good°
→  Tracy:    Anthin' else
→  David:    No nothin's happening
      Tracy:    Ok:ay.
      David     Okay
      Tracy     Bye
      David:    Bye
```

Topic initial elicitors therefore allow for both a drastic movement out of a closing by providing opportunities to introduce a new topic which will occasion further talk or they may occasion minimal movements because, when a decline is produced, closure again becomes relevant, as both participants to the conversation have signalled that they have no further talk to introduce.

In-conversation objects

In-conversation objects are objects which are used to mark the receipt of prior talk and to provide for the speaker to continue (Button, 1987). They show that the speaker is available for talk and remains in the conversation, although s/he is not offering any new material for talk in the conversation.

(31) [Gail 1]
```
      Gail:    .hhh We' ll have a coffee.
      Shir:    Okay
→     Gail:    Mmhmm?
      Shir:    An' then we' ll go and get that book.
```

These sorts of objects can also be found where a closing-related component would be expected and therefore constitute a moving out of the closing. When this happens, rather than continue with the closing the next speaker may provide new material for the conversation. This means that the speaker is orienting to these tokens as signalling that the prior speaker is 'in-conversation' and is available for further talk and produces the talk required to continue the conversation, which may become quite extended before a closing is re-established, as in (32).

(32) [KS:SH:II]
```
      Kylie:   . . . and then we can get some m:ore of those
               picnic things a' the market.
      Sally:   Yeah.
      Kylie:   Okay?
→     Sally:   Uh::::m,
      Kylie:   Cos' they were really good.
      Sally:   Yeah an' so chea:p too.
      Kylie:   An' I could do with more y' know,
      Sally:   Yeah, they' re like always handy.
      Kylie:   Well then I' ll see yuh Sa' day.
      Sally:   Yeah see yuh then.
      Kylie:   Okay.
      Sally:   Okay.
      Kylie:   By:[:e,
      Sally:      [ Bye
```

In-conversation objects work in a similar way to topic initial elicitors. They do not offer any new material, but they indicate that the speaker is available for further talk. This means that they may occasion drastic movement if the next speaker chooses to produce more talk on the topic, and closing is therefore no longer relevant at that point in the conversation. Unlike topic initial elicitors, which are closing implicative if they are declined, in-conversation objects do not seem to be closing implicative as they simply signal continuation rather than enquire about the availability of topics for talk (Button, 1987) and rejection of an in-conversation object does not have the same unequivocal status of passing up an opportunity to introduce new material as has a topic initial elicitor.

(33) [KS:NB:I]
```
        Kylie:    Call me when you get in woncha?
        Norm:     Yeah.
        Kylie:    Okay then, Norm
        Norm:     'Kay
    →   Kylie:    Uh:m,
                  (0.4)
        Kylie:    So have a safe trip.
        Norm:     Yeah.
        Kylie:    An a goo' time.
        Norm:     Sure will.
        Kylie:    Right.
        Norm:     Alright.
        Kylie:    Bye bye
        Norm:     Bye
```

In extract (33), Norm does not continue with talk after Kylie's *u:hm* and in so doing passes up on further talk following the in-conversation object. While Kylie signals that she is still in the conversation, Norm's silence is a declining of further participation at this point. However, here the declining does not lead to closure and after a pause Kylie continues with further talk.

Solicitudes

Solicitudes are often found in closings and result in a movement out of the closing with the next speaker making some sort of response to the solicitude. This response is usually a minimal turn accepting the solicitude.

(34) [YS:LL]
```
        Lynn:     I'll see you soon
        Yvonne:   Okay Lynn=
        Lynn:     Okay
    →   Yvonne:   Have a good trip
    →   Lynn:     I: will hh.
        Yvonne:   Okay
    →   Lynn:     Okay give my love to Steve
    →   Yvonne:   Yeah I will
        Lynn:     Okay
        Yvonne:   Oka:[y
        Lynn:         [Byebye
        Yvonne:   Bye
```

Solicitudes usually constitute a minimal moving out of the closing as the closing will be reinitiated after the solicitude is completed. This is not always the case, however, and some solicitudes may be elaborated to such a point that a minimal response is no longer appropriate.

```
(35) [MK 2:IV]
       Mandy:    Yeah I' ll tell you what happens when I see
                 yuh
       Bryan:    .hh Okay
       Mandy:    Awrigh'
       Bryan:    [ Bye
  →    Mandy:    [ An' be careful drivin' home. Tom says the
  →              traffic' s real bad out there 'n' with the rain
  →              'n' all. In fac' he said he saw 'n accident on
  →              the way home.
       Bryan:    Yeah there' ll be a lot uh those tunight
                 [ I guess
       Mandy:    [ Yeah 's bad out now
       Bryan:    Yeah
       Mandy:    Okay so take care
       Bryan:    Yeah
       Mandy:    Okay
       Bryan:    A' righ' Mandy
       Mandy:    Bye,
       Bryan:    Bye
```

Reasons for call

Reasons for call may be reintroduced in closings and they may lead to turn on the topic by the next speaker or, as they are closing implicative, they may be followed by the initiation of the closing. Reasons for call usually produce a minimal move out of the closing.

```
(36) [GATT: 4:5]
       Gina:    So that' s goo::d
       Anna:    Yeah(h)
       Gina:    h-Kay
       Anna:    Okay
  →    Gina:    I just thought I' d call to let you know
       Anna:    Okay Gina,
       Gina:    Okay
       Anna:    Bye
       Gina:    Bye
```

Appreciations

An appreciation may refer either to an appreciation of a telephone call itself or it may refer to some other appreciable which is relevant to the conversation and both types may be found in moving out, although their sequential consequences appear to be different. In particular, an appreciation for the call may be inserted within a closing sequence without affecting the trajectory of the closing. Where this occurs, the closing continues as if no additional material has been inserted and closing does not have to be re-established. This means that the closing sequence becomes longer than the expected archetype of four components, but it remains a closing sequence.

```
(37) [Franco: I: 14:15]
       Clara:    Okay I' ll talk to yuh later
       Fran:     Yeah
       Clara:    Okay
   →   Fran:     Okay thanks for calling
       Clara:    Bye
       Fran:     Bye
```

This expanded but uninterrupted trajectory occurs where the appreciation is not acknowledged by the recipient. Where there is an acknowledgement, the closing is usually interrupted and the closing needs to be re-established, as in (38).

```
(38) [Franco: II: 14:15]
       Mavis:    Okay I' ll talk to yuh later
       Fran:     Yeah
       Mavis:    Okay
   →   Fran:     Okay thanks for calling
       Mavis:    I' s nice to talk to you.
       Fran:     Okay
       Mavis:    Okay
       Fran:     Bye
       Mavis:    Bye
```

Where the appreciation is a back reference to some other appreciable in the prior talk, the appreciation is typically acknowledged and produces a moving out of closing, after which the closing must be re-established.

```
(39) [Luisa]
       Rosa:     so I' ll talk to you about that later
       Luisa:    yeah sure
```

```
        Rosa:     okay
→      Luisa:     okay Rosa thanks again for picking up the
                  kids
        Rosa:     that's fine
        Luisa:    okay
        Rosa:     okay
        Luisa:    bye
        Rosa:     bye
```

Expanded closing sequences

It is possible for a closing sequence to be expanded in ways which are specific to a conversation and which do not constitute moving out for these conversations. This is the case in (40), a conversation between a couple who are living apart for work reasons.

```
(40) [Commute]
        Tom:      Talk to yuh tomorrow.
        Terry:    Okay.
        Tom:      Okay
→      Terry:     Love you.
→      Tom:       Love you too.
        Terry:    Bye.
        Tom:      Bye.
```

Here the endearments do not interrupt the closing and the pre-closing components are not redone before proceeding to the closing, rather these endearments seem to be included as a part of the leave-taking routine for these two participants in a particular conversational setting. The closing sequence is expanded by an endearment adjacency pair, which accomplishes interactional work for these participants, ratifying their ongoing relationship. This is a closing sequence designed by and for these recipients rather than being interactionally relevant for other participants or other conversations. Examples such as this highlight clearly that the sequential organization of conversational closing is achieved by participants rather than being a set routine through which all conversations must pass.

Conclusion

Conversational closings are interactionally delicate events which are achieved collaboratively by participants by deploying a set of sequential resources. These resources allow them to negotiate their respective orientations to the current conversation and to determine the relevance of continuation or closure of the conversation at various relevant points in the talk. The sequential structure of closings works to determine at various stages in the talk whether closing or continuing is the appropriate conversational undertaking and to allow possibilities for previously unmentioned mentionables to be raised in the talk. Closing, therefore, is achieved by passing up opportunities to do something other than closing rather than by providing specifically for closing as the activity which is currently being undertaken.

The interactional problem of extended turns

It was argued above that the basic organization of speaker change in conversation revolves around the first possible completion of a TCU as a transition relevance place – a place at which speaker change can legitimately occur. This feature of conversation produces an interactional problem for actions, such a telling stories and jokes, which by their nature cannot be completed in a single TCU and which must extend beyond the first possible completion if they are to be accomplished. The organization of speaker change would appear to make such actions impossible, as they would become vulnerable to speaker change before they could be completed. The interactional problem which faces speakers is how to create a space in which to undertake an action which requires an extended turn when the turn-taking system provides for the possibility of speaker change at the first possible completion of the TCU under way. This chapter will examine how speakers achieve orderly solutions to this interactional problem and create interactional spaces in which extended turns can be accomplished.

Stories

Stories in conversation are tellings which occur as multi-unit, extended turns at talk. They occur during interaction and their telling is accomplished collaboratively by the participants in the conversation. This means that the telling of a story is not simply the act of a speaker/narrator, but also the act of a story recipient. Moreover, stories do not occur incidentally in conversation, but rather are designed for the interaction in which they occur (Sacks, 1992). Stories are located within turn-by-turn talk. They are both preceded and followed by such talk. However, stories are not simply interruptions of turn-by-turn talk;

they articulate with it. They emerge from the turn-by-turn talk which precedes them and are also sequentially implicative for the turn-by-turn talk which follows them (Jefferson, 1978).

One important interactional issue for stories in conversation is how those stories come to be told. In some cases, stories may be told in response to a question by a prior speaker: that is, stories are elicited by the story recipient and their production is required as the answer SPP in an adjacency pair. In such contexts, the story recipient makes him/herself available as a story recipient by eliciting the story and the interactional work required of the story-teller to place the story in conversation is minimal. While some studies of story-telling have been based on such elicited stories (e.g. Labov and Waletsky, 1966), elicited stories are not the usual way stories are introduced into everyday conversation. Many stories are introduced by the tellers themselves, who have to deal with the interactional problems associated with placing a story in conversation and securing a recipient for the story.

In telling their story, story-tellers also have to deal with the legitimacy of the story for the current conversation. Story-tellers take a risk in that their story may not be accepted as relevant or newsworthy. Hearers' responses may be 'So what?' or 'What's the point?' (Labov and Fanshell, 1977; Polanyi, 1979; Sacks, 1992). The main constraint on whether or not a story may be legitimate in a particular conversation is that the story is unknown and of potential interest to the story recipient. If the story is unknown and of potential interest, the story is tellable in that conversation. A story which is tellable in one conversation may not be equally tellable in another because the story may already be known or the circumstances of the story may be inappropriate for a particular participant (Sacks, 1986).

Beginning and ending stories

The study of a story in conversation is not simply the study of the turn in which the story occurs. In order to understand how stories are placed in conversation it is important to examine the talk preceding the story itself, as much important and relevant interactional work is done before the story-telling itself. In addition, because stories are sequentially implicative, the interactional relevance of stories does not end with the end of the story turn, but continues into the following turns at talk. This means that the analysis of beginnings and endings of stories begins before the story is told and ends after the story turn has finished.

Stories are produced by reference to the talk which precedes them; that is, they are locally occasioned by the emerging turn-by-turn talk. Jefferson (1978) argues that this local occasioning has two possible trajectories:

1. the prior talk may remind a participant of a particular story, which may or may not be topically coherent with the turn-by-turn talk;
2. a story may be methodically introduced into the talk.

Where the teller is reminded of the story, it is usually preceded by a disjunct marker such as *oh, by the way* or *incidentally* (cf. Jefferson, 1978). This is shown in extract (1):

```
(1) [Lunch]
    Harry:    . . . an then c' d you send those up to Jane and
              Mar[y,
 → Joy:          [Oh: tha' r-, did you hear what happened
              to Ja::ne.
    Harry:    What?
    Joy:      She w' s working back late a couple a nights
              ago an' she heard this sound outside her
              office, [ Story]
```

In this extract, the *oh:* marks Joy's talk as having been triggered by Harry's prior talk and that the prior reference to Jane has recalled a possible tellable about her. At the same time, it marks a disjunction between the topic of Harry's talk and Joy's which has been prompted by the discovery of the possible telling. It is also possible that something outside the talk itself may prompt recall of a possible tellable, as in (2).

```
(2) [J:FN (Jefferson, 1978)]
              ((Three people walking together; someone
              passes them wearing a photograph teeshirt))
    Nettie:   Oh that teeshirt reminded me [ Story]
```

In extract (3), the story is topically coherent with the prior talk and is not marked as being triggered by the prior talk. Rather, the topic has been introduced methodically through the prior turns.

```
(3) [Park]
    Sue:      So whaddid yuh end up doin' on Sunday.
 → June:      We decided to have a picnic in the park.
    Sue:      Yeah?
```

```
        June:     Yeah. (I w' s fun.)
     →  Sue:      Yeah. I' s a great place for a picnic.
        June      Yeah.
                  (.)
     →  Sue:      Yeah. We went there f' r a picnic once an' i'
                  was the wo:rst.
        June:     What happened?
        Sue:      Well it looked like I was going to be a grea:t
                  day, i' w' z sunny n everything and we thought
                  it would be nice there by the river ...
                  [Story]
```

Here, Sue's question elicits the first mention of picnicking in the park, which is taken up by Sue in her later turn-by-turn talk before being introduced by Sue as a story preface, and eventually as the story. Here there is no sudden remembering of an event occasion by the prior talk, but rather continuing talk about the topic with frequent repetitions of the key elements *picnic* and *park*. These repetitions are embedded into the emerging talk and serve to locate the element of prior talk which has occasioned the story (Jefferson, 1978). It is also possible that both devices will be found in the emergence of a single story, as in (4).

```
(4) [Schenkein:I:7 (Jefferson, 1978)]
     Ellen:    tuh relax er during this last illness, on top
               of the antibiotics.
               (1.0)
  →  Ben:      W-well on top a' thee, cough medicine.
  →  Ellen:    Yeah, and the cough medici- incidentally.
               Did I tell you?
     Ben:      No.
     Ellen:    That the d- he told us to give Snookie
  →            a third of a teaspoon of uh: cough medicine.
               Cheracol, is there a- Is there a
               cou[gh me[dicine call' Cherac' l=
     Bill:        [Yeah.
     Ben:              [Yeah,
     Ellen:    =.hhh We happen' tuh have Vic' s Four Forty
               [Story]
```

Here, Ben's mention of cough medicine is followed up by a topically coherent embedded repetition of cough medicine in the next line, which is interrupted by a disjunct marker and the tellable for the story is introduced as having been triggered by the mention of cough syrup.

Both devices for introducing stories into talk involve indicating that the story is in some way relevant to the prior talk, either because it develops the turn-by-turn talk or because some element of the turn-by-turn talk has prompted the recall of the prior talk. These devices then deal with issues related to the relevance of a story at a particular point in a conversation; however, there is more involved in telling a story in conversation than the legitimacy of the story at a point in the unfolding talk. The story-teller needs also to undertake work to secure an interactional space in which the extended story turn can be told. Stories are usually preceded by a type of pre-telling, usually called a *story preface* (Sacks, 1992). Like other pre-tellings, story prefaces deal with issues of the tellability of a particular story. However, they perform additional interactional work. A speaker who wishes to tell a story requiring an extended turn not only has to deal with the issue of tellability, that is, whether or not the story can be told in this particular conversation, but also must deal with the interactional problem of securing the space in which to tell the story if it is a tellable. Story prefaces also deal with this problem. As with other pre-sequences, story prefaces consist of two turns at talk: the first by the intending teller, the second by the intended recipient (Sacks, 1974). The first turn projects a forthcoming story and the second turn aligns its speaker as a story recipient. Once these two turns have been completed, if the next speaker gives a go ahead response, s/he positions him/herself as a story recipient for this story (Jefferson, 1978). This means that the canonical form of a story beginning involves a three-turn structure:

1. a first turn with the story preface in which the story-teller projects a forthcoming story and indicates a position in the conversation as a potential story-teller;
2. a second turn in which another participant aligns as the story recipient;
3. a third turn in which the story is told.

Chapter 6 examined some formulaic pre-tellings which are also potentially usable as story prefaces; these are given again in (5):

(5)

guess	what	
(do) you know	who	± information
remember	when	
	where	

Story prefaces with question forms like *do you know what?* and *guess what?* are very effective ways of securing the next turn for a story because they are designed to get an SPP answer which is also a question: *what?*. They therefore require further talk from the speaker of the original question and provide not only for an opportunity to talk, but for an obligation to do so (Sacks, 1992: I: 256–7). However, many story prefaces do not have these formulaic forms but rather are designed for a specific story in a specific interaction. In addition, story prefaces may also include formulaic turns, such as:

(6)	did you hear about did I tell you about	+information

Where these forms are used, a *no* answer indicates that the story being proposed is a tellable in the conversation and orients to the issue of telling unknowns. This can be seen in extract (7), in which the *no* response leads directly to a story.

```
(7) [Gina and Hal]
    Gina:      ↑OH, did I tell you about what happened to me
               on Friday night?
    Hal:       No:.
    Gina:      [ Story]
```

If the information is unknown then the story is potentially tellable; however, if the story is known then it cannot be told in this conversation, as in (8).

```
(8) [Car conversation]
    Sasha:     an all- did he tell yuh about his problems
               with his wife an [ that
    Nick:                        [ yeah. oh I knew all about
               that anyway.
               (0.2)
    Nick:      an he's got this tattoo on his ↓che:st
```

Here, Nick's *yeah* means that Sasha's story about *his problems with his wife* is not a potential tellable for Nick and no story is produced. After a pause, Nick continues with related talk, but on a different topic.

Story prefaces may also be constructed using evaluative adjectives which characterize the nature of the story to be told, as in extracts (9) to (11).

(9) [S&S:1]
<pre>
    Sam: Someth' n' great happen' to me this morning.
    Sal: What?
    Sam: [Story]
</pre>

(10) [Trial]
<pre>
    Al: You wanna know th' wo:rs' thing th's ever
            happen to me?
    Ben: What¿
    Al: [Story]
</pre>

(11) [Dinner3]
<pre>
    Chris: You wanna hear something really amazing?
    Dan: What?
    Chris: [Story]
</pre>

In these cases, the go ahead response is *what* and in extracts (10) and (11) the *what* response is especially interesting because it replaces a possible *yes* response to the question. The *what* here orients quite strongly to the status of the prior turn as a story preface and the alignment of the speaker as a story recipient.

Story prefaces are not always formulaic, but may be designed in reference to a specific story and context as in the case of (12) and (13).

(12) [D:1:DC]
<pre>
    Donna: We h' d the worst weekend?
    Cath: What happened?
    Donna: [Story]
</pre>

(13) [G:26:5:53 (C. Goodwin, 1984)]
<pre>
    Ann: well- ((throat clear)) (0.4) we coulda used
            a liddle marijuana. tih get through the
            weekend.
    Beth: what h[appened.
    Ann: [[Story]
</pre>

Here the story preface takes the form of a formulation about an event which is unknown to the recipient and as such resembles a telling, although as a telling it is incomplete. The turn gives a small amount of information about an event, which could potentially allow the recipient to identify the event as known or unknown, and implies that there is more to be told about this event. The recipients' response *what happened?* indicates that the event is unknown and therefore tellable, and orients the speaker as a recipient for a story about the event.

Story prefaces may, therefore, be used to achieve a number of things relevant to the telling of a story:

1. they negotiate an interactional space in which the story can be told as a multi-unit turn;
2. they negotiate issues of tellability;
3. they provide some indication of roughly what the story is about.

All story prefaces are concerned with the first of these tasks and many are concerned with the second. However, prefaces of the sort *guess what?* provide little information which would be useful for a recipient to use in gauging whether the projected event was known or unknown. Those prefaces which include some evaluative information, such as the adjectives in extracts (9), (10), (11) and (12) or the evaluation implied by *we coulda used a liddle marijuana. tih get through the weekend* in extract (13), indicate roughly what the story is about. In so doing, these prefaces provide a type of interpretive framework which the recipient can use to understand the story and its import in the current conversation. These story prefaces, therefore, signal to the recipient roughly what it will take for the story to be completed and provide the recipient with a format in which to display that they have recognized the story as having been completed (Sacks, 1992: I: 766).

In opening an interactional space to allow for a multi-unit turn to be produced, story prefaces and their responses suspend the turn-taking system which allows for speaker change at the next possible completion. This suspension is temporary and the turn-taking system is restored on completion of the story. This raises a new interactional problem for participants: they need to be able to determine when the turn-taking system can legitimately be restored. As with the operation of the turn-taking system itself, this is also a question of completion. The turn-taking system is restored when participants recognize the story as being possibly complete. The recognizable completions of stories signal that a unit of talk is possibly complete, not because of the possible completion of a TCU, but because of the possible completion of a recognizable activity (Sacks, 1992: I: 682). Story prefaces play a role in this in that they may project roughly what it will take for the extended turn under way to be possibly complete (Sacks, 1992: II: 10). They do this when they characterize the story in some way. For example, a story about 'something wonderful' will not be seen to be properly complete until something occurs which is recognizable as 'wonderful'. In this way, the story preface provides a framework in which a recipient can attend to each next bit of the story as being possibly a final bit of the story.

On completion of a story, a response to the story from the recipient is relevant. This response firstly displays the recipient's understanding that the story is now over and secondly it involves a display of how the recipient has understood the story.

```
(14) [SSHHTJ:1:8]
     Heli:    [Story] an' now I just go li:ke all c-cold
              whenever I see a ssnake.
     Jo:      Sh::it Kerry I' da die::d.
```

Here, Jo's response displays an understanding that the prior story about encountering a snake at home was traumatic and shows a strong affective response. Where there is no response to the story, this is a noticeable absence and is repaired, as in (15), in which the speaker may solicit a relevant response (cf. Sacks, 1992: I: 766).

```
(15) [Pets]
     Tina:    [Story] but my father had to have her put
              down after.
              (0.2)
     Tina:    Wasn' that sa:d?
     Sally:   I' was awful.
```

In this extract Tina is telling a story about her pet dog who had to be destroyed. Her story is followed by a pause, after which she prompts an assessment from Sally. The lack of talk by Sally here is problematic, as she has failed to register the end of the story. Tina's question elicits an assessment which evaluates the story and in so doing shows a recognition that the story in now completed. In other cases, story-tellers may respond to such pauses by proposing that the story is incomplete at the pause and add a further component to the story as in (16).

```
(16) [Sue]
     Dina:    [Story] and in the end she got this really
              ugly bag th' t doesn' t go with anything.
              (0.4)
     Dina:    but she' s like so proud of it.
     Clara:   *o:h shi:t* that girl has no taste.
```

Here Dina's possible story ending is followed by a silence of 0.4 seconds after which she adds an increment to the turn, converting the pause from an inter-turn pause to an intra-turn pause. In so doing, the pause is converted from a missing response to the prior story to a pause during the ongoing story itself. After the added component, Clara produces a response which displays her understandings of the story and as the story as a now completed action.

(17) [JJ]
```
Jill:    [Story] an now I don' know what she's gonna
         do.
Jane:    O:H that's te:rr[ible.
Jill:                     [' S just awful.
```

In extract (17), Jane's turn includes an assessment *O:H that's terrible* which displays her understanding of the import of the telling of this story, an understanding which is ratified by Jill's assessment in the following line. Sometimes a recipient and a story-teller may not share the same understanding of the import of a story, as in extract (18). Here, A is relating to B a story of what happened when she advertised a house for rent.

(18) [(Sacks, 1992, II:10)]
```
A:    So I thought just for fun, I would uhm - uh,
      since I had this much time, I'd run a little
      ad myself?
B:    Uh huh,
A:    and maybe handle it myself if I could?
B:    Mm hm,
A:    and do you know I was just amazed, it was in
      last night, I was amazed at the responses I
      got.
B:    Mm hm,
A:    and uh its- I already have a (1.0) a deposit
      for it.
→ B:    Well good!
→ A:    Isn' t that something?
→ B:    Well I should say.
```

In this extract, Sacks (1992: II: 10) argues that B's *well good!* displays an understanding of the story as having been about how good it is to have rented the flat quickly. However, A's next turn displays a different understanding of the import of the story, as being something amazing rather than something good, and proposes a repair of B's understanding of the story. B repairs her understanding of the story in the next turn. An understanding of the story could potentially be developed from a hearing of the talk which makes up the story, however story prefaces not only provide information about what the story might contain but also provide a resource for designing the recipient's response to a story. A story about 'something wonderful' requires a response that shows the recipient's understanding of the event as 'wonderful'.

Jefferson (1978) has noted that recipients' talk after a story may be either directly continuous with and fitted to the story or may be tangential to the story. Where the talk is continuous there is no problem, as issues of understanding have been dealt with in the talk. However, where the talk is tangential it is potentially problematic as a display of understanding. Jefferson notes that in cases of tangential talk, storytellers do not explicitly challenge such talk, but rather propose that the story is not yet completed by adding further talk to the story.

```
(19) [Labov:T.A.:4r (Jefferson, 1978)]
     Rita:      She didn' have time tuh cook yesterday she
                got home la:te,
                (0.4)
     Rita:      So ah met' er et (Promtiers).
                (0.2)
     Rita:      She had a:, (0.3) a broi:led hambuhrger,
                (0.6) with no gravy awnit, (0.5) She hadda
                serving of cabbage, 'n she hadda salad.
                (0.3)
a→  Marge:     Very- It' s terrific I
                bec[ause I' m telling yih-]
b→  Rita:         [En   she   couldn'  ev] en fini-sh
                                          [:: i(h)t,]=
     Marge:                                [ There' s ]
     Marge:     =E:vrybody' s e[couraging[ her there. ]
c→  Rita:                        [enna cupp[ a ca:wfee. ]
```

Here, Marge initiates tangential talk at arrow a, after the story has reached a possible completion. In overlap, Rita produces a further component of the story *En she couldn' ev]en fini-sh[:: i(h)t*, during which Marge's tangential talk continues, at arrow c. Rita adds a further component to the story, backing up the list of things which the women being discussed ate. This shows that stories have a relationship with the sorts of talk which follows them, just as they have a relationship with the talk which precedes them. Jefferson (1978) argues that the ends of stories are sequentially implicative in two ways:

1. they can be a source for topically coherent talk and
2. a range of techniques are used to display a relationship between
    the story and the subsequent talk.

This means that stories not only project possible trajectories of talk, but that participants in the talk orient to the relevance of such coherent talk in designing their further talk.

Story structure

Stories have internal structures which are interactionally relevant for the telling. Goodwin (1984) has described the internal sub-components of stories as interactionally accomplished elements which participants use as resources for structuring and understanding their participation in story-telling. The subcomponents of story structure are described by Goodwin through an investigation of the telling of the story in extract (20).

```
(20) [(C. Goodwin, 1984)]
  1              (0.4)
  2  Ann:     well- ((throat clear)) (0.4) we coulda used
  3           a liddle marijuana. tih get through
  4           the weekend.
  5  Beth:    what h[appened.
  6  Ann:          [Karen has this new hou:se. en it's got
  7           all this like- (0.2) ssilvery:: g-go:ld
  8           wwa:llpaper,.hh (h)en D(h)o(h)n sa(h)ys,
  9           y' know this is th' first time we've seen this
 10           house.=fifty thousn dollars in Cherry
 11           Hill.=right?
 12              (0.4)
 13  Beth:    uh hu:h?
 14  Ann:     Do(h)n said. (0.3) dih-did they ma:ke you
 15           take this [ wa(h)llpa(h)p(h)er?
 16  Beth:              [ hh!
 17           er(h)di[dju pi(h)ck] =
 18  Beth:           [ Ahh huh huh] =
 19  Ann:     ={ [ i(h)t ou(h)t.
 20  Beth:    ={ [ huh huh huh  [ huh
 21  Don:                       [ uhh hih huh hu[h
 22  Ann:                                       [ UHWOOghgh
 23           HHH!= y' kno(h)w that wz
 24           [ like the firs' bad one.
 25  Beth:    [ uh:oh wo::w hh
 26              (0.2)
```

```
27  Don:   but I said it so innocuously y' know.
28  Ann:   yeh I'm sure they thought it wz- hnh hnh!
```

Goodwin (1984) has shown that this story has a basic internal structure made up of background information (lines 5–7) and a climax (lines 13–14) and this structure is interrupted at line 8, which begins a climax (*Do(h)n said.*) which is subsequently aborted and a parenthesis (lines 8–11) in which additional background information is inserted, before returning to the climax. This story is preceded by a story preface, in lines 1–2, and an acceptance of the preface in line 4. In the story, the background elements provide the necessary information that the recipient needs in order to be able to understand the climax as a climax, and to hear the climax as something relevant to the way in which the story is characterized in the story preface *we coulda used a liddle marijuana. tih get through the weekend,* that is a story about a problematic or difficult weekend. Sacks (1974, 1978) has made a similar observation about certain types of jokes which require a pattern to be established through the early talk in the joke in order to enable the punchline to be heard as humorous.

Goodwin (1984) argues that the division of the story into background and climax is oriented to by the participants as a resource for their participation in the story. Ann, the teller, marks the climax as distinctive by including laughter tokens. She does this in both the aborted attempt at the climax at line 8 and in the redoing of the climax at lines 13–14. In so doing she performs the climax differently from the background and as such interactionally displays the structuring of the story. She also indicates a dimension of the interpretive framework established by her story preface by indicating the story is to be heard as a humorous telling by deploying an invitation to laugh (Jefferson, 1979). In addition to this verbal marking of the story, Ann also marks the story structure non-verbally. She adopts a distinctive body position for the telling of the story with her hands clasped and her elbows placed on the table, while she leans forward and gazes at the recipient (Beth). She begins this position at the word *new* in line 5 and holds it until the word *out* in line 16 and as such holds this position for the duration of the story. She unclasps her hands during the parenthesis (lines 8–11) and then returns to the clasped hand position at the end of the parenthesis, ready to deliver the climax. There is similar marking in the pattern of eye gaze deployed by the teller and the recipient. In this extract, Ann secures Beth's gaze in the preface, as extract (21) shows:

(21) [(C. Goodwin, 1984)]
```
Ann:                                        . . . [ X_____
        Well- (- - -[-) we coulda used [ a liddle,
Beth:                      [ X_____
Ann:    _____                                    .[ X__
        =marijuana tih get through the wee[kend.
Beth:   _____
```

Here, Ann secures Beth's gaze as recipient for her talk, pausing after beginning her turn until eye gaze is established. However, during the background part of the story Beth withdraws her gaze and Anne does no interactional work to re-establish it.

(22) [(C. Goodwin, 1984)]
```
Ann:    _____
        Karen has this new hou:se. en it's got all this
Beth:   _____  , , ,         ((nod))
```

When Beth's gaze is withdrawn, the participants do not treat this as a violation of the rule that the teller should be speaking to a gazing recipient and there is no attempt to repair the lack of gaze. Instead the talk continues through the background of the story. Goodwin (1984) argues that gaze withdrawal is unproblematic at this point because of two features of the sequential organization of the talk. First, the recipient has already displayed recipiency for the story as a whole by gazing during the preface and the early part of the story and by explicitly requesting that the story be told through accepting the story preface. Secondly, the entry into an extended turn at talk has suspended the relevance of speaker transition at every next TCU and the gaze shift occurs at what is recognizably a first element rather than a last element in the talk. This means that the behaviours at this point indicate that participants are orienting to this part of the story as being in some way preliminary. Beth begins to do repair-oriented work for the gaze withdrawal just prior to the climax itself through a series of hitches and perturbations in her delivery of *silvery gold wallpaper*.

(23) [(C. Goodwin, 1984)]
```
Ann:    like- (0.2) ssilvery:: g-go:ld
        wwa:[llpaper,=
Beth:        [X_____
Ann:    =.hh (h)en D(h)o(h)n sa(h)ys,
Beth:   _____
```

Beth returns her gaze to Ann just before the beginning of the climax and continues to maintain her gaze through the laughter-marked delivery of the first try at the climax. In so doing, the participants orient to this talk as being different from the preceding talk and relevant to the possible completion of the extended turn at talk. However, this climax is aborted and the teller returns to relating background information and the recipient again withdraws her gaze from the speaker. Beth then requests greater engagement from her recipient with the tag question *right?* at line 10. In the new version of the climax, Beth accepts the invitation to laugh and in so doing displays her co-participation in the story-telling. Goodwin (1984) argues on the basis of this behaviour that the telling is organized by the actions of both the teller and the recipient and is not simply an accomplishment of the teller herself. In fact he further argues that the other participants in the conversation also orient to this story structure in the ways in which they coordinate their behaviours with the unfolding structure of Ann's talk.

The story structure which emerges is not a mechanical performance based on the emerging speech, but rather an interactional accomplishment of structure through the process of interaction. This means that interaction is precisely organized through systematic procedures that are not simply relevant to the talk but also play a role in constitution of the talk as a structured activity. The division of a story into background and climax is therefore an interactionally relevant story structure and some parts of the story will be heard by participants as talk which is incomplete as a telling and talk which is potentially complete, that is as a climax. The accomplishment of this structure through talk involves multiple TCUs in which talk is grammatically and intonationally complete, but which are not attended to by the participants as places at which speaker change is a relevant next action. Recipients in conversation routinely use devices which show their understanding of the talk under way as not complete. Continuers such as *mmhm* show that the story has been heard not yet to have reached a point of recognizable completion and that the recipient of the story is continuing his/her recipiency (Sacks, 1992: II: 9; Schegloff, 1982). Talk other than a continuer, especially assessments, show that the recognizable completion has been reached (Sacks, 1992: I: 766). Schegloff (1982) maintains that continuers such as *uh huh* both claim understanding of the talk under way and also display the nature of that understanding by declining to produce fuller talk in that position. Schegloff argues continuers are not so much turns at talk but rather cases of passing up turns at talk in order to display understanding of the action under way as not yet being complete. Continuers are heard as displays of continued states of recipiency in extended turns because they are hearable as the withholding of other possible forms of talk in such positions, especially as withholding repair initiation. That is, the deployment of a token such as *uh huh* or *mm hmm* demonstrates that no interactional work is required at this point in the unfolding talk to deal with problems of hearing and understanding. The withholding of repair indicates that the talk can proceed unproblematically. This in turn means that the accomplishment of a long turn at talk is not simply the production of such talk by a speaker, but also the continued orientation of a recipient to such production and the passing up of alternatives which could prevent the turn from continuing.

The discussion so far indicates that stories are interactionally accomplished actions which involve the collaboration of participants in the interaction in order to succeed. This means that stories in conversation are not simply the deployment of generic structures in the conversation, nor are they simply instances of teller's talk which can be analysed only as the linguistic production of a single participant in the interaction. However, stories also have a role in the development of further talk in the conversation and can have an affect beyond the turn in which they are produced.

Second stories

Sacks (1992: I: 706) has observed that 'given the telling of a story, other stories may be forthcoming'; however, it is also the case that not any story can follow any prior story. Next stories are characterizable as next stories in that they will have a shape determined by the prior story and they will be about something related to the prior story. Each story is constructed as being in second position to a prior story. Second stories are not second simply because they occur after first stories, they are also second in that they show relationships to first stories. That is, they show a relationship of relevance to the preceding story. These stories, therefore, not only do story-telling, but also are a way of showing understanding of a prior story. This relationship between first stories and second stories can be seen in the story beginning at line 32 in extract (24).

```
(24) [Melb:2]
  1  A:      We can' t decide whether we wanna go tuh
  2          Melb' ne or not fuh th' break.
  3  B:      O:↑h. Did I tell you wha' happened last time
```

```
4                    I went t' Melb' ne,
5    A:              Na:h wha' happen.
6    B:              Well we had a really a::wful time yuh know,
7                    i' was last March 'n John an' I decided we' d
8                    fly down, (w' ll) the plane left n' as we were
9                    takin' off well I started tuh get this fu:nny
10                   feelin' in my ears, [ and ] we were goin' up=
11   A:                                  [ mm?  ]
12   B:              =an' this feeling' just keeps gettin' wo:rse
13                   an wo:rse an it' s startin' to hu:rt.
14                   An' I said tuh John ↑there' s sumthin' wrong
15                   with the pla:ne. Well yuh know I' was the
16                   pressure an' air was lea:kin' [  out.] =
17   A:                                           [ yeah?]
18   B:              =An the pilot come on tuh say that we' re
19                   gunna hafta go back coz there' s this problem
20                   with the plane. So we turn back. and yuh know
22                   everyone is so sca:red,' n jus' holding their
23                   breath, hopin' that it would come out
24                   alright. Anyway we got back safe an we didn'
25                   need the oxygen masks 'r anything.
26                   But it was the worst trip of my life
27                   an' I sti:ll get nervous 'bout it when I get
28                   on planes.
29   A:              THat mus:t have been terrible.
30   B:              Yeah it was, but it came out alright.
31                   I mean yuh hear about much worse.
32→  A:              Yeah (I kno:w) I saw a story in the paper
33                   'bout a man who w' s almost sucked oudda the
34                   window of a pla[ne.
35   B:                             [hh.=
36   A:              =The window nexta him broke while
37                   they were flying an' the pressure sortta blew
38                   him through the hole,
39   B:              o:[:h¿]
40   A:                [An ] the person nexta him grabbed onta his
41                   legs an' lotsa other people too I think,
42                   an' they had tuh hold him until the plane
43                   could land (yih-) hanging outta the window
44                   all the time it musta been terrible but he
45                   got back alright, I guess he was pretty
                     lucky.
46   B:              Yeahh..
```

In this extract, there are two stories each about a problem occurring during an aeroplane flight. The first of the stories (lines 6–28) is a story of personal experience while the second (32–45) is a telling of a reported account of another's experience. The topics of the stories are similar and the second is triggered by the first. However, the similarity between second stories and prior stories is an interactionally achieved similarity (Sacks, 1992: II: 4–5). A recipient of a story has to show understanding of the story and needs to find something s/he can use in talk to do this. One way of doing this is to use 'things this reminds me of'; that is, to relate the story to elements of one's own personal experience. This means that when a recipient is listening to the teller, part of this listening will involve a search for some relationship between the story and one's own experience (Sacks, 1992: I: 768). In extract (24), the second story is framed as a reminder of a recalled story. The second story is designed as relevant to the first in that it takes as its topic problems occurring during flights, but is also tied to the story by the formulation *I mean yuh hear about much worse*. The story is simultaneously dealing with the topic developed by the prior talk and with the characterization of what something much worse could entail. The second story is also tied to the first at a level of greater detail in that both refer to instances of 'pressure' being the source of the problem and as the upshot of the story being characterized as *it came out alright* in the first story and as *he got back alright* in the second. As such, there are parallels of form as well as of content between the two stories (see also M. H. Goodwin, 1990).

Another feature of second stories is that they are often not preceded by interactional work to establish the story. In the case of extract (24), for example, the story is not launched by a story preface and accepting turn but rather in lines 32 onwards, the story begins immediately with an announcement of a reminding. Second stories do not need to announce the sort of action they are second to in order to be considered as cases of the activity to which they are second. They rely on their positioning after a prior activity and invoke the structure which has previously been made relevant. Second stories can therefore be simply delivered without the prior interactional work of establishing story-telling as a relevant activity in the conversation (Sacks, 1992: I: 683).

Stories of shared experience

Stories are not necessarily the work of a single speaker and other participants in the conversation may contribute to the talk (see for example, Ochs *et al.*, 1992; Sacks, 1974). It may be the case that others present at the telling were involved in the events related in the story, but even those who were not involved may insert additions, corrections, comments, questions, protests, etc. The role of teller is therefore potentially interactionally problematic, especially when two or more participants in the conversation share participation in the events being narrated. Stories of shared experience are problematic for two reasons: (1) there are two (or more) participants who are qualified to tell the story, (2) there are two (or more) people who are not possible recipients of the telling (Mandelbaum, 1989). The presence of two potential tellers leads to the possibility of competition for the role of 'narrator' of the story. These difficulties are addressed interactionally in conversations in which stories of shared experience are told. In some cases, the teller may involve another potential teller in the story by eliciting corroboration of the information told in the story through means of a repair initiation (C. Goodwin, 1987).

```
(25) [Car conversation]
     Sasha:    o:h. we saw some briyant ones recently, like
               um
               (1.0)
               oh what was that one about- (0.4) like Double
               In- (.) Indemnity=n like lots of movies from
               the  thirties  that  ha-  had  amazing  plot
               lines?
               (0.9)
               some of them were really full on: like um:
               (0.3) A Place in the Sun?
     Nick:     yeah.
     Sasha:    like this man: (0.8) was um (0.6) out in a
               boat and his wife drowned or something, and
→              (0.6) he did d-=was it he didn't do it (.)
               Elly¿
     Elvis:    yeah.
     Sasha:    he didn't do it but (0.2) he didn't say he
               didn't do it so he got (.) killed at the end,
               like hanged or something=but it was really
               [ full on
```

In this extract, Sasha's =*was it he didn't do it* (.) *Elly¿* provides an acknowledgement that Elvis, although not acting as a teller in this story, is qualified to tell the story. The repair initiation displays Elvis' access to the story and involves him in the telling. In this talk, Sasha displays that Elvis was a co-participant in the events being told and is a knowing recipient for this story, although he is not the addressed recipient. Alternatively, knowing recipients may claim knowledge and involvement by correcting details of the telling (Mandelbaum, 1989).

```
(26) [MU:1:20]
     Penny:    yih see he w' z readin' this book or s[ometh:i-
     Louise:                                          ['s a
               newspaper
     Penny:    yuh a newspaper and he didn' see . . .
```

In this extract, Louise initiates an other-initiated other-repair on the word *book* in Penny's talk. In so doing, she displays her own qualification to tell the story and her co-participation in the event and that she is a knowing recipient of the story. In these cases, the role of the knowing recipient is collaborative and secondary. That is, the knowing recipients support the telling of the story, but do not become tellers in their own right. However, it is possible that participants may compete to become tellers of a story and in this case the status of teller is contested by participants in the talk and this issue is managed locally by the participants.

In extract (27), three people in a car are driving home from a party: Sasha, Elvis and Nick. Sasha is driving. Sasha and Elvis are partners. Interactionally this raises the possibility that Sasha and Elvis have a store of shared experiences which are potential tellables with Nick as recipient.

```
(27) [Car conversation]
  1  Nick:    jus' go like follow this roa[d almost all=
  2  Elvis:                                [ yea:h
  3  Nick:    =the way through
  4  Sasha:   yep
  5  Elvis:   an' run intuh (.) buses
  6  Sasha:   o:h g[od Elvis    ] I thought we were dead=
  7  Elvis:        [heh huh huh]
  8  Sasha    =that day.
  9  Sasha:   that wa[s so 1-
 10  Elvis:          [that w' z the closest ca:ll man goin'
 11           throu-I' ll show yuh which [ w-
 12  Sasha:                              [ o:h I ne[ver=
 13  Elvis:                                        [ it' s=
 14  Sasha:   =been s:o-
 15  Elvis:   =the one right up (0.9) [ the ] top=
 16  Nick:                            [ ( ) ]
 17  Elvis:   of th[is
 18  Nick:        [ the ] top,
```

```
19 Elvis:   ye:p
20 Sasha:   h[e jus' goes-
21 Elvis:    [i' w' z fuckin' like THERE WAS A BUS
22 Elvis:   RIGHT THE:RE MAN, IN THAT FUCKIN' BLI:ND
23          spot, [ an' I ] =
24 Nick:          [ yeah,]
25 Elvis:   =looked th[rough an I didn' t see   ] =
26 Sasha:             [an he' s drivin' through]
27          [an' I' m jus screamin=             ]
28 Elvis:   =[anything so I wen' through
29 Sasha:   =my lung[s out
30 Elvis:           [ .hh an you jus screa:med
31          an I just stopped.=
30 Sasha:   =slammed on the brakes. in the middle of
31          th[e intersection.
32 Nick:      [didjou have the right of way?
33 Sasha:   no:.
34 Nick:    w' z it on a roundabout?
35 Sasha:   no he w' z at a give [ way si:gn.
36 Elvis:                        [ ih-w' z
37 Nick:    o:h right[yeah I know th] e one   y] eah.=
38 Elvis:            [huh   huh  huh]     yeah.]
39 Sasha:   =n' he starts takin' off an the bus is like
40          this n [ I' m jus' screa:min'
```

The story is occasioned by Nick's direction-giving which introduces into the conversation a location which is concerned with a potential tellable: an event shared by Sasha and Elvis. Elvis introduces the tellable in a way which appears to be designed for a knowing recipient: he invokes an event from their shared experience in such a way that the sharing of the experience is important in understanding the reference. Sasha responds to this as a recalling of the experience. The initial way this story is introduced, then, is through reminiscence between Sasha and Elvis as joint knowers of a story in which Nick has no part and, as an unknowing recipient, can have no part. The turns by Sasha and Elvis, however, are not produced simply in a conversation between themselves, but with an additional recipient. Elvis invokes a specific shared event and Sasha's response indicates that, in this event, there is something worth telling (Mandelbaum, 1989). The telling so far has been off the record and has not actually referred explicitly to the event being recalled. There is a potential for a story to be told here. Sasha's turn *that was so l-*, however, seems oriented to continuing with reminiscence.

Elvis in line 10 reforms the story as a tellable for Nick framing the story with the *closest call.* In so doing he provides an interpretative frame for Nick to be able to predict roughly what it will take for the story to be told and selects himself as teller: he has provided the story preface. He is now in a position in which he has used the same tellable as reminiscence with Sasha and as a story for Nick: two versions with different interactional import. At line 11, Elvis rushes through to provide background information for Nick, locating the event in space. At line 12, Sasha self-selects for a turn in overlap: this turn may be in overlap because of a mistiming caused by Elvis' rush through. Her turn is framed as an assessment which could be sequentially appropriate as a reminiscence with Elvis or as a contribution to a narrative addressed to Nick. At the end of the background information at line 18 – that is at the first possible position for the climax, which is the key tellable – Sasha self-selects as a teller of this part of the narrative. This turn is no longer even potentially designed as a reminiscence for a knowing recipient, but rather as a story designed for an unknowing recipient: the subject pronoun *he* is used rather than *you* and the talk is therefore designed to be about Elvis, not for him. Elvis also begins fractionally later, selecting himself as the teller of the same climax. Having begun second, the normal application on turn-taking should give the turn to Sasha. In this case, however, both speakers stop, Sasha with a cut-off; that is, a more marked stop.

At line 20, Elvis again self-selects as teller and relates part of the climax, with Nick as recipient. Elvis' delivery is loud and this appears to be an upgraded response to the previous overlapping talk following overlap resolution (Schegloff, 2000a and Chapter 4). At line 24, Sasha again self-selects as narrator, this time in overlap with Elvis. There are now two competing tellings co-occurring, relating different versions of the same event. The identity of the teller here is at stake, and neither speaker stops their utterance. In fact, Sasha emerges as the last speaker in resolution of the overlap. This is interactionally important as last speaker emerges as current speaker, and in this context as story-teller. Elvis overlaps the end of Sasha's turn and reformulates Sasha's talk, this time as a reminiscence designed for his knowing recipient (*you*). This talk integrates Sasha's talk into Elvis' own version of a narrative, and also invokes an earlier activity. It acknowledges, through reminiscence, Sasha's shared experience, while simultaneously transforming her talk into his own. He then adds a further element to the story. This element, however, is designed for either recipient as it both continues as reminiscence with Sasha, but also functions to advance the story for Nick. At this point, Elvis has emerged as the last speaker in the story, and potentially as the last teller of the story to Nick. However, Sasha then self-selects and again reformulates Elvis' addition and adds further information to emerge as the final speaker and the final teller. This turn becomes the last story turn, as Nick's question returns the interaction to turn-by-turn talk. Nick's question is not designed in a way which unambiguously selects a next speaker, although it does require further talk. The form 'you' is potentially problematic here (cf. Lerner, 1996b): it may encode 'the driver of the car' as a singular or 'the occupants in the car' as a plural. Sasha, replying here, treats it as being the occupants and continues with the status of teller she won at the end of the story. Nick's next question is again ambiguous in terms of speaker selection, potentially allowing either to become next speaker and again it is Sasha who self-selects, replying with a tellable about Elvis (*he*), although this time Elvis also self-selects in overlap but does not emerge as a current speaker.

This extract illustrates a number of things about story-telling. First, the event being studied here is not a single activity that participants are engaged in: it is not simply a story told to Nick by a story-teller. Stories are not self-contained generic units, but are interactionally accomplished events. There are in fact two different activities with different participation frameworks involved here: a) a story of shared experience invoked by Elvis with Sasha as the (knowing) addressed recipient and with the possibility of shifting the roles of teller and recipient, and (b) a story told to an unknowing addressed recipient about which the role of teller is disputed interactionally. It is not simply a question of one activity leading to the other in this conversation, but that both activities are possibly present through the talk. Secondly, the identity of teller is not a given in conversation but rather it is achieved interactionally. Where only a single teller has knowledge of the event being told, the identity of teller is interactionally unproblematic and a single teller is the normal outcome. In the case of stories involving experiences shared by some of the participants, the identity of story-teller is interactionally problematic; a single teller does not follow unproblematically for the launching of the story preface and speakership may be competed for through the talk. Thirdly, collaborative examples of story-telling, in which one knowing participant is a teller and the other plays a supportive role in the telling, are likewise interactionally achieved. That is, stories which run off with a single story-teller throughout do so because the other knowing recipient does not become or attempt to become a teller. One does not gain a right to tell a story as a sole narrator, one is given the opportunity to tell the story in this way.

Conclusion

This chapter began by arguing that stories are interactionally problematic because of the way in which the turn-taking system functions. In order to secure the space for multi-unit turns speakers have to negotiate a space in which this talk can happen, and this means they have to suspend the normal operation of turn-taking. The suspension of turn-taking is, however, not an exception to the turn-taking rules of conversation; rather, it is a special application of these rules. Firstly, stories are introduced through an operation of turn-taking through the story preface which is constructed with an orientation to the normal function of the system: story prefaces are constructed as single TCUs and provide for speaker change at their completion. This enactment of speaker change in this context, however, serves to suspend turn-taking as the normal consequence of a possible completion until the story is told. Secondly, during stories, story recipients display their orientation to turn-taking by passing up opportunities for talk through the use of continuers. Thirdly, the turn-taking system becomes relevant again at the moment the story is completed and comes into operation at the possible completion of the activity of story-telling. This means that, although turn-taking has been suspended, participants continue to orient to the turn-taking system in organizing their participation in the talk. Stories, therefore, are not simply told by tellers who in some sense take a long turn at talk; rather, they are collaboratively achieved by the participants through and in the telling of stories.

References

Atkinson, J. M. (1983), 'Two devices for generating audience approval: A comparative study of public discourse and texts', in K. Ehlich and H. van Riemsdijk (eds), *Connectedness in Sentence, Text and Discourse*. Cambridge: Cambridge University Press (pp. 370–409).

— (1984a), *Our Masters' Voices: The Language and Body Language of Politics*. London and New York: Methuen.

— (1984b), 'Public speaking and audience responses: some techniques for inviting applause', in J. M. Atkinson and J. Heritage (eds), *Structures of Social Interaction*. Cambridge: Cambridge University Press (pp. 370–409).

— (1985), 'Refusing invited applause: Preliminary observations from a case study of charismatic oratory', in T. A. van Dijk (ed.), *Handbook of Discourse Analysis*. London: Academic Press. (Vol. 3 *Discourse and Dialogue*, pp. 161–81).

Atkinson, J. M. and Drew, P. (1984), *Order in Court: The Organization of Verbal Interaction in Judicial Settings*. London: Macmillan.

Atkinson, J. M. and Heritage, J. (1984), 'Preference organisation', in J. M. Atkinson and J. Heritage (eds), *Structures of Social Interaction*. Cambridge: Cambridge University Press (pp. 53–6).

Beach, W. A. (1993), 'Transitional regularities for "casual" "Okay" usages'. *Journal of Pragmatics*, 19, 325–52.

Boden, D. (1990), 'The world as it happens: Ethnomethodology and conversation analysis', in G. Ritzer (ed.), *Frontiers of Social Theory: The New Synthesis*. New York: Columbia University Press (pp. 185–213).

— (1994), *The Business of Talk: Organizations in Action* Cambridge: Polity.

Burke, P. (1993), *The Art of Conversation*. Cambridge: Polity.

Button, G. (1987), 'Moving out of closings', in G. Button and J. R. E. Lee (eds), *Talk and Social Organization*. Clevedon, Avon: Multilingual Matters (pp. 101–51).

— (1991a), 'Conversation-in-a-series', in D. Boden and D. Zimmerman (eds), *Talk and Social Structure: Studies in Ethnomethodology and Conversation Analysis*. Cambridge: Polity Press (pp. 251–77).

— (1991b), 'On varieties of closings', in G. Psathas (ed.), *Studies in Ethnomethodology and Conversation Analysis*. Lanham, MA: University Press of America.

Button, G. and Casey, N. (1984), 'Generating topic: The use of topic initial elicitors', in J. M. Atkinson and J. Heritage (eds), *Structures of Social Interaction*. Cambridge: Cambridge University Press (pp. 167–90).

— (1985), 'Topic nomination and topic pursuit'. *Human Studies*, 8, 3–55.

Chomsky, N. (1965), *Aspects of a Theory of Syntax*. Cambridge, MA: MIT Press.

Clayman, S. and Maynard, D. (1995), 'Ethnomethodology and conversation analysis', in P. ten Have and G. Psathas (eds), *Situated Order: Studies in the Social Organization of Talk and Embodied Activities*. Washington, DC: University Press of America (pp. 1–30).

Coates, J. (1987), 'Epistemic modality and spoken discourse'. *Transactions of the Philological Society*, 85, 100–31.

Cook, G. (1990), 'Transcribing infinity: Problems of context presentation'. *Journal of Pragmatics*, 14, 1–24.

Crozet, C. and Liddicoat, A. J. (1998), 'Reconnaissance et ajustement dans l'interaction française', in B. Caron (ed.), *Proceedings of the XVIth International Congress of Linguists*. Oxford: Pergamon (Paper No. 325).

Davidson, J. (1984), 'Subsequent versions of invitations, offers, requests, and proposals dealing with potential or actual rejection', in J. M. Atkinson and J. Heritage (eds), *Structures of Social Interaction*. Cambridge: Cambridge University Press (pp. 102–28).

Drew, P. (1984), 'Speakers' reportings in invitation sequences', in J. M. Atkinson and J. Heritage (eds), *Structures of Social Interaction*. Cambridge: Cambridge University Press (pp. 129–51).

Drew, P. and Heritage, J. (eds), (1992), *Talk at Work: Interaction in Institutional Settings*. Cambridge: Cambridge University Press.

Drew, P. and Sorjonen, M.-L. (1997), 'Institutional dialogue', in T. A. van Dijk (ed.), *Discourse as Social Interaction*. London: Sage (pp. 92–118).

Drummond, K. (1989), 'A backward glance at interruptions'. *Western Journal of Speech Communication*, 53, 150–66.

Duranti, A. (1997), *Linguistic Anthropology*. Cambridge: Cambridge University Press.

Egbert, M. (1997), 'Schisming: The collaborative transformation from a single conversation to multiple conversations'. *Research on Language and Social Interaction*, 30, 1–50.

Ehlich, K. and Switala, B. (1976), 'Transkriptionssysteme – Eine exemplarische Übersicht'. *Studium Linguistik*, 2, 78–105.

Ford, C. and Thompson, S. A. (1996), 'Interactional units in conversation: syntactic, intonational, and pragmatic resources for the management of turns', in E. Ochs, E. A. Schegloff and S. A. Thompson (eds), *Interaction and Grammar*. Cambridge: Cambridge University Press (pp. 134–84).

Ford, C., Fox, B. and Thompson, S. A. (2001), 'Constituency and the grammar of turn increments' in C. Ford, B. Fox and S. A. Thompson (eds), *Language of Turn and Sequence*. Oxford: Oxford University Press (pp. 14–38).

Fox, B. A. (1987), 'Interactional reconstruction in real-time language processing'. *Cognitive Science*, 11, 365–87.

Gardner, R. (2001), *When Listeners Talk: Response Tokens and Listener Stance*. Amsterdam: John Benjamins.

— (2005), 'Acknowledging strong ties between utterances in talk: Connections through right as a response token', in I. Mushin (ed.), *Proceedings of the 2004 Conference of the Australian Linguistic Society*. Retrieved 2 September 2005, from www.dspace.library.usyd.edu.au:8080/handle/123456789/107.

Garfinkel, H. (1964), 'Studies in the routine grounds of everyday activities'. *Social Problems*, 11, 225–50.

— (1967), *Studies in Ethnomethodology*. Cambridge: Polity.

— (1988), 'Evidence for locally produced, naturally accountable phenomena of order, logic, reason, meaning, method, etc. in and as of the essential quiddity of immortal ordinary society (I of IV): An announcement of studies'. *Sociological Theory*, (6), 10–39.

Garfinkel, H. and Sacks, H. (1970), 'On formal structures of practical actions', in J. C. McKinney and E. A. Tiryakian (eds), *Theoretical Sociology*. New York: Appleton-Century-Crofts (pp. 337–66).

Gernsbacher, M. A. and Jesceniak, J. D. (2002), 'Cataphoric development in spoken discourse'. *Cognitive Psychology*, 29, 24–58.

Goffman, E. (1959), *The Presentation of Self in Everyday Life*. Doubleday Anchor.

— (1963), *Behaviour in Public Places: Notes on the Social Organisation of Gathering*. New York: Free Press.

— (1964), 'The neglected situation'. *American Anthropologist*, 6, (2), 133–6.

— (1967), *Interaction Ritual: Essay on Face-to-Face Behaviour*. New York: Doubleday Anchor.

— (1969), *Strategic Interaction*. Philedelphia, PA: University of Pennsylvania Press.

— (1971), *Relations in Public*. New York: Basic Books.

— (1981), *Forms of Talk*. Philadelphia, PA: University of Pennsylvania Press.

Goodwin, C. (1979), 'The interactive construction of a sentence in natural conversation', in G. Psathas (ed.), *Everyday Language: Studies in Ethnomethodology*. New York: Irvington (pp. 97–121).

— (1980), 'Restarts, pauses and the achievement of mutual gaze at turn-beginning'. *Sociological Inquiry*, 50, 272–302.

— (1981), *Conversational Organisation: Interactions between Speakers and Hearers*. New York: Academic.

— (1984), 'Notes on story structure and the organization of participation', in J. M. Atkinson and J. Heritage (eds), *Structures of Social Interaction*. Cambridge: Cambridge University Press (pp. 225–46).

— (1987), 'Forgetfulness as an interactive resource'. *Social Psychology Quarterly*, 50, (2), 115–31.

— (1996), 'Transparent vision', in E. Ochs, E. A. Schegloff and S. A. Thompson (eds), *Interaction and Grammar*. Cambridge: Cambridge University Press.

— (2002), 'Time in action'. *Current Anthropology*, 43.

— (2003), 'Pointing as situated practice', in S. Kita (ed.), *Pointing: Where Language, Culture and Cognition Meet*. Mahwah, NJ: Lawrence Erlbaum (pp. 217–41).

Goodwin, C. and Goodwin, M. H. (1992), 'Assessments and the construction of context', in A. Duranti and C. Goodwin (eds), *Rethinking Context: Language as an Interactive Phenomenon*. Cambridge: Cambridge University Press (pp. 151–89).

Goodwin, C. and Heritage, J. (1990), 'Conversation analysis'. *Annual Review of Anthropology*, 19, 283–307.

Goodwin, M. H. (1990), *He-Said-She-Said: Talk as Social Organisation among Black Children*. Bloomington and Indianapolis: University of Indiana Press.

Green, J., Franquiz, M. and Dixon, C. (1997), 'The myth of the objective transcript: Transcribing as a situated act'. *TESOL Quarterly*, 31, 172–6.

Gumperz, J. J. and Berenz, N. B. (1993), 'Transcribing conversational exchanges', in J. A. Edwards and M. D. Lampert (eds), *Talking Data: Transcription and Coding in Discourse Research*. Hillsdale, NJ: Lawrence Erlbaum (pp. 91–121).

Hanamura, N. (1998), 'Teaching telephone closings in Japanese: A comparison between textbook materials and actual conversation', in N. Bramley and N. Hanamura (eds), *Issues in the Teaching and Learning of Japanese*. Canberra: ALAA.

ten Have, P. (1991), 'Talk and institution: A reconsideration of the "assymetry" of doctor-patient communication', in D. Boden and D. Zimmerman (eds), *Talk and Social Structure: Studies in Ethnomethodology and Conversation Analysis*. Cambridge: Polity (pp. 138–63).

— (1999), *Doing Conversation Analysis: A Practical Guide* London: Sage.

Heath, C. (1984), 'Talk and recipiency: Sequential organisation in speech and body movement', in J. M. Atkinson and J. Heritage (eds), *Structures of Social Interaction*. Cambridge: Cambridge University Press (pp. 247–65).

Heath, C. and Luff, P. (1993), 'Explicating face-to-face interaction', in N. Gilbert (ed.), *Researching Social Life*. London: Sage (pp. 306–26).

Hepburn, A. (2004), 'Crying: Notes on description, transcription and interaction'. *Research on Language and Social Interaction*, 37, (3), 251–90.

Heritage, J. (1984a), 'A change of state token and aspects of its sequential placement', in J. M. Atkinson and J. Heritage (eds), *Structures of Social Interaction*. Cambridge: Cambridge University Press (pp. 299–345).

— (1984b), *Garfinkle and Ethnomethodology*. Cambridge: Polity Press.

— (1985), 'Analysing news interviews: Aspects of the production of talk for an overhearing audience', in T. A. van Dijk (ed.), *Handbook of Discourse Analysis*. London: Academic (Vol. 3, pp. 95–117).

— (1988), 'Explanations as accounts: A conversation analytic perspective', in C. Antaki (ed.), *Analysing Everyday Explanation: A Casebook of Methods*. London: Sage (pp. 127–44).

— (1989), 'Current developments in conversational analysis', in D. Roger and P. Bull (eds), *Conversation: An Interdisciplinary Perspective*. Clevedon: Multilingual Matters (pp. 21–47).

— (1995), 'Conversation analysis: Methodological aspects', in U. M. Quasthoff (ed.), *Aspects of Oral Communication*. Berlin: Mouton de Gruyter (pp. 391–414).

— (1998), 'Conversation analysis and institutional talk: Analysing data', in D. Silverman (ed.), *Qualitative Research: Theory, Method and Practice*. London: Sage (pp. 161–82).

— (2004), 'Conversation analysis and institutional talk', in R. Sanders and K. Fitch (eds), *Handbook of Language and Social Interaction*. Mahwah NJ: Lawrence Erlbaum (pp. 103–46).

Heritage, J. and Watson, D. R. (1979), 'Formulations as conversational objects', in G. Psathas (ed.), *Everyday Language: Studies in Ethnomethodology* Hillsdale, NJ: Lawrence Erlbaum (pp. 123–62).

Herringer, J. (1977), 'Pre-sequences and indirect speech acts', in E. Ochs Keenan and T. L. Bennett (eds), *Discourse Structure Across Time and Space*. Los Angeles: University of Southern California Linguistics Department (pp. 169–80).

Hopper, R. (1988), 'Speech, for instance: The exemplar in studies of conversation'. *Journal of Language and Social Psychology*, 7, 47–63.

— (1989), 'Speech in telephone openings: Emergent interaction v. routines'. *Western Journal of Speech Communication*, 53, 178–94.

— (1991), 'Hold the phone', in D. Boden and D. Zimmerman (eds), *Talk and Social Structure: Studies in Ethnomethodology and Conversation Analysis*. Cambridge: Polity Press (pp. 217–31).

— (1992), *Telephone Conversations* Bloomington: Indiana University Press.

Jackson, S. and Jacobs, S. (1980), 'Structure of conversational argument: Pragmatic bases for the enthymeme'. *The Quarterly Journal of Speech*, 66, 251–65.

Jefferson, G. (1972), 'Side sequences', in D. Sudnow (ed.), *Studies in Social Interaction*. New York: Free Press (pp. 294–338).

— (1973), 'A case of precision timing in ordinary conversation: Overlapped tag-positioned address terms in closing sequences'. *Semiotica*, 9, 47–96.

— (1978), 'Sequential aspects of storytelling', in J. Schenkein (ed.), *Studies in the Organization of Conversational Interaction*. New York: Academic (pp. 219–48).

— (1979), 'A technique of inviting laughter and its subsequent acceptance/declination', in G. Psathas (ed.), *Everyday Language: Studies in Ethnomethodology*. New York: Irvington (pp. 79–96).

— (1981), 'The abominable "ne?" A working paper exploring the post-response pursuit of response'. *Manchester University Department of Sociology Occasional Paper*, 6.

— (1983), *Issues in the Transcription of Naturally Occurring Talk: Caricature versus Capturing Pronunciational Particulars*. Tilburg: Tilburg University.

— (1984), 'On stepwise transition from talk about a trouble to inappropriately next-positioned matters', in J. M. Atkinson and J. Heritage (eds), *Structures of Social Interaction*. Cambridge: Cambridge University Press (pp. 191–222).

— (1985), 'An exercise in the transcription and analysis of laughter', in T. A. van Dijk (ed.), *Handbook of Discourse Analysis*. London: Academic (Vol. 3, pp. 25–34).

— (1987), 'On exposed and embedded correction in conversation', in G. Button and J. R. E. Lee (eds), *Talk and Social Organization*. Clevedon, Avon: Multilingual Matters (pp. 86–100).

— (1989), 'Preliminary notes on a possible metric which provides for a "standard maximum" silence of approximately one second in conversation', in D. Roger and P. Bull (eds), *Conversation: An Interdisciplinary Perspective*. Clevedon, Avon: Multilingual Matters (pp. 166–96).

— (1990), 'List construction as a task and interactional resource', in G. Psathas (ed.), *Interaction Competence*. Washington, DC: International Institute for Ethnomethodology and Conversation Analysis and University Press of America (pp. 63–92).

— (2004), 'Glossary of transcript symbols with an introduction', in G. H. Lerner (ed.), *Conversation Analysis: Studies from the First Generation*. Amsterdam: John Benjamins (pp. 13–31).

Jones, C. M. and Beach, W. A. (1995), 'Therapists' techniques for responding to unsolicited contributions from family members', in G. H. Morris and R. J. Chenail (eds), *The Talk of the Clinic: Explorations in the Analysis of Medical and Therapeutic Discourse*. Hillsdale, NJ: Lawrence Erlbaum.

Kasper, G. and Faerch, C. (1989), 'Internal and external modification in interlanguage request realisation', in S. Blum-Kulka, J. House and G. Kasper (eds), *Cross-Cultural Pragmatics: Requests and Apologies*. Norwood, NJ: Ablex (pp. 221–47).

Kendon, A. and Ferber, A. (1973), 'A description of some human greetings', in R. P. Michael and J. H. Crook (eds), *Comparative Ecology and Behaviour of Primates*. London: Academic Press (pp. 591–668).

Kwon, J. (2004), 'Expressing refusals in Korean and in American English'. *Multilingua*, 23, 339–64.

Labov, W. and Fanshell, D. (1977), *Therapeutic Discourse: Psychotherapy as Conversation*. New York: Academic.

Labov, W. and Waletsky, J. (1966), 'Narrative analysis: Oral versions of personal experience', in J. Helm (ed.), *Essays on the Verbal and Visual Arts*. Seattle, WA: University of Washington Press (pp. 12–44).

Lerner, G. H. (1991), 'On the syntax of sentences-in-progress'. *Language in Society*, 20, 441–58.

— (1996a), 'On the "semi-permeable" character of grammatical units in conversation: Conditional entry into the turn space of another speaker', in E. Ochs, E. A. Schegloff and S. A. Thompson (eds), *Interaction and Grammar*. Cambridge: Cambridge University Press (pp. 238–76).

— (1996b), 'On the place of linguistic resources in the organization of talk-in-interaction: "Second person" reference in multi-party conversation'. *Pragmatics*, 6, (3), 281–94.

— (2003), 'Selecting next speaker: The context-sensitive operation of a context-free organization'. *Language in Society*, 32, 177–201.

— (2004), 'Introductory remarks', in G. H. Lerner (ed.), *Conversation Analysis: Studies from the First Generation*. Amsterdam: John Benjamins (pp. 1–11).

Levinson, S. (1983), *Pragmatics*. Cambridge: Cambridge University Press.

Liddicoat, A. J. (1997), 'Interaction, social structure and second language use: A response to Firth and Wagner'. *Modern Language Journal*, 81, (3), 313–17.

— (2004), 'The projectability of turn construction units and the role of prediction in listening'. *Discourse Studies*, 6, (4), 449–71.

— (2005), 'Corpus planning: Syllabus and materials development', in E. Hinkel (ed.), *Handbook of Research in Second Language Teaching and Learning*. Mahwah, NJ: Lawrence Erlbaum (pp. 993–1012).

Liddicoat, A. J., Döpke, A., Brown, S. and Love, K. (1992), 'The effect of the institution: Openings in talkback radio'. *Text*, 12, (4), 541–62.

Mandelbaum, J. (1989), 'Interpersonal activities in conversational story-telling'. *Western Journal of Speech Communication*, 53, 114–26.

Merritt, M. (1976), 'On questions following questions (in service encounters)'. *Language in Society*, 5, 315–57.

Mishler, E. G. (1991), 'Representing discourse: The rhetoric of transcription'. *Journal of Narrative and Life History*, 1, 255–80.

Nofsinger, R. E. (1975), 'The demand ticket: A conversational device for getting the floor'. *Speech Monographs*, 42, (1), 1–9.

— (1991), *Everyday Conversation*. Newbury Park: Sage.

Ochs, E. (1979), 'Transcription as theory', in E. Ochs and B. Schieffelin (eds), *Developmental Pragmatics*. New York: Academic.

Ochs, E., Taylor, C., Rudolph, D. and Smith, R. (1992), 'Storytelling as a theory-building activity'. *Discourse Processes*, 15, 32–72.

Polanyi, L. (1979), 'So what's the point?' *Semiotica*, 25, 207–41.

Pomerantz, A. (1980), 'Telling my side: "Limited access" as a "fishing device"'. *Sociological Inquiry*, 50, 186–98.

— (1984), 'Agreeing and disagreeing with assessments: Some features of preferred/dispreferred turn shapes', in J. M. Atkinson and J. Heritage (eds), *Structures of Social Interaction*. Cambridge: Cambridge University Press (pp. 57–101).

— (1987), 'Descriptions in legal settings', in G. Button and J. R. E. Lee (eds), *Talk and Social Organization*. Clevedon, Avon: Multilingual Matters.

Pomerantz, A. and Fehr, B. J. (1997), 'Conversation analysis: An approach to the study of social action as sense making practices', in T. A. V. Dijk (ed.), *Discourse as Social Interaction*. London: Sage (pp. 64–91).

Psathas, G. (1986), 'Some sequential structures in direction-giving'. *Human Studies*, 9, (2–3), 231–46.

— (1990), 'Introduction: Methodological issues and recent developments in the study of naturally occuring interaction', in G. Psathas (ed.), *Interaction Competence*. Washington, DC: International Institute for

Ethnomethodology and Conversation Analysis and University Press of America (pp. 1–30).

— (1991), 'The structure of direction-giving in interaction', in D. Boden and D. Zimmerman (eds), *Talk and Social Structure: Studies in Ethnomethodology and Conversation Analysis.* Cambridge: Polity (pp. 197–216).

— (1995), *Conversation Analysis: The Study of Talk in Interaction.* Thousand Oaks: Sage.

Psathas, G. and Anderson, T. (1990), 'The "practices" of transcription in conversation analysis'. *Semiotica*, 78, 75–99.

Raymon, G. (2003), 'Grammar and social organization: Yes/no interrogatives and the structure of responding'. *American Sociological Review*, 68, (6), 939–67.

Rendle-Short, J. (1999), 'When "okay" is okay in computer science seminar talk'. *Australian Review of Applied Linguistics*, 22, (2), 19–35.

— (2002), *Talk and Action in the Computer Science Seminar.* Unpublished PhD, Australian National University, Canberra.

— (2003), 'So what does this show us? Analysis of the discourse marker "so" in monologic talk'. *Australian Review of Applied Linguistics*, 26, (2), 46–62.

Rose, P. and Duncan, S. (1995), 'Naive auditory identification and discrimination of similar voices by familiar listeners'. *Journal of Forensic Linguistics*, 2, (1), 1–17.

Sacks, H. (1973), 'On some puns: With some imitations', in R. W. Shui (ed.), *Report of the 23rd Annual Round Table Meeting on Linguistics and Language Studies.* Washington, DC: Georgetown University Press (pp. 135–44).

— (1974), 'An analysis of the course of a joke's telling in conversation', in R. Bauman and J. Scherzer (eds), *Explorations in the Ethnography of Speaking.* Cambridge: Cambridge University Press (pp. 337–53).

— (1975), 'Everyone has to lie', in M. Sounches and B. G. Blount (eds), *Sociocultural Dimensions of Language Use.* Clevedon, Avon: Multilingual Matters.

— (1978), 'Some technical considerations of a dirty joke', in J. Schenkein (ed.), *Studies in the Organization of Conversational Interaction.* New York: Academic (pp. 249–70).

— (1984), 'On doing "being ordinary" ', in J. M. Atkinson and J. Heritage (eds), *Structures of Social Interaction.* Cambridge: Cambridge University Press (pp. 413–29).

— (1986), 'Some considerations of a story told in ordinary conversation'. *Poetics*, 15, 127–38.

— (1987), 'On the preferences for agreement and contiguity in sequences in conversation', in G. Button and J. R. E. Lee (eds), *Talk and Social Organisation.* Clevedon, Avon: Multilingual Matters.

— (1992), *Lectures on Conversation.* Oxford: Basil Blackwell.

— (2004), 'An initial characterization of the organization of speaker turn-taking in conversation', in G. H. Lerner (ed.), *Conversation Analysis: Studies from the First Generation.* Amsterdam: John Benjamins (pp. 35–42).

Sacks, H. and Schegloff, E. A. (1979), 'Two preferences in the organisation of reference to persons in conversation and their interaction', in G. Psathas (ed.), *Everyday Language: Studies in Ethnomethodology*. Hillsdale, NJ: Lawrence Erlbaum (pp. 15–21).

Sacks, H., Schegloff, E. A. and Jefferson, G. (1974), 'A simplest systematics for the organisation of turn-taking for conversation'. *Language*, 50, 696–735.

Schegloff, E. A. (1968), 'Sequencing in conversational openings'. *American Anthropology*, 70, (6), 1075–95.

— (1972), 'Notes on conversational practice: Formulating place', in D. Sudnow (ed.), *Studies in Social Interaction*. New York: Free Press (pp. 75–119).

— (1979a), 'Identification and recognition in telephone conversation openings', in G. Psathas (ed.), *Everyday Language: Studies in Ethnomethodology*. New York: Irvington.

— (1979b), 'The relevance of repair for syntax-for-conversation', in T. Givón (ed.), *Discourse and Syntax*. New York: Academic.

— (1980), 'Preliminaries to preliminaries: "Can I ask you a question?" '. *Sociological Enquiry*, 50, 104–52.

— (1982), 'Discourse as an interactional achievement: Some uses of "uh huh" and other things that come between turns', in D. Tannen (ed.), *Georgetown University Roundtable on Linguistics*. Washington: Georgetown University Press (pp. 71–93).

— (1984), 'On some gestures' relation to talk', in J. M. Atkinson and J. Heritage (eds), *Structures of Social Interaction*. Cambridge: Cambridge University Press (pp. 266–96).

— (1986), 'The routine as achievement'. *Human Studies*, 9, (2–3), 111–51.

— (1987a), 'Analysing single episodes of interaction: An exercise in conversation analysis'. *Social Psychology Quarterly*, 50, (2), 101–14.

— (1987b), 'Some sources of misunderstanding in talk-in-interaction'. *Linguistics*, 25, (1), 201–18.

— (1988a), 'Goffman and the analysis of conversation', in P. Drew and A. Wooton (eds), *Erving Goffman: Exploring the Interaction Order*. Oxford: Polity Press (pp. 89–135).

— (1988b), 'On an actual virtual servo-mechanism for guessing bad news: A single-case conjecture'. *Social Problems*, 35, (4), 442–57.

— (1988c), 'Presequences and indirection: Apply speech act theory to ordinary conversation'. *Journal of Pragmatics*, 12, 55–62.

— (1990), 'On the organisation of sequences as a source of "coherence" in talk in interaction', in B. Dorval (ed.), *Conversational Organisation and its Development*. Norwood, NJ: Ablex.

— (1991), 'Issues of relevance for discourse analysis: Contingency in action, interaction and co-participant context', in E. H. Hovy and D. R. Scott (eds), *Computational and Conversational Discourse*. Berlin: Springer-Verlag (pp. 3–35).

— (1992a), 'In another context', in A. Duranti and C. Goodwin (eds), *Rethinking Context: Language as an Interactive Phenomenon*. Cambridge: Cambridge University Press (pp. 191–228).

— (1992b), 'Repair after next turn: The last structurally provided defense of intersubjectivity in conversation'. *American Journal of Sociology*, 97, (5), 1295–1345.

— (1993), 'Reflections on quantification in the study of conversation'. *Research on Language and Social Interaction*, 26, 99–128.

— (1995a), 'Discourse and an interactional achievement III: The omni-relevance of action'. *Research on language and Social Interaction*, 28, (3), 185–211.

— (1995b), *Sequence Organisation* Department of Sociology, UCLA: Unpublished paper.

— (1996a), 'Confirming allusions: Towards an empirical account of action'. *American Journal of Sociology*, 104, 161–216.

— (1996b), 'Turn organization: One intersection of grammar and inter-action', in E. Ochs, E. A. Schegloff and S. A. Thompson (eds), *Interaction and Grammar*. Cambridge: Cambridge University Press (pp. 52–133).

— (1997), 'Third turn repair', in G. R. Guy, C. Feagin, D. Schiffrin and J. Baugh (eds), *Towards a Social Science of Language: Papers in Honour of William Labov*. Amsterdam: John Benjamins (Vol. 2, pp. 31–40).

— (1999), '"Schegloff's texts" as "Billing's data": A critical reply'. *Discourse Processes*, 10, 558–72.

— (2000a), 'Overlapping talk and the organisation of turn-taking in conversation'. *Language in Society*, 29, (1), 1–63.

— (2000b), 'When "others" initiate repair'. *Applied Linguistics*, 21, (2), 205–43.

— (2002), 'Opening sequencing', in J. E. Katz and M. Aakhus (eds), *Perpetual Contact: Mobile Communication, Private Talk, Public Performance*. Cambridge: Cambridge University Press (pp. 325–85).

— (2005), 'On complainability'. *Social Problems*, 52, (4), 449–76.

Schegloff, E. A. and Sacks, H. (1973), 'Opening up closings'. *Semiotica*, 7, (289–327).

Schegloff, E. A., Jefferson, G. and Sacks, H. (1977), 'The preference for self-correction in the organisation of repair in conversation'. *Language*, 53, (361–82).

Schiffrin, D. (1987), *Discourse Markers*. Cambridge: Cambridge University Press.

Searle, J. (1975), 'Indirect speech acts', in P. Cole and J. Morgan (eds), *Syntax and Semantics*. New York: Academic Press (Vol. 3, Speech Acts).

Selting, M. (1998), 'TCUs and TRPs: The construction of units in conversational talk'. *InLiSt (Interaction and Linguistic Structures)*, 4, 1–48.

Sinclair, J. M. and Coulthard, M. (1975), *Towards and Analysis of Discourse*. London: Oxford University Press.

So'o, A. M. and Liddicoat, A. J. (2000), 'Telephone openings in Samoan'. *Australian Review of Applied Linguistics*, 23, (1), 95–108.

Sorjonen, M.-L. (1996), 'On repeats and responses in Finnish', in E. Och, E. A. Schegloff and S. A. Thompson (eds), *Interaction and Grammar*. Cambridge: Cambridge University Press (pp. 277–327).

Streeck, J. and Hartge, U. (1992), 'Previews: Gestures at the transition place', in P. Auer and A. di Luzio (eds), *The Contextualization of Language*. Amsterdam: John Benjamins (pp. 135–57).

Terasaki, A. K. (1976), 'Pre-announcement sequences in conversation', in *Social Science Working Paper 99*. Irvine, CA: University of California, Irvine, School of Social Science.

— (2004), 'Pre-announcement sequences in conversation', in G. H. Lerner (ed.), *Conversation Analysis: Studies from the First Generation*. Amsterdam: John Benjamins (pp. 171–233).

Watson, D. R. (1997), 'Some general reflections on "categorization" and "sequence" in the analysis of conversation', in S. Hester and P. Eglin (eds), *Culture in Action: Studies in Membership Category Analysis*. Washington DC: University Press of America (pp. 40–76).

Wooffitt, R. (2005), *Conversation Analysis and Discourse Analysis: A Comparative and Critical Introduction*. London: Sage.

Zimmerman, D. H. (1984), 'Talk and its occasion: The case of calling the police', in D. Schiffrin (ed.), *Meaning, Form and Use in Context: Linguistic Applications. Georgetown University Round Table on Language and Linguistics 1984*. Washington, DC: Georgetown University Press (pp. 201–8).

Index